CHURCH ORDER
IN THE NEW TESTAMENT

STUDIES IN BIBLICAL THEOLOGY

CHURCH ORDER
IN THE
NEW TESTAMENT

EDUARD SCHWEIZER

SCM PRESS LTD
56 BLOOMSBURY STREET
LONDON

Translated by Frank Clarke from the German
GEMEINDE UND GEMEINDEORDNUNG IM NEUEN TESTAMENT
(Zwingli-Verlag, Zurich, 1959)

FIRST PUBLISHED IN ENGLISH 1961
© SCM PRESS LTD 1961
PRINTED IN GREAT BRITAIN BY
W. & J. MACKAY & CO LTD, CHATHAM

CONTENTS

Contents

PREFACE

A flood of literature has been published on our subject. It is no longer possible completely to master the whole of it, and I can only hope that I have not overlooked something that proves to be the most important work of all.* A particularly important piece of research by H. von Campenhausen appeared in 1953 (see n. 46). In view of all the work that has been done, I had grave doubts whether it was necessary to put forward my own attempt. If I have done so, it is because readers of my first essay, *Das Leben des Herrn in der Gemeinde und ihren Diensten* (Zürich, 1946, out of print for several years) repeatedly told me that the book had helped them in the actual building up of the Church. So here I have tried to listen carefully to the testimony of the various New Testament writers. I consider it the first task of an interpreter not to do violence to the text, but to read it humbly and attentively, even when it shows conceptions too different to be easily equated. My concern is not mainly the historical investigation of the Church's development, but rather the theological problem of how the New Testament Church understood itself, and how it expressed that understanding in its order. The purely historical question, therefore, about the form of the Church at different times and places, while admittedly necessary, need be asked only in so far as the actual shaping of the Church is always evidence of the concept of its own nature to which it testifies. Thus the arrangement of the New Testament writings is determined primarily by the theological kinship of their idea of the Church, and only secondarily by chronological or geographical considerations. The Pastoral Letters, for instance, appear in Part IB, because they are much closer to the theological conception of Luke than to that of Paul, although they are dependent on Paul in other respects.

*For the older literature see especially the survey by Linton (n. 7); for the newer see W. G. Kümmel in the *TR*, New Series (14, 1942, 81 ff., 155 ff.; 17, 1948, 3 ff., 103 ff.; 18, 1950, 1 ff.; 22, 1954, 138 ff., 191 ff.). The discussion to be found in my book of 1946 of work prior to that date is repeated here only in exceptional cases.

7

The New Testament therefore stands in the centre, and other contemporaneous writings, of equal value on purely historical grounds, are investigated rather more briefly in a special section.

I try uniformly to translate the New Testament term *ekklesia* by 'church', in order to emphasize that linguistically the New Testament cannot distinguish, as we do, between the local and the universal Church. 'Congregation' would certainly be closer to the Greek word. Like the German *Gemeinde*, it would be appropriate because it is used, like the Greek term, both in a religious and in a secular sense. In English, however, it would be so unusual as a designation of the universal Church, that we have to choose 'church', always remembering that in the New Testament the term means especially the local community.

The German word *Heilsgeschichte* is virtually untranslatable. It is rendered here by 'God's plan of salvation', which seems to be the best English equivalent. However, the reader should keep in mind that *Heilsgeschichte* (literally 'salvation-history') also stresses that this plan of God comes into being within concrete earthly history. It is in the political and social history of the nation of Israel, in the first instance, that the rule of God over all history becomes visible.

Thirdly, German distinguishes between *Dienst* and *Amt*, between a ministry or service entrusted to every member of the Church, and an official ministry requiring some special rank like that of an ordained priest. In this book 'ministry' is used in the first of these senses unless otherwise stated.

May I ask my readers to be kind enough to quote according to chapters and sections ? They are exactly the same as in the German edition. Why should we make it so difficult to check quotations at a time when so many books appear in translations ? This is especially difficult if we quote according to pages, since usually each library contains only an edition in the language of its own country. I quote by chapters and sections in all my cross-references. As these are indicated at the top of every page, it is, I suppose, as easy for the reader to look them up as if the number of the page were given. Thus any quotation from the German text can be checked equally easily in the English text, and vice versa.

Finally I must apologize for the comparatively numerous

quotations from my own works. They have been made only to give an adequate basis to statements for which I have produced more detailed support elsewhere.

I can only dedicate the book again to my wife, whose presence through the years has in large part made it possible for me to write it.

Zürich,   EDUARD SCHWEIZER
8 June 1960

ABBREVIATIONS

Ap. Min.: *The Apostolic Ministry*, ed. K. E. Kirk, 1946
Background: *The Background of the New Testament and its Eschatology: in honour of C. H. Dodd*, ed. W. D. Davies and D. Daube, 1956
BJRL: *Bulletin of the John Rylands Library*
Buch v.d. Kirche: *Ein Buch von der Kirche*, ed. G. Aulén and others, 1951
CJT: *Canadian Journal of Theology*
ET: English translation
EvTh: *Evangelische Theologie*
ExpT: *Expository Times*
JBL: *Journal of Biblical Literature*
JTS: *Journal of Theological Studies*
Min. and Sacr.: *The Ministry and Sacraments*, ed. R. Dunkerley and A. C. Headlam, 1937
NtlStud: *Neutestamentliche Studien für R. Bultmann* (*ZNW* Beiheft 21), 1954
NTS: *New Testament Studies*
RAC: *Reallexikon für Antike und Christentum*, 1950 ff.
RB: *Revue Biblique*
RevSR: *Revue des Sciences Religieuses*
RGG: *Religion in Geschichte und Gegenwart*, 1956 ff.
RHPR: *Revue d'Histoire et de Philosophie Religieuse*
SAH: *Sitzungsberichte der Akademie der Wissenschaften zu Heidelberg*, philol. Klasse
SBT: Studies in Biblical Theology
SJT: *Scottish Journal of Theology*
ST: *Studia Theologica*
Str-B: H. Strack and P. Billerbeck, *Kommentar zum NT aus Talmud und Midrasch* I–IV, 1922–8
StudPaul: *Studia Paulina in honorem J. de Zwaan*, ed. J. N. Sevenster and W. C. van Unnik, 1953
TWNT: *Theologisches Wörterbuch zum NT*, ed. G. Kittel, 1933 ff.
TLZ: *Theologische Literaturzeitung*
TR: *Theologische Rundschau*

Abbreviations

TQ: *Theologische Quartalschrift*
TU: Texte und Untersuchungen
ZAW: *Zeitschrift für die alttestamentliche Wissenschaft*
ZKG: *Zeitschrift für die Kirchengeschichte*
ZKT: *Zeitschrift für katholische Theologie*
ZNW: *Zeitschrift für die neutestamentliche Wissenschaft*
ZTK: *Zeitschrift für Theologie und Kirche*
ZWT: *Zeitschrift für wissenschaftliche Theologie*

For references to the Qumran texts see the abbreviations in
D. Barthélemy and J. T. Milik, *Qumran Cave I*, 1955, pp. 46 f.
Figures refer to column and line; for the *Damascus Document*
R. H. Charles' chapters and verses (*Apocrypha and Pseudepigrapha*
II, 1913, pp. 799 ff.) are added in square brackets.

11

PART ONE

THE DIVERSITY OF
THE NEW TESTAMENT CHURCH

I

THE AUTHORITY OF SCRIPTURE FOR THE
ORDERING OF THE CHURCH

a. There is no such thing as *the* New Testament Church order.
Even in New Testament times circumstances were very varied,[1]
and it may be vital for the ecumenical dialogue that we should
admit this.[2] Does this mean that every Church order, from the
Quakers' to the Roman Catholics', is equally justified in taking
its stand on the New Testament?[3]

The answer to this question depends on the way in which we
regard the New Testament as an authority. Its content would be
misunderstood if we regarded its Church order as a *law* that we
had to imitate.[4] For even in the New Testament the ordering of

[1]J. K. S. Reid, *The Biblical Doctrine of the Ministry*, 1955, 31, shows that
today this at least is plain, that what is found in the New Testament is open
to more than one interpretation.
[2]Is it really only Free Church scholars who feel impelled to grant this (so
W. D. Davies, *A Normative Pattern of Church Life in the New Testament: Fact
or Fancy?*, London (ca. 1950), 11 f.)? B. H. Streeter, *The Primitive Church*,
1930 (especially 67 ff.), strongly emphasizes the diversity, but the other view
is certainly shown as a reaction in G. Dix, 'The Ministry in the Early Church'
(in *Ap. Min.* 183–303), 290 f.
[3]Cf. Davies, 10 f., but he clearly qualifies this on p. 22. On the problem
see E. Schweizer, 'Die Urchristenheit als ökumenische Gemeinschaft' (*EvTh*
11, 1950/51, 273 ff. = *Die Einheit der Kirche und die Sekten*, 1957, 10 ff.).
[4]It is quite true that an office like that of the Pope, which is burdened with
the duty of political representation and the pomp associated with it, is difficult to imagine if regard is had to the pronouncements of the New Testament;
but it is not on that account fundamentally impossible. *If* a real service of
humility, which could not otherwise be given, had become possible through
it, it might have become an indispensable form in other circumstances (Reid, 3).

the church in Jerusalem is not a law for the church in Corinth; and Luke, who was the first to reflect on the question of the Church's historical development, seems consciously to distinguish between the time when the Church began and the later time, and to see different laws operating in the two periods.[5] Still less can we take our stand on Old Testament laws.[6]

This does not mean, however, that Church order is a matter of indifference, or is to be dictated simply by the existing practical, political, or economic conditions.[7] The New Testament's pronouncements on Church order are to be read as a *gospel*—that is, Church order is to be regarded as a part of the proclamation in which the Church's witness is expressed, as it is in its preaching. There may be times when this kind of proclamation is better heard and regarded by the world than are any words; and for that reason this part of the Church's witness too must be given clearly and plainly.[8] Certainly the church that lacks order does not cease to be a church, but its service is impaired. In the following pages, therefore, we are not concerned only with the purely historical question of events recorded in the New Testament, as if by doing so we should then have in our hands the material for building up a present-day church. We are concerned with the much more difficult question of recognizing in the actual ordering of the New Testament Church, and in what is said about it, the theological

[5]H. Conzelmann, *The Theology of St Luke*, ET 1960, 210 ff.
[6]So T. W. Manson, *The Church's Ministry*, 1948, 12 ff.; Reid, 10 f. against A. M. Farrer, 'The Ministry in the New Testament' (in *Ap. Min.* 113–82). On this cf. 16d.
[7]Cf. O. Linton, *Das Problem der Urkirche in der neueren Forschung,* Diss. Lund 1932, 25 (also 27 f.): according to Lutheran teaching scriptural principles are confined to doctrine; they are extended to constitutional questions only among the Reformed Churches. See especially R. Sohm, *Kirchenrecht* II, 1923, 142, 169; also I, 1892, 593 f., 600, 611 f.: all external order, it is argued, is a matter of indifference from a religious point of view and therefore belongs to the civil authority; and apostasy consists in transferring questions of order from the reigning princes to an ecclesiastical consistory. Further, if order must be deduced from God's word (II 64; I 23 n. 2, 583), it is only a voluntary and loving accommodation for the sake of unity (I 23, 25 n. 2; but cf. also Linton 47 for Harnack's view). But see e.g. Manson 85.
[8]This is strongly emphasized by Karl Barth, *Church Dogmatics* IV/2, ET 1958, 676 ff., especially 682 ff. The struggle of the Confessional Church in Germany has shown that a Church order not in accord with biblical testimony is exposed to any exercise of arbitrary power by the state (cf. H. Gollwitzer, 'Amt und "Führertum" in der Kirche', *EvTh* 1, 1934/5, 79 ff.).

concerns that caused it to take that form and no other. So when we ask about the Church's order, we must also try to understand the Church's essential nature.

b. As regards method, we have to proceed from the texts, and first of all to consider the different witnesses separately. In doing so we ask what statements they make about the nature of the Church, what can be discerned about the actual order, and whether the Church has succeeded in giving a clear testimony of its essential nature in its actual shaping. We can then try in Part Two to set out what is common to the New Testament as a whole.

But in what sense is this counter-question about the New Testament of any value? Has not the position been radically changed since the Reformation period by our present knowledge of the early Jewish sources, and above all those of the early Church? Do not these now make it possible for us to interpret New Testament pronouncements that are in themselves ambiguous?[9] It goes without saying that no scholar can read the New Testament today without constantly keeping before him the Jewish background and the further development of early Christianity; but as regards method he must be quite clear what this means for him.

c. First, he must not, of course, arbitrarily select the documents by which he wants to interpret the New Testament. It might indeed be that gnostic or other heretical documents showed a better understanding of the New Testament than did those recognized as orthodox. It is even more important for the exegete constantly to bear in mind that an idea taken from Judaism, for instance, by Jesus or the Church may be completely recast. That is certainly true of the idea of the 'Messiah'. We shall therefore have to be careful not to jump to the conclusion that if a certain interpretation can be shown to have been current in Judaism and the early Catholic Church, it must therefore have been adopted by Jesus and the early Church. If scholastic thought dominates the theology of the end of the middle ages and Protestant orthodoxy after Luther, that does not mean that it is to decide our interpretation of Luther. If, for instance, in painting, before a great artist there was a bad average style which re-establishes itself in his school after him, it does not follow that the artist and his own

[9]So Dix, *Ap.Min.* 289.

15

pupils painted like that. Nor, on the other hand, can it be objected
that there was such a strong contrast between Church and synagogue that Christianity could not have taken over anything
Jewish after the year 70.[10]

It can be shown how, in that very period between 70 and 135,
the Church was quite open to Jewish influences on many points;[11]
even the history of fasting proves that the Jewish practice was
taken point by point as a model in the Church after New Testament times.[12] The same is true of the doctrine of the inspiration
of Scripture[13] together with the exact fixing of the canon[14] and the
importance of oral tradition,[15] of the Church's pre-existence,[16] of
saints' tombs,[17] of altars,[18] of the works of supererogation of which
the Church can give its members the benefit,[19] of the intercession
of the saints which saves from hell,[20] of taking over the Jewish
Apocrypha and its doctrines in general, and perhaps also of the
idea of purgatory.[21] We may say, too, that the rabbinical succession,
for which Rabbi Judah suffered martyrdom at the beginning of
the second century, when he ordained young candidates, so that
the chain should not be broken,[22] lives on in the apostolic succes-

[10]Dix, *Ap.Min.* 228.

[11]L. Goppelt, *Christentum und Judentum im ersten und zweiten Jahrhundert,* 1954
(summarily 315–18); O. S. Rankin, *Journal of Jewish Studies* I, 1948, 27 ff.;
cf. also G. Delling, *Der Gottesdienst im Neuen Testament,* 1952, 89 f. for practices
connected with worship (also for the introduction of the reading of the Old
Testament, G. Kunze in *Leiturgia* II, 1955, 94 f.; A. Niebergall, 193 f.).

[12] J. Behm, *TWNT* IV 929 ff., 934 f.: regular fasting on Monday and
Thursday for Jews, Wednesday and Friday for Christians; prohibition of
fasting on the Sabbath and Sunday respectively; fasting as a preparation for
revelation or for receiving the Spirit, as a reinforcement of prayer, as a
meritorious act or an atoning sacrifice.

[13]*TWNT* VI 452. 29 ff., cf. e.g. Philo, *Vit. Mos.* II 37; Irenaeus, *Haer.*
III 21. 4.

[14]A. Schlatter, *Geschichte Israels,* 1906, 283; J. Jeremias, *Heiligengräber in
Jesu Umwelt,* 1958, 133 ff.

[15]K. Schubert, *Die Religion des nachbiblischen Judentums,* 1955, 6 ff.

[16]See 19b and n. 582.

[17]Schlatter, *op. cit.* 241 f.; Jeremias, *Heiligengräber* 5, 114 ff., 126 ff. T. W.
Manson, 'Martyrs and Martyrdom', *BJRL* 39, 1957, 482, discusses the
reverse influence in the fourth century.

[18]In the New Testament there is only a heavenly altar; but as early as
Heb. 13.10 we see the longing for the Jewish earthly altar.

[19]W. Bousset and H. Gressmann, *Die Religion des Judentums,* 1926, 198 f.

[20]Schlatter, *op. cit.* 241.

[21]*Vita Adae* 47 (cf. Enoch 22.10); Str-B IV 1043 ff.

[22]H. Bietenhard in *Judaica* 4, 1948, 178 (*Sanhedrin* 14a, *Aboda zara* 8b).

sion.[23] This process is quite natural, and is constantly repeated. The introduction of the ceremony of confirmation in the Protestant churches was greatly influenced by the Roman Catholic confirmation ceremony, although it was at a time when the opposition between them was very strong. Thus, too, whenever Protestantism sees itself confronted by a strong Roman Catholic Church, it likes to magnify the dignity and authority of its own bishops, to show that it is at no disadvantage. In the New Testament the Letter to the Hebrews proves that in the Church of the second or third generation[24] the hankering after the Jewish cult could be very strong, and that the writer has to stress that the Church too has a high priest, an altar, an oblation, and a tabernacle.[25]

The method of simply arguing back from the sources of about the year 200 to New Testament times is therefore inadmissible,[26] even if pre-Christian Jewish examples can be quoted.

d. A second consideration as to method is bound up with the first. There is undoubtedly development. New relationships and new questions demand new solutions. Right up to the parousia, indeed, the Church is constantly developing;[27] and so we cannot simply brush aside as unwarranted the objection that Paul's churches represented a provisional initial stage and only gradually developed into clear and orderly institutions.[28] But when we say that there is development here, it does not mean that the development is constant and along one continuous line. Even in the New Testament it is by no means the case that a time of as yet unregulated enthusiasm is followed by a period of consolidation and order:[29] the Johannine Letters indicate quite a different

[23]Cf. G. Strecker, 'Christentum und Judentum in den ersten beiden Jahrhunderten', *EvTh* 16, 1955/56, 476.

[24]Heb. 2.3; 13.7.

[25]C. F. D. Moule in *JTS* n.s. 1, 1950, 36 ff., though he gives a date just before 70.

[26]Against Dix, *Ap. Min.* 191, it may be remarked that the principle of arguing 'back from the known to the unknown' is highly questionable. Cf. below.

[27]L. Cerfaux, *The Church in the Theology of St Paul*, ET 1959, 185.

[28]F. M. Braun, *Neues Licht auf die Kirche*, 1946, 166.

[29]O. Kuss, in *Theol. Quartalschrift* 135, 1955, 35–37, 52–54, thinks that it was only the postponement of the parousia that showed the need of order, while the special character of the Pauline churches was of a provisional kind, made possible only by the belief that the end was near, and not acceptable later.

development from the Pastoral Letters. Of course we believe that God's Spirit is at work in the Church;[30] but the great question is *where* he is to be seen in it. There are those who assume as a matter of course that the history of the official Church represents this manifestation of the Holy Spirit. Many, however, want to limit this to the first centuries.[31] Others, again, see such manifestation only in the heretics, those figures on the fringe, repeatedly emerging, moved by the Spirit, wanting to shake and rouse the Church, but mostly expelled or condemned.[32] Both assumptions are highly questionable, because God's Spirit does not bind itself either to an official Church or to strange outsiders, but may work or refrain from working here or there. In any case, belief in the living Spirit of God through the centuries does not mean belief in unmistakable progress in one direction.

e. We may clarify this by taking an example. There is no doubt that Graeco-Roman culture is still effective in western countries; but not through a continual increase of understanding. It has been misunderstood and allowed to fall into oblivion, and people have come back to it again. But even where there was a living appreciation of it, there was always a return to the original documents; every epoch had to reinterpret them for itself. The appreciation of Greek culture during the Renaissance or in Goethe's time may help us to interpret it for ourselves, but it is certainly not just a preliminary stage of our comprehension in an unbroken line. What follows in these pages is to be regarded as an attempt to return to the source; we therefore concentrate on the New Testament, while keeping constantly before us the sources outside it.

What has been said will prevent this essay from being misunderstood as if it were a matter of conserving and reproducing the New Testament Church.[33] A return to the source can have meaning only if what we discern there is recast in the light of the present time and situation. There is no question, therefore, of a

[30]Farrer, *Ap. Min.* 178. On the rise of the idea of providence in this connection cf. E. Brunner, *The Misunderstanding of the Church*, ET 1952, p. 41.

[31]R. Williams (Bishop of Leicester) in *Theology* 61, 1958, 161; also Kuss 172 ff.

[32]W. Bauer, *Rechtgläubigkeit und Ketzerei im ältesten Christentum*, 1934; cf. also W. Nigg, *Das Buch der Ketzer*, 1949.

[33]G. Dix, *Jew and Greek*, 1953, 67, says quite rightly that a mere preservation of the 'original' means ossification and heresy.

static Christianity;[34] a mere repetition of New Testament formulae or regulations no more guarantees the Church's authenticity[35] than does the continuance of the same line of development within a given tradition.

Church history will help in the task of interpretation, but it is not a second source of revelation. It is an interpretation, which is to be heard with the greatest respect, but which cannot absolve us from constantly returning to the source; for the history of the Church can just as easily be the history of a constantly renewed understanding as of a constantly repeated misunderstanding. A real church, therefore, can exist only where, having regard to the problems, dangers, and promises of the existing situation, and listening in humility to previous history, we seek enlightenment afresh in the New Testament, not for a legalistic reproduction of its details, but to heed, in the light of the gospel, the message that it contains.

[34]This must certainly be conceded to Farrer, 179. If, therefore, he wants to break off any discussion with one who asserts that the written word of the New Testament is enough, it is to be hoped that he does not do so just yet.

[35]To express this epigrammatically: In the year 40 the primitive Church would have decided for Arius, not for Athanasius; but that does not alter the fact that, in view of the problems that developed up to the fourth century, only Athanasius, and not Arius, held to what the primitive Church actually thought (Dix, *Jew and Greek* 80 f.).

A. Jesus' Conception of the Church

2

JESUS

IT is difficult to be sure of the historical data, because the words and the story of Jesus came through a long tradition till they were fixed in the New Testament writings that have been handed down to us. Thus it is often not possible to say with certainty what can be traced back to Jesus himself, and what has been transformed or re-formed by the Church. Some points, however, are clear.

a. Jesus proclaims the coming of the kingdom of God. This idea denotes—much more strongly than the title 'Messiah'—a dimension of the future and the hereafter. God will cause his kingdom to break into the world without human aid. Indeed for Jesus it is imminent, but clearly in the future.[36] He never speaks of building or advancing the kingdom; men can only receive it, inherit it, obtain it by entreaty, enter into it,[37] for *God* will give it to them to possess.[38] The present time is the time of the call, and so by his words and deeds Jesus calls all Israel, and beyond Israel people of other nations,[39] to the coming kingdom of God.

Thus Jesus lives entirely within the national and religious associations of Israel, and knows no Church separate from all Israel.[40] This is certainly true for the period of his work on earth.

[36]W. G. Kümmel, *Promise and Fulfilment*, ET (SBT 23), 1957, 19 ff. Cf. e.g. Mark 1.15; Matt. 6.10; 10.7; Luke 22.16–18.
[37]K. L. Schmidt, *TWNT* I 588 ff. (ET, *Basileia* (Bible Key Words 7), 1957, 49 ff.). Cf. e.g. Mark 10.15; Matt. 25.34; 6.10; 5.20.
[38]Cf. e.g. Luke 12.32; 22.29. Even Matt. 11.12 does not say that the disciples obtain the kingdom by fighting (so A. Schweitzer, *Geschichte der Leben-Jesu Forschung*,[6] 1951, 404; *The Quest of the Historical Jesus*, 1911, 357), but that its enemies fight against it (cf. Matt. 13.19; G. Schrenk, *TWNT* I 610. 23 ff.; Kümmel, *Promise and Fulfilment*, 122 f.). F. W. Danker, *JBL* 77, 1958, 231 ff., thinks that in this sentence Jesus quoted a dictum of the Pharisees, by which they characterized his message.
[39]J. Jeremias, *Jesus' Promise to the Nations*, ET (SBT 24), 1958.
[40]So too Brunner, *The Misunderstanding of the Church* 19.

There is no sign to distinguish those who gather round Jesus from the other Israelites—neither a rite such as the baptism of John, nor a set creed[41] such as that daily recited by faithful Israel, 'Hear, O Israel. . . .' (Deut. 6.4), nor a given place of assembly like the monastery at Qumran by the Dead Sea, nor a common rule such as the *Manual of Discipline*. Jesus gives his disciples no special name and no special rite (Mark 2.18). There is nothing to distinguish his group of disciples from other people, except the fact that they have been reached by his word,[42] and that therefore they are in a special way, and more than all others, called to suffering, to a life in which they are no longer to try to get their own way, but are to be prepared to go under for other people (Mark 8.34 f.; John 12.25 f.). A few walk with him, but that too is no sign. Many who have heard his call do not walk with him (Mark 5.19 f.; 9.38), and many follow him who do not belong to him at all (Mark 3.7 f.; 5.24; 11.8 f., etc.).

b. Whether Jesus expected such a church to be formed for the time after his death is disputed.[43] The facts are as follows. In the four Gospels the word 'church' occurs only in Matt. 16.18 and 18.17. The second passage is in a context that reflects the experiences of the later Church, and the verse cannot, from its content, have originated with Jesus.[44] Matt. 16.18 can be traced, as has been shown by the long and as yet unfinished discussion,[45] to an

[41]According to the oldest account, Mark 8.27 ff., Peter's confession is not refused, but Jesus does not assent to it either, and corrects it four times in vv. 30, 31, 32 f. and 34 ff.

[42]N. A. Dahl, *Das Volk Gottes*, 1941, 161: 'A separate synagogue without synagogue and *Halacha*, an apocalyptic circle without apocalypse, a messianic movement without zealotism'—a baptismal movement without a baptist! R. Schreiber, *Der neue Bund im Spätjudentum und Urchristentum* (Diss. Tübingen 1955, not printed) thinks on the contrary that Jesus set up a new community with eschatological claims in contrast to the existing people of the covenant (*TLZ* 81, 1956, 696).

[43]On the discussion see W. G. Kümmel, *Kirchenbegriff und Geschichtsbewusstsein in der Urgemeinde und bei Jesus*, 1943; 'Jesus und die Anfänge der Kirche', *ST* 7, 1953, 1 ff.; on the other hand Kuss, *TQS* 135, 43 n. 20. An intermediate position is taken by A. Oepke, *Das neue Gottesvolk*, 1950, 155 ff.: Jesus foresees the break and expects a renewed people of God (but not an obedient 'remnant'). Cf. K. Stendahl, *RGG* III 1302.

[44]Cf. e.g. R. Bultmann, *Die Geschichte der synoptischen Tradition*, 1931, 151, 156, and the 1958 supplement. (ET in preparation.)

[45]Finally collected *ibid.*, supplement 21. However, M. Kaiser, *Die Einheit der Kirchengewalt nach dem Zeugnis des NT und der apostolischen Väter*, 1956, 45, thinks that the authenticity is still unshaken.

Aramaic word—that is, to the Aramaic-speaking Church[46] or to
Jesus himself. The latter certainly seems to me most unlikely, as
it would be a solitary expression, without parallels, handed down
to us only from Matthew, and one, moreover, that can hardly
have been used in the context in which it appears there.[47] Besides,
Jesus' own words about the coming Church must have been
specially important for it, and preserved by it.[48] We should at
least be obliged, with Cullmann, to transfer the saying to Jesus'
last days on earth; but there too there are difficulties about fitting
it in.[49] It might be thought that Jesus was thinking of the future
Church when he instituted the Lord's Supper; but at the most
that means that after his death his group of disciples will meet
again in his name for a common meal, and it does not imply an
exclusive church that separates itself from the rest of Israel.
Indeed, it may be supposed that the actual words instituting the
Supper do not, after all, go back to Jesus.[50]

This would be in accord with the fact that other titles of the
Church, such as 'the people of God', 'Israel', 'the saints',[51] are not
used in the first three Gospels to describe the disciples.[52] 'Israel'
denotes simply all Israel, not just the obedient remnant that listens
to Jesus' call. So we can only point to the words about the 'flock'
(Luke 12.32; Mark 14.27). The second passage, however, is
purely an image for the scattering of the disciples, so that only

[46]H. v. Campenhausen, *Kirchliches Amt und geistliche Vollmacht*, 1953, 19,
142, thinks of Syria, unless indeed it is a tendentious formation of a Peter-
faction.
[47]O. Cullmann, *Peter: Disciple—Apostle—Martyr*, ET 1953, 170 ff.
[48]On the whole discussion cf. v. Campenhausen, 140 ff.
[49]Cullmann, *Peter* 182 ff., which also deals with the discussion. He thinks
of the situation referred to in Luke 22.31 ff. There is, however, as he himself
sees, the difficulty that the wording does not agree; but Matt. 16.17 f. is so
different in tone that there is hardly room for it *beside* Luke 22.32a, 34.
But if we have to choose, the tone of Luke 22.31 ff. fits incomparably better
into the situation then existing.
[50]Cf. Ed. Schweizer, 'Abendmahl im NT', *RGG* I 15. But even if they did,
it is not certain that what was in his mind was a church severing itself from
the rest of Israel. It might also be understood as spiritual food for a band of
messengers on their journey. Cf. n. 84.
[51]I Peter speaks forcefully about the Church, without using the word.
[52]Ἅγιοι does not appear at all. The designation of Jerusalem as ἁγία πόλις
(Matt. 4.5; 27.53) is a Matthean turn of speech. Neither λαός nor ἔθνος
occurs in the synoptic sayings of Jesus, and a passage like Matt. 1.21, which
speaks of 'his (Jesus') people' is a late interpretation that originated in the
Church.

one quotation remains.[53] If the word goes back to Jesus, it describes the group of those who allow themselves to be reached by his word and are chosen for the kingdom of God. In that sense, of course, Jesus will never be without a Church. To that the term 'Son of man' by which he chose to characterize himself may also be relevant.[54] It is also possible that Jesus expected persecution for his disciples, and therefore had in mind that they would attract attention by their preaching or by their solidarity with him, and be regarded as the adherents of a definite movement. But there is nothing in the old tradition to indicate that he had more in mind than that certain of his followers were so exposing themselves, possibly in groups of two or three. Of the Holy Spirit, baptism, and church assemblies Jesus never spoke.

c. What concern lies behind these striking facts? They must be put side by side with another, equally striking: Jesus avoided all the usual titles that might describe the importance of his person.[55] He understood his life as a way of obedience involving lowliness and suffering, in the light of the ways of all righteous men, of all God's servants who had already followed the way of obedience in Israel; but he did not call himself 'God's servant'. He did, indeed, stand in a new and unique relation to God, and prayed to him as 'Father' in a quite remarkable way;[56] but he did not call

[53]For a discussion of these passages cf. F. M. Braun, *Neues Licht auf die Kirche*, 61 ff.

[54]Cf. Ed. Schweizer, 'Der Menschensohn', *ZNW* 50, 1959, 185 ff.; 119 'The Son of Man', *JBL* 79, 1960, 119 ff. The interpretation of F. Kattenbusch, 'Der Quellort der Kirchenidee', *Festgabe für A. Harnack*, 1921, 143 ff., has its roots here. The corporate interpretation of the idea 'Son of man' has been particularly stressed by T. W. Manson (cf. A. J. B. Higgins in *NT Essays: Studies in Memory of T. W. Manson*, 1959, 119 ff.). But on the other hand see Kümmel, *Kirchenbegriff* 33 f. And O. Cullmann, *The Christology of the New Testament*, ET, 1959, 155 f., rightly emphasizes that such an interpretation is at best faintly echoed in Jesus' use of the term.

[55]Cullmann, *Christology* 117 ff., has particularly emphasized this for the title 'Christ'. In any case, Jesus never expressly said that he was 'God's servant', even if some scholars (e.g. Cullmann, *Christology* 60 ff.) think that he consciously regarded himself as such. The title 'Son of God' he certainly used very seldom (*ibid.* 275 ff.); in fact in my opinion he avoided it entirely. All this is not to say that Jesus did *not* regard himself as Christ, servant of God, and Son of God; but it probably does mean that he consciously refused to have his activity classified under the usual titles (on this see especially Cullmann, *Christology* 326; Schweizer, *Union Seminary Quarterly Review* 15, 281 ff.).

[56]J. Jeremias, *TLZ* 79, 1954, 213 f. and in *Synoptische Studien* (für A. Wikenhauser), 1953, 86 ff.

himself the 'Son of God'. He claimed to be more than all the
kings and prophets, more indeed than the Baptist, the man who
marked the end of the old order; but he did not call himself
'Messiah'. When he spoke of himself as the 'Son of man' (though
whether he did so is disputed),[57] he used an expression that had
not then become firmly established and was therefore open to
different interpretations, and so he did not exempt his audience
from making a considered decision. Did he mean by it, according
to the Aramaic usage of the term, simply that he was some poor
'man' or other? Did he mean that figure, exalted to the presence
of God, of whom Dan. 7.13 f. speaks? And is he himself the 'Son
of man', or, as might be supposed from some passages (Mark
8.38; 14.62), is it someone else? Jesus calls on men to accept his
words and works, to repent, and to allow God to come back into
their lives. Who Jesus is can therefore be discerned only by those
who follow him, whether in an outwardly visible community or
without it in obedience to his word.

Jesus therefore wishes to keep men from deceiving themselves
into thinking that they can avoid meeting him by simply adopting
a formula, a name, a doctrine, or a method. He does not merely
seek reforms, however radical; and so he opposes neither the
priesthood nor the sacrificial cult nor the organization of the
Sanhedrin. He therefore founds no new Church; for there is no
salvation even by entering a religious society, however radically
transformed. Even the best reform of Church order still does not
achieve conversion to God. Israel must meet God in the life and
work of Jesus; all else can follow only from that.

d. But here we find a second concern: Jesus lays claim to all
Israel. No one is written off and thereby enabled in some degree
to make his mind easy by feeling that he is not among those who
are called. All the barriers erected by others are torn down—
barriers behind which the tax-collectors, prostitutes, lepers, and
in general those unversed in the law had gradually become used
to leading an irreligious life and not belonging to the pious elect.
Even the Roman centurion and the Canaanite woman are called.

---

[57]Ph. Vielhauer in *Festschrift für G. Dehn*, 1955, 51 ff., and H. Conzelmann
in *ZTK* 54, 1957, 277 ff., are of the opinion that the idea was produced by the
Church; for a different view see Cullmann, *Christology* 155; Schweizer, *ZNW*
50, 1959, 185 ff., *JBL* 79, 1960, 119 ff.

So the band of disciples remains a fully open circle; wherever the disciples want to close it, and to have it laid down that so-and-so does not belong to them, they are sharply rebuked (Mark 9.38–40; 10.13–16).[58]

e. We shall have to ask whether this open circle necessarily holds good only for the period before Easter, and is replaced by a community of a different category. But if any continuity at all exists between the group of disciples and the post-Easter Church,[59] then at least these two concerns must be taken over into the ordering of the Church after Easter. The Church must be kept from the heresy that adherence to a religious community, a cult, an orthodox creed or a certain way of living, is in itself enough for salvation, without the need for everyone to have that new and decisive meeting with the living God, who calls him in the words and work of Jesus. And the Church must never forget to regard itself as a band of messengers for all people, must never 'write off' any areas. If it is correct at all—the question will have to be asked later—for the 'Church' and the 'world' to become separated visibly and terminologically, then at least something of the conception of Jesus' disciples, who live, without any walls, face to face with the 'world', will have to be kept.[60]

f. Yet that is to see only one side of the matter, for the kingdom of God preached by Jesus is not simply something that may be viewed from a distance. The apocalyptic writer can observe its coming as if it were a film being run off before his eyes; but that is made impossible for anyone who listens to Jesus. In contrast to all Jewish apocalyptic writing, not only is there no detailed description of the future,[61] but above all the intervening length of

[58]Another question is that of God's time. For Jesus too there is a time for Israel and a time for the nations. Although I do not think that words such as Matt. 10.5 f., 23 are authentic words of Jesus, passages like Matt. 8.11, put beside the fact of his activity in Palestine, point in that direction. But waiting for God's time does not mean that people are to be shut off from salvation—Jesus' attitude to the Gentiles shows that too.

[59]It is, of course, clear that the evangelists take questions of the post-Easter Church straight back into the circle of the disciples, and are of the opinion that the order that Jesus lays down for that circle is likewise valid as a matter of course for the Church of their time (for Luke, however, see 1a).

[60]This is also stressed by L. Simon in *Foi et Vie* 55, 1957, 394 f., 401 f., and even more strongly by H. D. Wendland in *Gottesdienstliche Gemeinde und weltliche Christenheit*, 1958, 8.

[61]This has been worked out especially by Kümmel, *Promise and Fulfilment* 88 ff.

time can no longer be calculated. This not only means a further drastic change of Jewish expectations in the sense that Jesus has shortened the intervening time still more; it means that anyone who is reached by Jesus' call can no longer meditate at all on how short or how long that interval is likely to be—there is no room for any expectation, either of a short wait or of a long one. For indeed, in Jesus' call the coming kingdom of God presses on the hearer so hard that it demands his answer *now*. In the 'Now' of the call and in the hearer's 'Yes' or 'No' is contained the judgment to which the Son of man will testify at the Last Judgment and which God will pronounce (Mark 8.38; Matt. 10.32 f.; Luke 12.8 f.).[62] So the future kingdom of God already comes upon the hearers in the very moment when they see and hear (Luke 11.20; 17.20 f.). 'Blessed are the eyes which see what you see!' (Luke 10.23 f.). The signs of the time are no longer all manner of events still to be speculated upon and calculated. Jesus himself in all his works is *the* sign (Luke 11.29–32; 12.54–56). Already the fall and rising again are taking place, judgment and mercy are present (Luke 2.34; Matt. 10.13 f.), and on those who shut their eyes to such a sign a judgment is already being passed that will one day prove more terrible than that passed on Sodom and Gomorrah (Matt. 10.15; 11.20–24; 12.41 f.).

That the final decisions are being taken here is illustrated by the fact that men leave not only fishing-boats and tax-collector's table, but even home and family, so as to follow Jesus. To be sure, there is no set rule—one is called away from his family and occupation, another is sent back to them (Mark 1.16 ff.; 5.19); one has to give up his wealth, another has to use it in service (Mark 10.21; Luke 19.8; cf. 10.38). Such a surrender of possessions is therefore not an ascetic achievement that could guarantee entrance into God's kingdom, nor is it an escape out of the world into a special sanctified sphere. On the contrary, Jesus again and again puts people among the questions and decisions of everyday life, which arise in marriage and family and in intercourse with one's neighbour.[63] But undoubtedly decisions are made that have concrete

---

[62]B. S. Easton, *Early Christianity*, 1955, 124 ff., who rightly stresses that Jesus founds no Church, refers to the 'present kingdom of God'. This, however, is open to misunderstanding.

[63]Cf. G. Bornkamm, *Jesus of Nazareth*, ET 1960, 96 ff., particularly 98 f. and 109.

results. The stories of the disciples' call may have been transformed later into ideal scenes; and the conversation with the rich man, in which following seems more important than fulfilling all the commandments, is certainly no verbatim report.[64] Yet there is no doubt that Jesus did call disciples to follow him, and that in a general way he demanded an obedience that in certain circumstances involves the sacrifice of family, possessions, and even life itself.[65]

g. Thus life is shaped in the light of the coming kingdom; but it is shaped in such a way that no law, no yardstick that man can apply, has the authority or the ability to measure it. In *God's* judgment, indeed, the city that rejected Jesus' call is no longer the same city as before. Jesus' beatitudes and woes effect a separation; but this is not plain for everyone to see. Even though the band of disciples and the kingdom of God are clearly related, they are just as clearly distinct. There is nothing whatever to suggest that Jesus sees in the circle of disciples anything in the nature of an advance model of the coming kingdom; they have been promised entrance into the future glory, but that glory is not yet represented among them.[66] What we can grasp historically, then, beside the fact that the disciples have left home, occupation, and family, is really only incomprehension, lack of faith, betrayal, and denial.[67] Again it must be asked what kind of concern there is behind this side of Jesus' work, which repeatedly produces such decisions and allows separations to be seen as signs, although no one can properly separate the saved and the lost, and exclaim, 'Lo, here . . . or there'.

h. If it is true, as has been said above, that there is at least continuity between the disciples and the post-Easter Church, then a Church would be unthinkable in which it was not clear that what finally matters is assent to or rejection of Jesus' deeds

[64]But cf. W. Zimmerli, *EvTh* 19, 1959, 97.
[65]The word ἀκολουθεῖν (1) is firmly fixed in tradition, and (2) acquired a completely new content as opposed to Hellenism, the Old Testament, and later Judaism (E. Schweizer, *Erniedrigung und Erhöhung bei Jesus und seinen Nachfolgern*, 1955, 8; ET, *Lordship and Discipleship*, [SBT 28], 1960, 12).
[66]Kümmel, *Kirchenbegriff* 28–30; *Jesus* 5–7.
[67]Does this really just cease with Easter, because it was only from then on that they belonged to the redeemed (J. Coutts, *JTS* n.s. 8, 1957, 111 ff.)? *Luke* is certainly concerned to make the period of the apostles appear as unobjectionable as possible; but we still have to remember Gal. 2.11 ff.

and words. Freedom from a sense of obligation has no place in the Church; and although this assent or rejection cannot be measured by human beings, it will prove to be a very real factor in practical behaviour, above all in living together with other people.

We may now sum up both aspects: a Church that is to be the successor of the group of disciples must certainly not succumb to the temptation to mark itself off, on account of any special qualities that can be tested, measured, or weighed by men, as holy, in contrast to those who do not display such qualities. But, as a group to which Jesus' words and deeds have struck home, it will live as a new creation. No one, for instance, not even the Church itself, will be able to measure the intensity of its love; but it *will* love. No one, not even the Church itself, will be able to define its boundaries; but that boundary *will* exist.

i. Before we go any further, we have to examine whether the group of Jesus' disciples is in any way the precursor of the later Church, and not simply of the office-bearers in it. Here too we find that a good deal is obscure; we know too little of how those who visibly followed Jesus stood in relation to those who accepted his call without walking with him. Both ways were obviously possible. This much, however, is clear: it is natural that those who accompanied Jesus played a part in the later Church. But of that group of disciples as a school for Church leaders there was certainly never any thought.[68] That is suggested by the fact that in the older strata of the Jesus-tradition the later Church and its order and doctrine do not appear at all[69]—that it is in fact quite open to question whether the twelve were ever leaders of the primitive Church.[70]

k. That Jesus gathered twelve disciples round him, besides a much bigger circle that followed him at least temporarily, is probably historical;[71] but they were not 'apostles';[72] they were

[68]In T. W. Manson's excellent little book *Ministry and Priesthood*, 1958, 18 f., both are stressed: Jesus teaches his disciples simply by their being in his company. That will still be important for the later Church. But in that company Jesus is not only the teacher but also the teaching.
[69]See 2a.
[70]v. Campenhausen 15 f.; see 3n.
[71]It may be said against J. Weiss, *The History of Primitive Christianity*, ET 1937, 47 f., that a statement quoted by Paul (I Cor. 15.5, regarded by Weiss,

those who would sit on twelve thrones in the coming kingdom of God (Luke 22.30).[73] It is possible that Jesus sent them out while he was working on earth,[74] and that the saying about 'fishers of men' did originate with Jesus.[75] But the same is also true of others outside that circle. Many became witnesses of his works and messengers of his call, with or without any direct summons to that effect. How could a distinction be drawn between Jesus' messengers and his usual followers? The twelve, like others, are messengers to non-believing Israel. They never appear as the teachers of a Church of believers in process of formation;[76] they never

24, as a gloss) gives 'the twelve' as witnesses of the resurrection. If that were a pre-dating of their status in the later Church, it is hardly imaginable that Judas would have been included in their number (cf. also Kümmel, *Kirchenbegriff* 30 f.). Moreover, there is a broad tradition about the twelve as they accompanied Jesus, whereas they do not seem to have played any part in the direction of the Church in Jerusalem (see 3n).

[72]See 24a, 26d. The ἐξουσία given to them lives on in the Pauline χάρισμα (O. Michel in *Deutsche Theologie* 9, 1942, 135, n. 4).

[73]In this form probably earlier than Matt. 19.28 (H. Schürmann, *Jesu Abschiedsrede Lk. 22.21–38*, 1957, 51 ff.). Even in Acts we can hear echoes of the original eschatological significance of the apostles. Would that be the reason why the place of Judas, who had lost that throne in the kingdom of God, was filled (Acts 1.15 ff., and see J. Renié, *RB* 55, 1948, 43 ff.; P. Gaechter, *ZKT* 71, 1949, 318 ff.), but not that of James the son of Zebedee (Acts 12.2; C. T. Craig, *The One Church in the Light of the NT*, 1951, 61)? For the eschatological significance of the apostolate for Paul, cf. II Cor. 11.2 (M. Goguel in *Min. and Sacr.* 308), and especially O. Cullmann, 'Eschatology and Missions in the NT' in *Background* 409 ff. His exposition of II Thess. 2.6 f. certainly seems to me to break down on I Thess. 4.17 (cf. n. 288): if Paul expects the parousia, he cannot be already 'caught up' before then.

[74]See the discussion of this question in V. Taylor, *The Gospel according to St Mark*, 1952, 302 f.; the same view is taken by C. K. Barrett, 'The Apostles in and after the NT', in *Svensk Exegetisk Årsbok* 21, 1956, 46.

[75]Cf. C. W. F. Smith in *Harvard Theol. Rev.* 52, 1959, 187 ff. The fact that they are commissioning words in Mark and Q (the form of this supposed tradition common to Matthew and Luke will not be discussed here), as well as in the material peculiar to Matthew and Luke, is certainly no final proof, as of course such words were urgent for the Church and its missionary task. Later they were at least developed and added to. Nevertheless some of them bear the character peculiar to Jesus' works of final urgency in the face of the God who is coming and no longer waiting.

[76]As an instance, if any, we might think of Luke 22.32. But in the first place the words are addressed only to Peter, and give him a special place among his 'brethren'—probably the other eleven (or ten). Secondly, it is reported only by Luke, and can scarcely go back to Jesus.

introduce others to the secrets of Jesus' doctrine; they never have to provide for order and discipline among those who are obedient to him.[77] Jesus certainly on occasion says things to the twelve, or to a few of his intimates among them, that he does not say to the crowd. There is no need to doubt that this happened[78]—it would be difficult to imagine that it never happened. Even if it occurred to Jesus that such sayings would some day be passed on by the disciples, he did not envisage this otherwise than as an urgent call to repentance, addressed to a people that would not as yet let itself be called. Even the Church, which has now long been living in a catechetical tradition, and knows that it is tied to the mediating of its message by the testimony of the apostles, does not describe the twelve as the bearers of Jesus' teaching to the people, or his few intimates as its bearers to the wider circle of the twelve.

Nor can we see what would have been gained if it could be shown that Jesus had consciously schooled the twelve as the guardians of tradition for a later Church.[79] For in that case he would simply sink to the level of a rabbi who wants to go on teaching his doctrine through his pupils. In that case, too, it would certainly be found that that subsequent teaching would succumb to historical laws, and would be bound in the course of its transmission through its chain of guardians to lose something of its original character and become weaker and weaker as time went on.[80] Even, therefore, if Jesus had thought of further activity

[77]Are we to think of Mark 6.35 ff. (and parallels)? But nothing is demanded of the disciples, except to hand on the bread. Luke (9.14) goes only a little further, and John (6.10, 12 f.) follows him the same way. But there too the disciples are drawn after the pattern of later deacons (or possibly as a pre-figuration of the later missionaries to the Gentiles: G. H. Boobyer in *SJT* 6, 1953, 77 ff.). In any case it gives no picture for Jesus' time. Still less is to be got from Mark 10.13 (*pace* E. Lohmeyer, *Das Evangelium des Markus*, 1937, 203).

[78]It is certainly not *merely* a mirror of the later catechetical instruction (for this cf. G. Schille, *NTS* 4, 1957/8, 13 ff.).

[79]So H. Riesenfeld, *The Gospel Tradition and its Beginnings*, 1957, 16 ff.; Easton 127 is much more guarded.

[80]Among Jesus' sayings there is no teaching about his dying and being raised from the dead, even if a few short references to them may be authentic; and there is hardly anything about the coming Church, baptism, and the Holy Spirit. The tradition spreads demonstrably and in abundant measure from one Gospel to another, and even from I Cor. 15.5 ff. to the beginnings of our Gospels. Isolated sayings, or even parables, of Jesus are transformed

by his disciples on these lines in a Church that developed later, the group of the twelve during his earthly life presents a picture not of a body of leaders, but of a few men who are trying to live with this Jesus and to go to meet the coming kingdom. If Jesus saw in them the people who would one day play a special part in that kingdom, it thereby becomes clear at once how he makes his claim to all Israel—the twelve then make his call to the people of the biblical twelve tribes apparent. That would certainly be the Israel of the last days, for the historical twelve tribes had long since disappeared. But it is this Israel of the last days only by accepting Jesus' call and experiencing the breaking in of the kingdom, not by establishing itself under the leadership of the twelve as a Church separate from the rest of Israel; thus in that circle of disciples there can be no self-sufficiency. It is the circle of those who now know about the coming kingdom and are living in its light, and for that very reason understand that they are messengers who have to call all Israel to repentance and will one day judge it in the future kingdom.

l. Finally we have to ask whether anything of the essential character of this group of disciples, which represents on the one hand the community of those who have been genuinely reached by Jesus' words and works, and on the other hand the band of messengers to 'the many', is expressed in the ordering of its life. Here, of course, we must be particularly cautious, as the important part that such order was bound to play in the later Church could easily lead to the production of sayings purporting to be the Lord's. We can therefore only touch here on a few fundamental points.

The negative conclusions are clear. The distinction between priests and laity plays no part at all;[81] in fact, to put it even more explicitly: God's grace is shown in the very fact that Jesus calls men to service, particularly those whose capacity for it was denied

---

or put into quite different contexts (J. Jeremias, *The Parables of Jesus*, ET 1954, 21 ff.). All this shows an essentially different picture from the rabbinic tradition.

[81]Even if the late tradition that John the son of Zebedee was a priest (see the passages collected by E. Stauffer, *New Testament Theology*, ET 1955, n. 68) were correct, there would not be the least evidence in the New Testament that the fact was of any consequence.

by the Pharisees (Mark 2.14).[82] Thus, on principle, everyone is engaged in service, and there is no point in distinguishing between ordinary believers and those called to service; how could one do so in a band of people whose fundamental service is readiness for suffering and self-sacrifice?

Nor, therefore, is there any hierarchy among Jesus' disciples. Indeed, such an idea is turned into its paradoxical opposite: 'Whoever would be great among you must be your servant, and whoever would be first among you must be your slave.'[83] It cannot be otherwise, for Jesus himself is among them 'as one who serves'.[84] This, however, hardly means that we can find here a polemic against the Jewish hierarchy. It is true that the ambition of the scribes, as of the Gentile rulers, is castigated (Mark 10.42; 12.38 f.; Luke 11.43), and the disciples are to avoid the title 'rabbi' among themselves (Matt. 23.8).[85] But the Jewish order as such is nowhere attacked, neither the priesthood nor the elders nor the Sanhedrin; on the contrary, it seems that Jesus expressly recognized the priesthood.[86] In both respects Jesus' band of disciples differs from the community of Qumran, which marks itself off sharply from the Jerusalem priesthood, and has a strictly ordered hierarchy in which the priest is entitled to certain definite privileges.[87] Both these differences are only the expression of what

[82]This is also reflected in sayings such as Mark 10.24, 26, 32; Luke 5.8–10; Matt. 10.8; cf. G. Bertram, *TWNT* III 5 f.
[83]There are six variations of this saying; see n. 645.
[84]Luke 22.27. The saying is difficult to judge. It interrupts the original continuity from v. 18 to v. 28, but it is hardly intelligible except in the concrete situation of meals taken in common by Jesus and his disciples. It seems, with vv. 15–18 and 28–30, to belong to a stratum in which the Last Supper was regarded only from this point of view of service by Jesus and of the eschatological promise (as it is then unfolded in John 13 and 14–16 in a characteristically Johannine way); cf. Schweizer, *RGG* I 15. Was it handed down independently as a saying of our Lord? For the whole subject cf. Schürmann, *Jesu Abschiedsrede* 79 ff.
[85]This last saying at least is a product of the Church, and already assumes the existence of Christian rabbis (see 4g).
[86]Mark 1.44; Luke 17.14. Of course we must allow for the fact that polemical words of Jesus against Judaism may have been suppressed at a time when the Church was at pains to regard itself as a group within Israel. But in first place, the words against the Pharisees did not disappear, but were even developed further, and secondly, under the pressure of persecution (Gal. 1.23; I Thess. 2.16 f.; Acts 8.1 ff.; 12.1 ff.) there was also the opposite tendency, to give them prominence.
[87]See nn. 640 and 644.

has been said above: Jesus is not concerned merely with a reform of Judaism.

m. On the other hand, however, Jesus' work is not an endorsement and justification of the order of Judaism. A band of Galileans leaves its homeland. They do not move out of Judaism, either into a monastery by the Dead Sea or to Damascus. They go to Jerusalem, of all places, not to worship in the temple, but rather to cause trouble in it,[88] not to fit into the priestly or pharisaic order, but rather to allow themselves to be destroyed by it. The end of the journey is the cross on which Jesus is executed— outwardly the victory of priesthood and pharisaism, but in fact the end of both. For in the cross it can be seen that God takes a different and very surprising way. Later on, Paul will reflect on why the cross is the end of all pharisaic legal righteousness, and the Letter to the Hebrews on why it is the end of all priestly sacrificial offering. For the present only one thing is obvious: what matters is either pharisaic obedience to the law and priestly order, whose victory is seen by all the world in Jesus' death, or Jesus, among whose disciples the chief can only be the servant of all. On Good Friday all the world, not excluding Jesus' disciples, chose the first alternative. It was clear that the disciples, in their impotence and poverty, without the old order of Pharisees and priests, law and sacrifice, and without a new order such as that set up by the people of Qumran, were bound to go under and go to pieces. Such idealism is not apt for life in this world. But Jesus deliberately and publicly took that very way. He did everything to attain no success, no growth, and no fortifying of the Church, but to allow himself and his followers to be broken in pieces—for the world.[89]

[88]The cleansing of the temple not only demands a reform of the temple service, but touches its very basis (cf. Luke 19.44 before 45 f.). The saying about the destruction of the temple (Mark 13.2; Luke 13.35)—a saying that is qualified in various ways in the tradition (Mark 14.57 f.; Matt. 26.61; John 2.21)—probably goes back to Jesus too, even if we cannot now be certain of its original form.
[89]See 23d.

B. The Primitive Community's Conception of the Church, and the Development of this Conception

3

THE PRIMITIVE CHURCH IN JERUSALEM

a. But Jesus appeared to his disciples.[90] This made it clear that God had decided in his favour—had given judgment for him, not for his opponents (and his faint-hearted disciples). There is much to be said for the view that this implied from the very beginning knowledge of the enthronement of the exalted Jesus as Lord of the Church.[91] How soon this faith took on definite forms and was expressed in a definite terminology is difficult to say, because we know nothing, comparatively speaking, of the earliest period of the primitive Church.[92] Two facts, however, are established that reveal two sides of this faith.

b. One fact is that the primitive Church continued in its Jewish national and religious associations—this means that it regarded as valid the priesthood, the sacrificial system, the synagogue services, and the law.[93] The kingdom of God remained

[90]The eleven were certainly among these. We do not know whether, e.g., the 'more than five hundred' of I Cor. 15.6 were already followers of Jesus before his death. The example of the Lord's brother James (I Cor. 15.7) shows that the appearance was also seen by one who previously, according to everything that we know, had stood completely aloof (Mark 3.21, 31 ff.).

[91]E. Schweizer, *Erniedrigung* 93 ff.; *Lordship* 32 ff.; *ZNW* 50, 1959, 202 ff.

[92]In spite of Bo Reicke's faith in the value of Acts as a source (*Glaube und Leben der Urgemeinde*, 1957, 5 ff.), it must be said that Acts is very incomplete, and is often constructed in accordance with a picture of its own. It is true that where we can check it (Acts 11.30; 15.1 ff.; Gal. 2.1 ff., etc.) we sometimes find that details are transmitted quite correctly, but on the other hand there are serious discrepancies on important points. Luke, like the other evangelists, can now tell us hardly anything about the Easter events (I Cor. 15.5 ff.), only a few anecdotes about the long stay in Ephesus, and nothing about the intervening journey to Corinth.

[93]Acts' picture is confirmed here by such passages as Matt. 5.23; 23.2 f.; 24.20, and by the fact that a general damning of the Church by Judaism does not occur till comparatively late. Thus it is certain that at least part of the primitive Church lived on as a group within Israel. Cf. W. L. Knox, *St Paul and the Church of Jerusalem*, 1925, 1–4; G. Harder in *TLZ* 85, 1960, 153 f.

in the future, and it was not for them to bring it in by reforms. All Israel, not just one severed group, was called to God's kingdom. Thus continuity between Israel and the open circle of Jesus' disciples was preserved; they were still a band of messengers.

We do not know how soon the Church began to assume terms relating to its own special character; but even at a later stage these still indicate that the primitive Church, in clear contrast to the Qumran group,[94] to Philo, and to the Mishnah,[95] still regarded itself as Israel, never as a religious association that might become a separate group alongside others.[96] Even the solution that presented itself to the Qumran group, to regard itself as the nucleus

[94]*ēdāh* in 1QM, 1QSa, 1QSb denotes almost exclusively the Israelite national community (so also in 1Q22 1 f., *Damasc.* 7.20 [Charles, *Apoc. and Pseudepig.*, 9.9]); but usually in the *Damascus Document* the community of the Essenes is meant (on this see L. Rost, *Die Vorstufen von Kirche und Synagoge im Alten Testament*, 1938, 140; Dahl, *Das Volk Gottes* 129 ff.). *ēdāh* often defines the circle or the community, e.g. the eschatological band of the elect, which the teacher of righteousness will build for God (4QpPs 37 2.16; 4QpIs^d 1.3, etc.). *Sōd*, which becomes a religious idea only by apposition, is often parallel to *ēdāh* in that sense (e.g. 1QS 11.7 ff.). Besides that there is *ēṣāh* (1QS 2.23, 25; 8.19, 21; 1QM 3.4; 1QH 6.5; *Damasc.* 20.25 [9.48B]) and *yaḥad* (very frequently in 1QS; also 1QpHab 12.4; 4QPatr Bless 1.5; 4QpIs^d 1.2; 1Q14 10.8 as a designation of the Essene community; 1QM 14.4; 1QH 3.22 f.; 11.14; fragm. 10.6 in the sense of 'community'). *qāhāl* on the other hand occurs only with the meaning 'assembly, summons', and even in that sense not often (for the congregation at divine service 1Q 29 5-7.3; *Damasc.* 7.17; 12.6 [9.7; 14.6]). Cf. O. Betz in *ZNW* 48, 1957, 57 f.; H. N. Richardson, *JBL* 76, 1957, 108 ff. It designates, however, in 1QSa the eschatological Israel of the Messianic time; cf. Stendahl, *RGG* III 1928.

For the collation of the evidence in concordance form (in completion of my own notes) I am indebted to Dr Eiss, *Assistent* to Professor K. G. Kuhn in Heidelberg. As Professor Kuhn's Concordance of the Qumran text is not yet available, I am extremely grateful for his generous help.

[95]Here *qāhāl*/ἐκκλησία is used only for the past time of salvation; for the present time Philo adopts the terminology of the Greek societies, the Mishnah *ṣibbūr* (Rost 145 ff.; Dahl 67).

[96]συναγωγή, which goes back to *ēdāh*, which became important after the exile (Rost 32 f., 59, 133 ff.; Dahl 67 ff.) appears only in James 2.2 (cf. Heb. 10.25), where, however, it means 'assembly'. ἐκκλησία, like οἱ ἄγιοι, οἱ ἐκλεκτοί, and of course all such designations as 'Israel' or 'the people of God', means the community elected as part of God's plan of salvation, the community defined in the Old Testament as *qāhāl Yahweh*, 'Yahweh's levy' or similar terms (cf. also O. Michel, *Das Zeugnis des NT von der Gemeinde*, 1941, 5 ff.). It is, however, unlikely that the title 'the saints' once denoted the church of Jerusalem or Jewish Christianity together with the apostles in contrast to the Gentile Christians (to which interpretation Cerfaux 100 returns), although it can hardly be doubted that the primitive church in

round which the rest of Israel would one day gather at the time of salvation, was not adequate.[97] Both are impossible for the primitive Church. It cannot, as a better nucleus with a higher status, separate itself from the 'fringe members';[98] nor can it still regard as the real Israel, even for the coming time of salvation, the Israel that rejected Jesus and his call to repentance. That is far more decisive than certain parallels that exist as a matter of course between two religious groups living at the same time in the same district and both stemming from the Old Testament and from Judaism.[99]

c. The second fact is that the primitive Church settled in Jerusalem.[100] That is most surprising, especially if, as still seems to

---

Jerusalem so called itself, and that the name was perhaps only gradually taken over by others, even though that happened before Paul (Kümmel, *Kirchenbegriff* 16). The Church, therefore, emphatically claims to represent nothing other than all Israel. See 23a.

[97]See L. Rost, *TLZ* 82, 1957, 668 ff. on the conception of 1QSa; cf. 1QH 40. 8.

[98]The decisive difference as opposed to Qumran (see n. 640) is that Jesus does not adopt the idea of a faithful, pious 'remnant' (J. Jeremias, *ExpT* 70, 1958, 68 f.; cf. Oepke, *Das neue Gottesvolk* 165), but promises the kingdom of God to tax-collectors and prostitutes, children, and chance hearers (Mark 2.14 ff., slightly corrected by Luke 5.32; Luke 7.44, frequently softened in exegesis: E. Klostermann, *Das Lukasevangelium*, 1929, 94; Mark 10.14, misunderstood in Herm. *Sim.* IX 29.1; Mark 3.34, already corrected in Mark 3.35, but also Matt. 12.49, altered even more in Luke 8.21).

[99]For this cf. e.g. S. E. Johnson, *ZAW* 66, 1954, 107 ff.; poverty is highly valued (but see n. 107); God's Spirit is important (but it is only in Jesus' Church that we hear of glossolalia and the like); twelve laymen (hardly nine, as M. Weise, *ZNW* 49, 1958, 120 n. 11 thinks) and three priests lead the community (but the three priests are wanting in the New Testament, and the twelve 'laymen' are chosen by Jesus as rulers for the eschatological future); priests enter the new group (but in the primitive Church they play no part at all); the 'many' appear in the assembly (but in Qumran it is clear that they are arranged according to their rank and subordinated to the hierarchy); the temple cult is repudiated (but in Qumran they believe in the Old Testament sacrifices, and in the primitive Church the cult is not repudiated, although it is no longer fundamental). See further 24i.

[100]It remains very unlikely that two churches existed from the beginning, one in Jerusalem and one in Galilee (E. Lohmeyer, *Galiläa und Jerusalem*, 1936, 100 f.; cf. e.g. Dahl 188 ff.; Oepke 183 ff., both of whom assume only various nuances within the Church). The theological differences quoted by Lohmeyer appear in combination even in Judaism ('Son of man' and 'Messiah' in Enoch) or can be traced to the various groups in Jerusalem (see 3h; n. 126). Above all, Paul knows only one Church (Gal. 1.18; 2.1 ff.). It might

me probable, the disciples retreated to Galilee after Jesus' arrest.[101] But even if that had not been the case, one would have expected the disciples to return to their families and perhaps work as missionaries in Galilee, for there too they could have worked in continuity with God's previous acts for the salvation of Israel.[102] Nor is a pilgrimage to the Jewish feast of Pentecost in Jerusalem an adequate explanation.[103] Even if that took place, at least the disciples' remaining there would necessarily be based theologically on the revelation of the Spirit.

In that change of locality the fact that we have already seen appears again, viz., that the primitive Church claims, like the disciples of the earthly Jesus, to be Israel—nothing else. It will not let itself be pushed away into the position of a Galilean sect. There the disciples would presumably have remained unmolested, as well as finding their homes and occupations again. But here the other side of the matter also becomes clear: the primitive Church learns more and more to realize that it is the true Israel. Jerusalem and the temple 'belong' to it. It knows, indeed, that

be thought that during the Jewish war the Church moved to Galilee as the land of the parousia (W. Marxsen, *Der Evangelist Markus*, 1956, 112 ff.); but there is contrary evidence, not only in the account of its withdrawal to Pella, but also in the analysis of Mark 13 (H. Conzelmann, *ZNW* 50, 1959, 210 ff.) and the references to the resurrection (not the parousia).

[101]Otherwise in H. v. Campenhausen, *Der Ablauf der Ostereignisse und das leere Grab*, *SAH* 1952, No. 4, 35; H. Conzelmann, *RGG* I, 699. Otherwise too in Marxsen 73 ff., who regards Mark 16.7 as a reference to the parousia which was expected in Mark's time to take place in Galilee. It was only thus that Matthew would have concluded that the appearances were in Galilee. Independently of that, however, John 21.1 ff. and the *Gospel of Peter* 59 f. show traditions of appearances in Galilee. The usual view, that the disciples went back to Galilee and that the appearances took place there, is supported by the fact that the tradition of the empty grave is in no way linked with it. That tradition, however, is probably very old, not only because of the conventional reference to the 'third day' (on which therefore something must have happened), but above all because the original version obviously knew of only one woman as a witness (thus John 20.1; but in the Synoptists too Mary Magdalene is the only one whose name is certain). That would hardly be possible in the case of legends created later. No one was there to make any further report or check, as the disciples were then already on the way to Galilee, so this was not supplemented before Luke 24.24 and John 20.2 ff.
[102]It is by this that Reicke 15 f. explains the return to Jerusalem.
[103]G. Kretschmar, *ZKG* 66, 1955, 251 ff.

there is behind it an act of God which is greater than the deliverance out of Egypt, even though that deliverance called Israel into life. If, therefore, the continuance in the temple and synagogue shows that the Church is no revolutionary party, but wants to go on being Israel, then its settling in Jerusalem shows that it regards itself as the new Israel, the Israel of the last days.

d. In both ways it proves at first to be a continuation of Jesus' group of disciples. With a certain naïvety the situation after Easter is treated as was that of the disciple whom the earthly Jesus had met, and so the words about following are handed on, not, of course, as mere historical reminiscences. Jesus, now exalted, still determines their way, first, no doubt, in the Easter appearances. Again he has ordained that they give up their homes and occupations, this time for good.[104] The working of the Spirit[105] is a continuation of their experience of the earthly and the exalted Jesus.[106] There is also a widespread renunciation of possessions by members of the community who had seen no appearances.[107] The working of the Spirit, too, is taken as a sign of the coming kingdom of God;[108] and in the eschatological rejoicing that was characteristic of the primitive Church's common meals the exultation of the disciples continues.[109] Again, therefore, there are

[104]So in a passage like Mark 10.29 f. (also 3.35) the Church appears as an equivalent, as a spiritual family, in which God is Father to the disciples (11.25, probably therefore omitted in 10.30, despite 10.29; cf. J. M. Robinson, *The Problem of History in Mark* [SBT 21], 1957, 81).

[105]The primitive Church was familiar with manifestations of the Spirit; cf. *TWNT* VI 402, n. 462, and 3 o below. This may be maintained in opposition to the one-sided approach in K. Holl, 'Der Kirchenbegriff des Paulus in seinem Verhältnis zu dem der Urgemeinde' (*Sitzungsberichte der Akad. der Wissenschaften zu Berlin* 1921, 920 ff. = K. Holl, *Gesammelte Aufsätze* II, 1928, 44 ff.), which is also adopted in J. L. Leuba's approach, *New Testament Pattern*, ET 1953, 95. It is therefore impossible to represent the apostles as the only essential bearers of the Spirit (Leuba 105). In view of Acts 10.13-15; 11.1 f., it cannot be maintained, even for Luke, that the Holy Spirit never dominates and judges the apostolic tradition.

[106]Cf. Mark 3.28-30; Matt. 12.28-32.

[107]It is clear that it was no legally enacted communism: Acts 4.36 f. (related as being an exception), 5.4 (unless we agree with F. Scheidweiler's conjecture, *ZNW* 49, 1958, 137) and 4.32 assume private property, which, however, is repeatedly put at the disposal of others. This is probably historical, and distinguishes the Church from Qumran by its freedom of action.

[108]Acts 2.17 ff. (especially if the correction of the OT text 'in the last days' is original; otherwise E. Haenchen, *ZTK* 51, 1954, 172); Heb. 6.4 f.

[109]Acts 2.46; R. Bultmann, *TWNT* I 19 f.

two things to be seen: the order of the coming kingdom takes shape in various signs, and yet the Church remains quite unrevolutionary in its old forms, because it expects nothing from reforms but everything from the coming kingdom and the call that it is already uttering.

e. But yet the differences must not be overlooked. Through Jesus' crucifixion and resurrection facts have been created that give the time after Easter a new character. On the one hand Israel has taken a decision by rejecting Jesus. That cannot be taken to mean that the primitive Church can look down in judgment on the others; for the whole tradition agrees that not only Israel but also the band of disciples failed, and that the Gentiles too shared in that rejection.[110] The question is, however, whether that guilt should be recognized or not. On the other hand, with Jesus' resurrection God has bestowed on the Church the new possibility of life, though again not as the exclusive possession of the faithful. For it is just this that is new in contrast to all other examples:[111] the death and exaltation of the suffering Righteous One implies not the final judgment on his godless persecutors, but the offer of mercy and salvation.[112] By this the relation of the Church to Israel has become no different from that of the disciples; but it has all entered the stage of extreme urgency.

f. Of course, we may say that what separates the primitive Church from Judaism is Christology. After Jesus' crucifixion there can only be seen in it the proof either of God's rejection of him, or of God's conclusive action. After the Easter appearances there can only be seen in them either the fantastic hallucinations of disordered minds, or God's act in which he said his 'Yes' to that same Jesus. And yet that does not give the answer. If there had simply been pronouncements of dogma introducing only a new object of faith, the Church would hardly have been persecuted.[113] Rabbi Akiba remained a most respected Jewish teacher, although

---

[110]Luke and John tone both these down, but cannot eliminate them.

[111]The Maccabaean martyrs too died vicariously; but they were killed by Israel's enemies, and their death benefited Israel only.

[112]It makes no difference here whether one regards Jesus' dying as an expiatory death or as the way of the suffering Righteous One, whose resurrection calls all Israel to repentance.

[113]Peter's confession of faith, reconstructed by Easton 104 f., would still be quite possible within Judaism.

he greeted Bar Cochba as the Messiah.[114] The Enoch circles remained within Judaism, although they believed in a son of man enthroned in heaven, whose glory would some day be shared by the righteous who obeyed him. It was often asserted within Judaism that Enoch, Elijah, and others down to quite recent times had been caught up into heaven, had risen from the dead, and were God's son and God's servant.[115] In all purely dogmatic questions Judaism remained extremely tolerant.[116] With all these pronouncements, therefore, the relation of the Church to Israel would not have become fundamentally different from that of Jesus' group of disciples, which, of course, also embraced a certain profession of faith; the claim would at the most have entered a stage of greater urgency. But the question whether the Church is a mistaken development, which Jesus did not want at all, or the fulfilment of his whole life and work,[117] depends on the question what the knowledge of the crucifixion and resurrection of Jesus means for the *life* of the primitive Church, and whether that life is or is not intelligible and necessary as a continuation of the life of the group of disciples.

g. What is perhaps most striking is that repentance is now associated with baptism. We do not know how early the latter was practised, and whether its use by a single group gradually became general; but in any case we cannot now point to any time in which it was not practised.[118] Nor do we know where it originated; we have no word from Jesus about that.[119] The only

[114]Ph. Menoud, *L'Eglise naissante et le Judaïsme*, 1952, 25 ff. He, however, stresses the novelty of the Christological profession of faith.

[115]Wisd. 2.13, 16, 18; 4.10–17; 5.1–5; Mark 6.14, 16; also Jub. 4.23; 10.17; II (4) Esd. 14.9, 49; Enoch 71.14 etc.

[116]Judaism is orthopraxy, not orthodoxy (Schubert, *Die Religion des nachbiblischen Judentums* 26). Cf. for instance the absolute freedom of ideas about life after death, where the denial of any future life, and belief in bodily resurrection directly after death or not till the end of the world, are just as possible as the idea of a future life of the soul, together with all imaginable combinations between those possibilities, or the manifold views about spirits, angels, archangels, mediators between God and man, or devils and princes of devils.

[117]Michel, *Zeugnis* 80 ff., referring to Loisy and others.

[118]*TWNT* VI 411. 25 f. (= *Spirit of God* (Bible Key Words 9), 1960, 52).

[119]Matt. 28.19 is certainly a late passage; the New Testament Church baptized in the name of Jesus, not in that of the Father and of the Son and of the Holy Spirit. It seems that the latter formula was usual only in the sphere of Matthew and the *Didache* (on the question of an interpolation see *TWNT* VI 399, n. 440). Mark 10.38; Luke 12.50 (O. Cullmann, *Baptism in the NT*,

obvious explanation is that the primitive Church took over the baptism of John.[120]

But did not that cause the open circle of Jesus' disciples to become something quite different, namely a Church? True, the practice of baptism means at first simply that repentance is now, if possible, even more serious and pressing. For from henceforth the facts of Jesus' execution and resurrection make all neutrality impossible; anyone who sees in them God's action of the last days is left no choice but to say 'No' to the official judgment of Judaism on Jesus. That compulsion already follows from the persecution of Jesus' followers, which sets in very quickly.[121] So here too it becomes clear that the dividing 'No' is ratified by suffering; what separates the Church from Israel is willingness to be destroyed. Thus baptism is the profession of belonging to a despised band recognized by neither side, and not to a successful Church. That must never be forgotten. For anyone to accept baptism is visible witness to this Jesus. The binding force of the call demands in that sitation an answer that is also binding.

Above all, however, baptism does not exclude anyone from Israel in its religious and national sense, any more than John's baptism did previously; baptized people still take part in the service of the temple and synagogue.[122] Jesus' intention would be betrayed only if the Church held that every baptized person was saved and every unbaptized person lost; even the late addition in Mark 16.16 does not assert that. The matter would be rather different if baptism had been regarded from the very first as conferring the Spirit, so that the possession of the Spirit clearly divided the members of the Church fron Judaism;[123] but that may

---

ET (SBT 1), 1950, 19 f.) could in any case not have established historically the custom of baptism, even if a theological connection existed.

[120]A marked divergence of these two groups was probably followed after Jesus' death by a drawing together, perhaps because some of the Baptist's disciples went over to the Church (C. H. Kraeling, *John the Baptist*, 1951, 158 ff., 171 ff.).
[121]Gal. 1.22; I Cor. 15.9.
[122]This is proved by the passages mentioned in n. 93. It is quite uncertain whether in the primitive Church or in certain parts of it the opinion prevailed that one could be saved *only* by baptism; there is no conclusive evidence on this point.
[123]This is stressed by Easton 128 f.

not yet have been the view of the Church, however highly it valued the experience of the Spirit, for Mark and Matthew hardly point anywhere to a general bestowal of the Spirit on the Church, and Mark 13.11 assumes such a thing only in special situations.[124]

h. This development was necessary from yet another angle. Even in Jesus' earthly activities there was an invitation to union, and it now enters its decisive phase; indeed, the knowledge of the risen Lord exalted at God's right hand is bound to take shape in communal life with others. This is realized in the 'breaking of bread', in the common meals with the risen Lord and the brethren together,[125] but also in the fact that in everyday matters people put their possessions at each other's disposal.

But even this does not yet imply a sharply defined unity of which it could be declared *extra ecclesiam nulla salus.* For, unless the tradition is quite misleading, there was, even in those first years before Paul was called, a Hellenistic group existing without any very close connection with the primitive Church that formed round the twelve.[126]

i. How, then, does the breach between the old and the new Israel, between Judaism and the Church of Christ, come about? We could give a purely historical answer by saying that the breach takes place in suffering, the Church remaining within Israel till it is expelled. This happens to the Hellenist group round Stephen[127]

---

[124]*TWNT* VI 396. 5 ff.; 400. 16 ff. (= *Spirit of God* 27 ff., 33 ff.). For the Roman Catholic view see N. Adler, *Taufe und Handauflegung*, 1951, 93 ff.

[125]See n. 109; and on Luke 22.15–18, 28–30 as an old report of the Lord's Supper, n. 84. That does not, any more than similar Jewish fellowship meals, exclude the participants from the service of the temple and synagogue.

[126]That the apostles remain in Jerusalem (Acts 8.1) and that neither they nor the Church forming round them appear at all in 7.1 ff., shows that the persecution was directed only against the group of Hellenists (Knox, *Church of Jerusalem* 49 n. 6; further E. Haenchen, *Die Apostelgeschichte*, 1956, 255 ff.; otherwise J. Munck, *Paul and the Salvation of Mankind*, ET 1959, 220 f.). On the Hellenist synagogue(s) in Jerusalem see P. Carrington, *The Early Christian Church* I, 1957, 47, and the illustration facing p. 65.

[127]On this cf. O. Cullmann in *NTS* 5, 1958/9, 157 ff. and 'Secte de Qumran. Héllenistes des Actes et quatrième Évangile' in *Les manuscrits de la mer morte*, 1957, 61 ff.; further *JBL* 74, 1955, 220 ff.; M. Simon, *Les premiers Chrétiens*, 1952, 44 ff. and *St Stephen and the Hellenists,* 1958; against him C. F. D. Moule in *ExpT* 70, 1959, 100 ff., who in substance defends the Acts narrative, though he considers Simon's thesis possible. For the connection between Qumran and the Letter to the Hebrews cf. C. Spicq in *Revue de Qumran* 1,

quite early. It is repeated, probably in the year 44,[128] in the case of Peter, and is completed, perhaps in the year 62, by the death of James and the Church's withdrawal to Pella[129] soon afterwards, when the imminent catastrophe and the destruction of the temple were already hanging over Jerusalem.[130] But that, of course, must not be taken as an attempt to apportion guilt; we have to determine the course of events purely historically, without deciding whether the blame lay in the challenge of the Church's attitude or in the answer of Judaism. As far as we can now see, the decisive part is always played by the question of the observance of the law. The blow at Stephen and his group is the result of their rejection of the temple and the law.[131] The fact that Peter has to flee from

---

1959, 365–90. The importance of the Hellenists is also stressed by L. Cerfaux in *Ephemerides Theol. Lovanienses* 16, 1939, 5 ff., especially 29 ff. On the 'seven' see 5i and 26f.

[128]The statements in Acts 12.1 ff. fit in very well with the fact that Agrippa relied on the Pharisees' support for his rule and was complaisant towards them.
[129]See n. 100.
[130]The picture would be essentially different if a reliable historical source could be discovered behind the Pseudo-Clementines, as H. J. Schoeps (*Zeitschr. für Religions- und Geistesgeschichte* 10, 1958, 1 ff.) thinks. In that case James would stand at the head of the Church from the beginning, and the apostles would be subordinated to him, as would be a teaching body of 70 or 72 people ordained by him. Afterwards James would have represented approximately the general line of Stephen's speech, and the first persecution would be instituted by Paul, and would have to be put in about the year 40 (p. 12). At first we should agree that such a source certainly might be more reliable than Acts, although the very complicated relations involved in the origins of the Pseudo-Clementines (R. Bultmann in *Gnomon* 26, 1954, 179 ff.) do not exactly favour that view (see Schoeps 4 ff.). But everything that we know from the Pauline letters tells against it. The statements in Gal. 1.18; 2.1 as to times make it impossible to put the calling of Paul so late, and Gal. 1.18; 2.9 exclude a monarchical position for James. They only show his gradually mounting influence, and this agrees with the account of Acts. G. Strecker's view is discussed most recently by G. Harder in *TLZ* 85, 1960, 153 f. Against Schoeps cf. also J. Munck, *NTS* 6, 1959/60, 103 ff.
[131]This is shown by Stephen's speech, so that Acts 6.13 f. is presumably not false evidence. Behind that attitude there already lies a fairly long development. In 1QS 8.5 f.; 9.3–6 the Qumran community is regarded as a 'holy house' and 'the Holy of Holies' for Israel (cf. A. F. J. Klijn, 'Stephen's Speech—Acts VII.2–53', *NTS* 4, 1957/8, 30 f.; D. Flusser in *Scripta Hierosolymitana* IV, 1958, 229 ff.). There is probably a similar idea behind Mark 14.58. It can be seen further in passages like I Cor. 3.16; 6.19; II Cor. 6.16 f.; Eph. 2.20 f.; I Peter 2.5; 4.17; *Barn.* 4.11; 6.15; 16.7–9; Ignatius, etc. (cf. O. Michel, *TWNT* IV 890 ff.; W. Nauck, *EvTh* 13, 1953, 362 ff. and *Die Tradition und der Charakter des 1 Johannesbriefes*, 1957, 48).

Jerusalem, while James[132] can go on working unmolested, is almost certainly bound up with their different attitudes to the question of the law.[133] And finally, in the year 62, James himself is executed as a law-breaker.[134] Thus there was still at least part of the Church holding out in Jerusalem and in Israel as a national and religious community, bearing persecution till God himself let loose the catastrophe on Jerusalem.[135]

k. But at the same time it must be said that the breach was bound to become outwardly apparent, quite apart from the moral question whether a group like that led by Stephen, or a radical group of Pharisees such as influenced Agrippa, did not push things too far. For it is clear that from the very beginning the Church no longer really lives on temple sacrifice[136] and observance of the law, even if it takes part in them. It hears the Old Testament in the synagogue, and from that it hears God's call; but it hears that call because Jesus' words and Jesus' death have opened the Old Testament to it. It takes part in the Passover, and is thereby reminded of God's redeeming action in Egypt; but that is made actual for it by what it experiences in its own small circle at the Lord's Supper. This involves no cut and dried dogmatics. To anyone who allows himself to be reached by Jesus' call to a childlike life of love, all casuistical fulfilment of the law, enabling him to calculate his debit and credit before God, is made impossible. Anyone who is willing to accompany Jesus on the lowly path to which future exaltation is promised no longer expects salvation from temple sacrifice or from the teaching of the law. Least of all is that possible for one who hears in that call from God,

[132]On him cf. P. Gaechter, *ZKT* 76, 1954, 129 ff.
[133]Cf. Gal. 2.11 f. and especially Cullmann, *Peter* 65 ff. And in Acts 15.1 ff. and Gal. 2.1 ff. the question of the law was the central question.
[134]Josephus, *Ant.* XX 9.1 (200).
[135]If C. C. Torrey, 'The Aramaic Period of the Nascent Christian Church', *ZNW* 44, 1952/3, 205 ff., were right, the Church would till A.D. 70 have leaned very strongly towards Jewish Christianity. Of course it is true that we must not overestimate the Pauline influence merely because his letters are preserved for us as the most important documents of the early Church; but there are in them and outside them such strongly marked traditions intelligible only as coming from the Greek language and Greek thought, that this thesis is untenable, at any rate in so one-sided a form.
[136]On the spiritualizing of temple and sacrifice cf. Cerfaux, *The Church in . . . St Paul* 145 ff.

who gives him a new task and a new way, the offer of God's mercy in the last days.[137]

If Jesus' earthly activity has actually made the breach complete, something of it gradually becomes visible. Yet the Church does not take the decision into its own hands; it remains in Israel. It learns that God can reject members of the Church (Acts 5.1 ff.) and choose their persecutors (Acts 9.1 ff.). And above all it does not deny that even those groups that think and act differently on important matters[138] are members of the one Church in which the salvation of the last days is present, even if those groups are often only very loosely joined to it—e.g. the group round Stephen, and the Pauline churches.

l. Nor is the decision made by the Church's imposing any new condition of acceptance into its membership—what separates it from Israel is the dropping of a condition. Again and again the question of the law gives an impetus to separation. The Church shuts itself off from Judaism by opening itself to the nations; in fact, the great missionary movement is certainly not simply Paul's work (Phil. 1.15 ff.; Rom. 16.7; Col. 1.6). Neither the church in Rome nor the one in Antioch was founded by him. Probably the mission is at first meant only for the Jews of the Diaspora, and 'God-fearing' Gentiles are received incidentally; but presumably this also holds good for the beginning of the Pauline apostolate. It may even be supposed that the primitive Church did not demand circumcision of non-Jewish applicants for baptism (Gal. 2.3). In any case the first formulation of the 'Pauline' message, Gal. 2.16, appears not only in a typically Jewish expression of thought, but also as a basis that Paul assumes to be at least as self-evident to Peter as to himself.[139] It is therefore not peculiar to the Pauline message that what actually separates the Church from Judaism is the question of the law, for Paul was merely the one who most

[137]We might here ask with Johnson, *ZAW* 66, 1954, 119 f., whether it may not be that the real fulfilment of what Jesus had in view is Paul, and not the primitive Church in Jerusalem—not at any rate as reproduced by Matthew.

[138]See n. 177.

[139]Cullmann, *Peter* 50 f.; Dix, *Jew and Greek* 30 ff., 52 f. Gentile Christianity regards itself as having been founded by the twelve, not by Paul: see Rev. 21.14; I *Clem.* 42; Polyc. *Phil.* 6; *Barn.* 5, 8; *Did.* intr. (Dix, *op. cit.* 58; the Pastorals otherwise).

clearly thought out and formulated theologically what took shape in the history of the primitive Church. Thus, paradoxically, it is precisely the continued openness of the circle of disciples that eventually determined the separation from Judaism. There would therefore be a wrong development wherever the Church re-erected the walls, even if the required righteousness based on the law were replaced by the *sacrificium intellectus* and the assent to dogmatic formulae—that is, if orthopraxy were replaced by orthodoxy. The Church fulfils and continues the disciples' circle wherever it *lives* entirely by the *grace* that appeared in Jesus of Nazareth. Both these emphases must therefore be expressed by its ordering: that it lives on that *grace*, not on its own reforms, morals, or dogmatics, and that it really *lives* on the grace in all the manifestations of its life, so that something of that new life may be seen.

m. The circumstances vary greatly.[140] While one group within the Church still holds fast to attendance at the temple, observance of the Sabbath, indeed to the authority not only of the law but also of the rabbinic tradition,[141] another declares its opposition to temple and law;[142] and it becomes clear, even at the time of the Council at Jerusalem, that circumcision is not being demanded of the Gentile Christians, while the Jewish Christian section, or at least the greater part of it, goes on practising it as a matter of course.[143] In the same way there are wide divergencies in the amount of attention paid to the food ordinances.[144]

We have to make the same reservation about the little that we know of the organization of the primitive Church, as here too the circumstances probably varied greatly. But there are two things to be said, as in the case of Jesus' band of disciples. The tradition shows nowhere any revolutionary attempt to build up a rival organization beside Israel; even the most radical group round Stephen contends only in support of the Old Testament, regarding the rejection of the temple as fidelity to the history, properly understood, of God's dealings with Israel—no deviation from the Old Testament is even suggested anywhere.

[140] So too Carrington 39 f.
[141] Matt. 5.23; cf. 17.27; 24.20 (an addition to Mark's version); 5.18; 23.2 f. See 4a.
[142] See 3h, i, and Knox, *Church of Jerusalem* 8 f.
[143] See n. 177.
[144] Gal. 2.12 f.

At first, therefore, the Church has no new order, but goes on living in the established Jewish forms;[145] Christian rabbis[146] and elders[147] only show that the old Jewish order is continued as a matter of course. That they say 'Yes' and not 'No' to Jesus of Nazareth implies at first only a divergence of doctrine that does not yet affect their place within Israel. It is almost certain, too, that priests joined the Church;[148] but what is very important is that they never play a special part there, as distinct from the laity, nor presumably do they renounce the temple service. Thus the order of the primitive Church makes it evident that it expects salvation neither from a reform of the old order nor from its revolutionary abolition. It is not till after 44 that some rigidity creeps in—the time when James takes over the leadership more definitely. Here kinship with Jesus of Nazareth gradually comes to be regarded as the decisive factor in the qualification for the leadership of the Church.[149] With that, the provisional order of a community that expected the conversion of all Israel and the end of this world becomes a constitutive one, and the Church something like a provisional kingdom of God.[150] But this rigidity also means the end of a degeneration that had become sterile.

n. On the other hand there also becomes apparent something of the new nature of the order in which the Church is living. The traditional regulations live on, just because they are no longer essential. That can be seen most clearly in the case of the priests, who now perform no special duties in the Church and have no special position. But it is also true of the rabbis. Although tendencies towards casuistical thinking are found,[151] Jesus' radical

[145]Strongly emphasized by Streeter, *The Primitive Church* 73. The newness of the Church is not expressed in these forms (R. Bultmann in *CJT* 1, 1955, 74).
[146]See 4a and n. 218.
[147]See 5i and 26f.
[148]Acts 6.7.
[149]Euseb. *Hist. eccl.* I 7.14; III 11; 20.6; 32.6; also Gregory Bar-Hebraeus *Chron.* III 22 f. Does Luke 4.16–30; 5.1–11 still reflect something of a rivalry between a Peter-group and a James-group (Conzelmann, *Luke* 43)?
[150]M. Goguel in *Min. and Sacr.* 310 ff.; cf. Knox 79 ff.; 87 n. 20.
[151]Matt. 19.9 (cf. Mark 10.11; Luke 16.18, but cf. H. Baltensweiler, *TZ* 15, 1959, 340 ff.); 5.29 f. (cf. Mark 9.43 ff.); 10.41 (inserted between vv. 40 and 42); perhaps 5.33 ff. (cf. James 5.12) and 18.15–22 (cf. Luke 17.3 f.); on this see E. Schweizer, 'Matt. 5.17–20, Anmerkungen zum Gesetzesverständnis des Matt.', *TLZ* 27, 1952, 484 n. 3.

utterances on the question of the law are quoted and taught, even
in the most legally-minded group of the Church; sometimes they
are softened and made 'practicable',[152] but they still stand over the
Church.

A particularly obvious sign of the new order under which the
Church is living is the position of the twelve.[153] It is true that we
do not now know what kind of part they played. It is certain that
they were not apostles in the sense of missionaries; we do not
hear of missionary journeys till a later time, and even then we have
reliable evidence only about Peter.[154] Probably they were not even
leaders of the Church.[155] But it will appear later that they were also
not apostles in the sense of Jewish plenipotentiaries.[156] Their
importance for the primitive Church lies in the fact that they are
chosen by Jesus[157] as representatives of Israel of the last days, and
will one day play an essential part in God's kingdom.[158] For that
very reason they exercise an authority that needs no formal certifi-
cation or legal definition. They are the witnesses of the Exalted

[152]See also *Did.* 1.
[153]See 2k.
[154]In Gal. 2.8 he is named alone. In I Cor. 9.5 (cf. 1.12) there still appear
with him only 'the brothers of the Lord'. For Paul the rest of the 'apostles'
presumably do not belong to the twelve (I Cor. 15.5/7; Rom. 16.7). Acts
knows nothing of missionary journeys by the twelve; on the contrary, the
apostles here remain in Jerusalem, while others begin with the missionary
work. On the absence of the idea of 'apostle' in the older synoptic tradition
see 24a and 26d.
[155]In Gal. 1.18 Paul mentions only Cephas (and James the Lord's brother);
in 2.2, 6 he refers to the δοχοῦντες, who are enumerated in 2.9: James,
Cephas, and John. These also seem to have been called 'pillars' already,
for in view of the Jewish parallels (n. 774) it is very unlikely that this was
merely a witticism by Paul (R. Annand, *ExpT* 67, 1956, 178). It is true that
Acts sees in them the directing body of the primitive Church. E. Stauffer
(*TLZ* 77, 1952, 201 ff.) sees here an after-effect of Jewish law (Acts 1.12–26);
but this *pericope*, if it is historical at all, can be better explained from the point
of view of the purely eschatological significance of the twelve. Against the
assumption in Acts there is also, besides the Pauline passages, the fact that
after Peter's withdrawal (in the year 44?) there is no longer anyone there to
lead the Church, and so the leadership passes to James and the 'elders'.
[156]See 24i.
[157]See 2k. But even if this were not historical, and they had therefore not
been chosen by the Lord till after he had risen, this would not essentially
change their importance for the primitive Church.
[158]Luke 22.30 (nn. 73 and 84); C. K. Barrett, 'Paul and the "Pillar"
Apostles' in *Stud Paul* (especially 16, 19); *The Apostles* 31 f.; v. Campenhausen,
Kirchliches Amt 16 f.

One, living signs of the coming kingdom, and so, as a matter of course, the Church takes special notice of what they say; but it may well be that only Peter, probably supported by one or two others, undertakes the direction of affairs.[159] That the appearances of Jesus also play a considerable part is shown by the importance soon attained by the Lord's brother James.[160] This probably shows, too, that the testimony about the earthly Jesus by those who had seen and heard him is not very vital for the primitive Church, and that Paul was not alone in his attitude on that point.[161]

o. We find some obscurity as to the position of the seven. All that we can be sure of is that they were not, as Acts reports them, deacons subordinate to the twelve.[162] According to what little we find in the tradition, they stand out as men who have the gift of missionary preaching and a special insight into the new nature of the Church.[163] Even more important is the role of prophets in the primitive Church. For a long time it was usual to draw a sharp dividing line between the church of Jerusalem which was ordered by law and the Pauline churches which were moved by the Spirit.[164] But that view is untenable, even if we allow for all the differences.[165] There is ample evidence of the co-existence of

[159]Cf. Jesus' intimate companions in the Synoptic tradition (Mark 1.29; 5.37; 9.2; 13.3; 14.33; also Acts 3.1 ff.; 8.14; Gal. 2.9).

[160]I Cor. 15.7; Gal. 1.19; 2.9. It is unlikely, both in view of 1.19 and for chronological reasons, that the last passage refers to the son of Zebedee: against K. Heussi, *TLZ* 77, 1952, 67 ff. (see also J. Dupont, *RB* 64, 1957, 38) cf. H. Katzenmeyer, *Internat. Kirchl. Zeitschr.* 1952, 178 ff.; B. Häsler, *TLZ* 82, 1957, 393 f. Nor, in view of Mark 3.31 ff.; John 7.5, can the identification of James the Lord's brother with James the disciple, the son of Alpheus (Leuba, *NT Pattern* 59), be maintained. Cf. G. Klein, *ZTK* 57, 1960, 275 ff.

[161]Gal. 1.1, 11 ff.; I Cor. 15.5 ff.; II Cor. 11.5; 12.11 f.

[162]We see here how unreliable Acts is as a historical source for these questions. We hear of Stephen immediately afterwards, with great emphasis, performing the very service that according to 6.4 the apostles have reserved to themselves. Later, in the We-passages, Philip is called not deacon but evangelist (21.8). The names also seem to indicate Greek-speaking men, so that it might be supposed that the Aramaic-speaking majority would accept only Hellenists to look after the poor. Cf. 3h (n. 126).

[163]Acts 6.3, 5, 8–10, 11, 13 f.; 7.2 ff.; 8.4 ff.; 21.8.

[164]Holl, 'Kirchenbegriff des Paulus' 920 ff. (44 ff.); M. Goguel, *The Birth of Christianity*, ET 1953, 95 ff.; *L'église primitive*, 1947, 23 ff., 96 ff.; *Les premiers temps de l'église*, 1949, 53.

[165]W. Mundle in *ZNW* 22, 1923, 20 ff.; F. M. Braun, *Neues Licht auf die Kirche* 44 ff.; Ph. Menoud, *L'église et les ministères*, 1949, 13 ff.; Michel, *Zeugnis* 32 ff.; Munck, *Paul* 287 ff. (cf. 69 ff.); others mentioned in *TWNT* VI 402, n. 462 (cf. *Spirit of God* 36 n. 4); see n. 105 above.

apostles and prophets;[166] and even if the origin of that juxtaposition
is uncertain, it is remarkable that the only prophets of which Acts
knows in any detail come from Judaea or adjoining districts.[167]
From the removal of the Galileans to Jerusalem until the withdrawal to Pella, the way of the Church was essentially determined
by the directions of the Spirit through prophets and other
members of the Church.[168] It is not here a matter of playing off
against each other the breath of the Spirit and the legal ordinance;
the prophetic claim itself creates new law,[169] and the fact that the
primitive Church largely continued to live in the old Jewish order
proves that it saw no inconsistency in doing so. What is vital,
however, is that the old order was no longer regarded as legally
binding—it had become to a certain extent loose and open. The
prophet, a Church member called by the Spirit, can again become
the decisive voice in everything. On the other hand, the supernaturalness of a phenomenon is not an indispensable condition.
The facts that James was Jesus' brother, and that the twelve were
companions of the earthly Jesus, are not overlooked; and such
natural circumstances play a particularly large part where the
elders appear in the Church order.

Thus it may be said that decisions are made in the primitive
Church by those who give directions with authority, and that the
leadership is in the hands of those who can really exercise it.
Whether such authority rests on natural causes, such as, for instance, greater age or association with the earthly Jesus, or on
supernatural causes such as the gift of prophetic insight, is an
entirely subordinate and irrelevant question. The only important
thing is that such authority is its own justification, and is not
provided by any formal appointment.[170]

[166]Luke 11.49 (cf. Matt. 10.40 f.); with I Cor. 12.28 f. (Eph. 4.11) cf. also
the un-Pauline formula in Eph. 2.20; 3.5 and Rev. (esp. 18.20).
[167]Acts 21.4.9; E. Schweizer in *TWNT* VI 402, n. 462; cf. *Spirit of God*
36 n. 4; *Erniedrigung* 77 f.
[168]Acts 9.10; 10.3 ff., 10 ff.; 11.28; 13.2; 16.6 ff.; 20.22 f.; 21.4, 9, 10 f. and
Gal. 2.2; Euseb. *Hist. eccl.* III 5.3; Epiphanius, *Haer.* 29.7; *Mens. et pond.* 15.
[169]E. Käsemann, 'Sätze heiligen Rechtes im NT', *NTS* 1, 1954/5, 248 ff.;
and in more detail in *ZTK* 57, 1960, 162 ff.
[170]Whether there are any rites of investiture or not cannot be decided for
certain (see 25b, c), as our sources do not tell us (see n. 162). For Peter see
2b, for the twelve also 2k.

4

MATTHEW'S CHURCH

a. Where the author of the first Gospel lived is uncertain. As his church lived for a considerable time within Jewish society, but was affected by such Hellenist influences as are to be particularly expected in the Diaspora, Syria, perhaps the borderland of Phoenicia,[171] is the likeliest place.[172] In that case we have a glimpse here of a church that was entirely characterized by Judaism growing in Diaspora territory. The ascertainment of the facts is, of course, made difficult by the need to distinguish between what Matthew himself saw and the material that he took over.

This is shown particularly clearly in the analysis of Matt. 23.[173] While Matthew himself represents the standpoint that the tradition of the scribes is in contradiction to the law, there is apparent behind the material that he had gathered together here a narrowly Jewish Christian group[174] which fully accepted the dogmatic doctrines of the scribes and reproached others with not observing them (vv. 2 f.[175]). A rather more advanced stage can be discerned in the tradition in vv. 13.31; it still shows the relationships that existed before the year 70, but the separation between Jews and Jewish Christians is already becoming clearer.[176] For Matthew

[171]So G. D. Kilpatrick, *The Origins of the Gospel according to St Matthew*, 1946, 124 ff.

[172]It tells against Jerusalem and its immediate neighbourhood that Peter plays such a central part, while James the Lord's brother does not come into the picture at all.

[173]Haenchen, *ZTK* 48, 1951, 38–63.

[174]The question whether the Judaizers of Galatians come from Jerusalem or not is open to argument. In favour of it we have Gal. 2.12, *pace* Munck 102 f., and Acts 21.20, unless we agree with Munck's conjecture (240 f.) that it refers to Jews and not Jewish Christians. But we must concede to Munck (242 ff.) that Jewish narrowness may have been most prominently shown outside Jerusalem, perhaps in Syria.

[175]These verses cannot belong to the same stratum as v. 8 (Haenchen 43).

[176]Haenchen 51 f. The liability to pay tithes of mint and cummin is still regarded as quite lawful, unless it involves the neglect of much more important things (vv. 23 f.).

himself it is already complete. That certainly does not mean that the Church is no longer living in the order taken over from Judaism. The observance of the Sabbath is still regarded as one of the most important commandments,[177] and the temple tax is paid.[178] Indeed, Matthew can at least still accept the saying that 'till heaven and earth pass away, not an iota, not a dot, will pass from the law', although he probably re-interprets it.[179]

b. What is changed, however, in the Church as Matthew himself knows it, in contrast with the beginnings of the primitive Church, is the experience of persecution by Israel (10.17–25) and of the mission to the Gentiles, probably specially impressive in Syria (8.11; 24.14). Above all, however, there is also the consciousness of lengthening time. More than four decades have already passed since Jesus' death and resurrection. That must not be understood to mean that the non-occurrence of the parousia is the central problem; it certainly does occupy the Church's attention,[180] but in fact the centre of the stage is taken by the problem of obedience to the law. Owing to the increasing passage of time, ethical exhortation and the expectation of the end have moved apart.[181] At the same time, because of the persecution by Israel,

[177] 'Sabbath' (Matt. 24.20) is additional to Mark. From Gal. 2.1 ff. (see R. Meyer, *TWNT* VI 86. 3 ff.); Acts 15.1 ff.; 21.18 ff. we learn that the primitive Church contained a group that held circumcision to be necessary for salvation, besides another that wanted to retain it only for Jewish Christians. More important is Gal. 2.11 ff., because we see there an attempt under the influence of Jerusalem (James) to impose the Jewish food ordinances on the Jewish Christians in the Diaspora churches too.

[178] Matt. 17.27.

[179] Against Bultmann, *Synopt. Tradition* 146 f., I consider v. 18 a separate saying, circulating by itself and taken up by Matthew when he put together vv. 17–20. It is 'fulfilled' in the Church's obedience to the law (see 4b).

[180] This is apparent in 25.1–13. The parable must have been so understood from the beginning, because the bridegroom represents the Messiah, the wedding represents the eschatological day of salvation, and the long wait is essential to the parable. But the fact that the delay is not a problem is apparent from the fact that Matthew can calmly set the parable side by side with 24.48, where it is the long period of waiting, not the short one, that proves to be an illusion, because the master comes much more quickly than the lazy servant expects. Cf. E. Grässer, *Das Problem der Parusieverzögerung in den synoptischen Evangelien und in der Apostelgeschichte*, 1957, 86 ff.

[181] This becomes particularly clear in Matthew. Chs. 5–7 on the one hand and 24 f. on the other are in self-contained blocks, no longer directly connected with each other. From the call in view of the approaching crisis, as we find in the Q-section Luke 12.49–13.9, there comes e.g. into the first

there has arisen the need to reflect on the relation of the age of the Church to that of Israel before Jesus. From both of these the Church learnt to regard itself as the group of obedient people. On the one hand, fulfilment of the law is the standard by which Israel will one day be judged, by which, that is to say, the true Israel will be separated from the false. On the other hand, Jesus' new interpretation of the law is, within the plan of God's salvation, the fulfilment of the Old Testament law;[182] and it is in possessing the right interpreter of the law that the Church becomes separated from Israel.[183] The prophetic principle that God desires mercy and not sacrifice is inserted by Matthew into the context that was handed down to him (Matt. 9.13; 12.7). The command to love one's neighbour comprises the whole law; this too is inserted in 19.19; and in 22.39, as distinct from the tradition in Mark, it is described as 'like [the first commandment]'. The *pericope* 15.1–20 shows, too, how anxious Matthew is to make it clear that Jesus' disciples do not reject the law on principle, but may at most overstep its bounds in a special case.[184] Possibly

---

block a passage such as Luke 12.57–59, which becomes in Matt. 5.25 a permanently valid ethical precept, while a picture such as that of Luke 13.6–9 appears again in Matt. 24.32 f. as a purely apocalyptic warning. Cf. Jeremias, *Parables* 35 f. and J. A. T. Robinson, *Jesus and his Coming*, 1957, 64 ff. (esp. 70 ff.). The reference to the coming judgment certainly appears also in 7.13 ff., and both the mission charge in 10.1 ff. and the passage on Church order in 18.1 ff. contain references to the eschatological kingdom. But the relation of present and future time is hardly thought out theologically beyond the expectation (which was already valid for Judaism) of reward and punishment. And we may even ask with Haenchen (47) whether the 'kingdom' does not in practice mean the Church.

[182]Schweizer, *TLZ* 77, 1952, 481 ff.

[183]For proof see G. Bornkamm, *TLZ* 79, 1954, 342 f. and in *Background* 244 ff. (an ET of this essay will appear shortly in the same series as the present work). A comparison of 4.17 with 3.2, and of 7.19 with 3.10, shows that the Baptist himself (whose baptism does not take place 'for the forgiveness of sins': cf. 3.1 with Mark 1.4) is seen as a teacher of righteousness (cf. 21.32). It is true that he is the one who prepares, not the one who fulfils (3.3 beside 3.2, and 4.16 beside 4.17). By the one 'teacher' (23.8) Matthew certainly means Jesus, and he repeatedly justifies Jesus by referring to the law of Moses.

[184]This is shown by B. H. Branscomb, *Jesus and the Law*, 1930, 160; cf. παραβαίνουσιν (15.2) instead of περιπατοῦσιν (Mark 7.5); the opponents are 'hypocrites' (15.7); only they themselves, not their tradition, are threatened with extermination by God (15.13 f.); finally the conclusion shows (15.20b) that Matthew is concerned with the explanation of a particular case.

the section 19.1–12 also shows that Matthew or his church, through a misunderstanding of the tradition, tries to reduce the gap between the Jewish and the Christian interpretation of the law.[185] This church is obviously much concerned to carry out the commandments. In the plan of salvation the Church is the fulfilment of Israel, because it is only in the Church that Israel can attain the real fulfilment of the law in the simplicity of love.

For that very reason we see again and again in relation to Jesus' radical claim a slight infiltration of casuistry. The commands must be made 'practicable', so that the Church may be kept from a theological speculation that forgets action.[186] But the new element is not merely that the Church really does whatever the rabbis teach. It does it, too, without 'hypocrisy'. For the Matthean church this expression sums up the essentially wrong attitude,[187] and it consists in seeking the praise of men, instead of that of God.[188] That, indeed, may not be an adequate statement of the case, since the childlikeness and love that Jesus wanted from his hearers puts out of court any sidelong glances towards God for reward. However much those virtues know about the promise of heavenly reward, they cannot, even in thought, lay any claim to it. Yet it shows that the Church is conscious that it is obeying the law in a new way; and for it that new way can be found only through Jesus.

c. It is not easy to define the significance of this new understanding. Matthew can speak of the 'faith' which alone gives entry into the kingdom of God (8.10–12[189]). According to 21.32 it consists in obedience rendered to the doctrine of righteousness preached by the Baptist; and so 'faith' proves in the first

[185]So H. Greeven, *Zeitschr. f. evang. Ethik* 1, 1957, 110 ff.: πρός in Mark 10.5 means 'with regard to = against', i.e. as accusing evidence of their hardness of heart! Only Matthew could have made out of that a concession that was already there in the law.
[186]The best-known addition is that in Matt. 5.32; 19.9 in relation to Mark 10.11; Luke 16.18; see also n. 151. On 5.21–48 see V. Hasler, *TZ* 15, 1959, 90–106.
[187]In 15.7; 22.18 it is inserted by Matthew; in 24.51 it replaces Luke's ἄπιστοι. Cf. 6.2, 5, 16; 7.5; 23.13 ff., 23, 25, 27 ff.
[188]23.5a (presumably a piece of Matthew's editing: Haenchen 42); 6.1 ff.
[189]Here the stock word 'faith' comes from the tradition, but the connection with v. 11, making faith the deciding criterion, might well be put down to Matthew's account.

place to be attachment to the new teacher of the law. That is also
shown at the end of the Gospel, where the presence of the risen
Lord is spoken of (28.20). But here, in contrast to all the parallel
passages, the end of the world is expressly introduced as a limiting
factor. [190] For this presence of the risen Lord is promised to the
disciples who teach Jesus' commandments to all nations; and
Jesus is therefore present in his Church as the teacher[191] of the new
righteousness according to the law. That is also why Matthew,
like Mark, still hardly speaks of the Spirit's presence in the
Church; it is not the Church, but only Jesus himself, who is
manifested by the Spirit of God living anew.[192] However, it must
not be forgotten that that teacher of the law has himself taken the
way that his Church can take only by following him. Only because he himself, free from all 'hypocrisy', has walked on earth
in lowliness, humility, and meekness, and takes his disciples with
him as the 'little ones' on his way, is there any possibility at all of
obedience.[193] It is precisely as the helper of the 'little ones' that he
is also, in future, the Judge of the world, to whom since Easter
all power has been given.

d. What does that mean for this community's idea of the
Church? It is clear that it regards itself as Israel. The question
where the real Israel is to be found runs through the whole
Gospel,[194] and it is answered by the reference to the right fulfilling
of the law. But as this is possible only in freedom from all
'hypocrisy', the Church is the band of 'little ones' who, in following the meek and humble King of lowliness, and being taught
by his interpretation of the law, go their way. Again it is a way
of suffering, in which the Church is ready to sacrifice itself

[190]'World' should probably be regarded as temporal, not spatial. In credal
formulae such as Phil. 2.9 ff.; I Tim. 3.16; Rom. 1.4, it is quite typical that
where the exaltation is central, no end to this is envisaged. This view may
have its roots in apocalyptic prophecy in the early Church of Palestine and
Syria, as is supposed by E. Käsemann, *ZTK* 57, 1960, 162 ff.
[191]See 23.8b, and Haenchen 44 on it.
[192]*TWNT* VI 402. 18 ff. = *Spirit of God* 35 f.
[193]G. Bornkamm has shown this excellently in *Background* 246 f. Cf. 3.13 ff.;
11.29. It may even be asked whether Matthew did not change the Messiah
riding on a horse (see the dictionaries for πῶλος, Mark 11.2 ff.) to the
King of lowliness 'humble and riding . . . on a colt the foal of an ass' in
Zech. 9.9. But cf. H. W. Kuhn, *ZNW* 50, 1959, 82 ff.; O. Michel, *NTS* 6,
1959/60, 82 f.
[194]'His [Jesus'] people' (1.21) are 'my [God's] people' (2.6).

(5.3–12, 38–48). Here, therefore, the act of following remains
central, and so an essential idea of Jesus' circle of disciples is
taken over; but the question arises whether and how far that idea
has been changed by the Church's new situation.

At first the Church maintains the openness of the disciples'
circle by not shutting itself off from the Gentiles. That is precisely
the reproach against the scribes—that they set up a barrier against
them.[195] But there is another form of Church openness, peculiar to
Matthew: the Church appears in his Gospel as a *corpus mixtum*.
Only the Last Judgment will reveal who is really chosen for
God's kingdom.[196] It is only in Matthew, too, that there is handed
down to us that moving account of that last separation, according to which the very people who are chosen do not know that
they have served Jesus (25.31 ff.). Equally surprising is the statement that the bad (put first!) and the good are admitted to the
feast (22.10). But it is here that the Church's new position is
shown. Jesus was not afraid that the tax-collectors and prostitutes
whom he called could misunderstand his call as cheap grace. But
the Church already knows such cases, and so it (or Matthew)
inserts vv. 11–13,[197] although in this parable a guest cannot be
expected to have a wedding garment handy.[198] But then the same
thing is said here as in the other two pictures: only the Last
Judgment shows who has really responded to Jesus' call.[199]

e. It is only with this proviso that the Church is seen here as the
band of people who are obedient to God's law as interpreted by

[195] 23.13 (Haenchen 46 f.). That point of view, however, was only gradually
achieved. Matt. 10.5 f., 23 testifies to the battles that were fought on the
question.
[196] 13.36 ff. According to v. 38 the field is the world. It may be asked whether
it is not meant here to denote the extent of the area in which the Church
exists (26.13). But even if 'world' had the negative character of estrangement
from God (16.26; 18.7?), that would mean that within this world there is no
possibility that human eyes can separate the Church from the world, or the
good people from the bad. Cf. Jeremias, *Parables* 64, 155 ff.; Grässer,
Parusieverzögerung 145 ff.
[197] Jeremias, *Parables* 37 ff.
[198] We might think of the custom of having festal garments provided by the
host (cf. II Kings 10.22; Rev. 19.8; Gen. 45.22; Judg. 14.12); but there is
nothing about that here (J. Schniewind, *Das Evang. nach. Matt.*, 1937, *ad
loc.*), and moreover, there is no evidence of this in Jesus' time (Jeremias,
Die Gleichnisse Jesu,[4] 1956, 39).
[199] That is not to deny that such obedience is in the last resort a gift, and
in view of such passages as 11.27–30 it is clearly true for Matthew too.

Jesus' teaching and meekness of life. It is the band of followers who are determined on thorough-going obedience, who share Jesus' insecurity and dishonour, but who can also be certain of his protection in the storm.[200] Matthew therefore uses 'church', at least in 18.17, to mean not simply the band of the elect, but the band of those actually gathered together. And yet is not the demand made here to establish a pure church from which all unrepentant sinners are excluded? In any case, even if the rule that is here handed down may for once have been so understood,[201] Matthew inserted it between 18.10–14 and 21–35, thus clearly interpreting it as an admonition to do everything possible to lose none of the 'little ones', but to go after every single one and forgive him. It is true that, as in 22.11–13, there is no lessening of the seriousness with which the Church repeatedly has to be called to repentance. But there is not set up the ideal of a church cleansed from all sin; on the contrary, it is expected that repentance is possible and necessary within the Church.[202] Thus the disciples' failure and their reproof by Jesus are stressed rather than softened in comparison with Mark.[203]

Yet it is clear that the breach between Judaism and the Church has already become irreparable.[204] God has left the temple,[205] in place of which there is now a 'Church of Jesus' founded on the rock Peter (16.18). Here too the choice of language[206] shows that

[200]Matthew has developed Mark's story about the miraculous calming of the storm (4.36–41) into teaching about following Jesus (8.23–27), as he expressly connects with it the two passages in 8.18–22 about following, and has introduced the story with the statement that the disciples (obviously in contrast to the people previously mentioned) now really followed Jesus into the boat, which has thus actually become for Matthew an image of the Church (G. Bornkamm, *Jahrbuch der Theol. Schule Bethel*, 1948, 49 ff.; ET in preparation; see n. 183). Dan O. Via, 'The Church as the Body of Christ in the Gospel of Matthew', *SJT* 11, 1958, 271–8, shows how this Church is the messianic community with which Christ identifies himself, in which he is present, and which carries out his ministry in virtue of his presence.

[201]On this see 6f and 23e.

[202]Cf. also R. Bohren, *Das Problem der Kirchenzucht im NT* (Diss. Basel 1950) 96, 102 ff., which, however, stresses that 18.17 also marks the end of such an attempt.

[203]14.30 f.; 16.22 f.; 17.16 f.; 26.56; 27.3–5; on the other hand 20.20.

[204]There is no longer a Jewish scribe who is 'not far from the kingdom of God' (Mark 12.34), but only one who wants to 'test' Jesus (Matt. 22.35).

[205]23.38; Haenchen 55 f.

[206]See 3b.

Church Order in the New Testament

the Church intends to be nothing less than Israel, the true Israel.[207]
The fact that Gentiles too are received into it (8.11 f.), does not
contradict this, for it is this very fact that shows it to be the real
Israel of God. The 'better righteousness', which exceeds that of
the scribes (5.20) because it is ready to sacrifice itself in suffering,
shows the presence of God's people. The vineyard will therefore
be given to a nation producing the fruits of it, as Matthew says
(21.41–45), particularizing Mark's brief allusion; and it is the son
who at first said 'No' who does his father's will (21.28–32).
While official Israel rejects Jesus, the band of children and insignificant people praises him (21.14–16).

f. The results of this interpretation of the Church are shown in
its order. The saying handed down only by Matthew (16.18 f.)[208]
shows how this Church traces its tradition most particularly to
Peter, who appears as the one who holds the keys of the kingdom
of heaven, and as such can 'bind' and 'loose'. Before we go into
that, it must be realized that in 18.18 the same authority to 'bind'
and 'loose' is conferred on the whole Church.[209] It is no doubt the
same saying, handed down here in a different form. 16.19
represents the more heavily edited version,[210] though that fact does
not determine whether the older form addresses Peter in the
singular or the whole Church in the plural. The following considerations make the former the more probable.[211] But we must
first ask how Matthew regarded the co-existence of the two. He
certainly sees in 16.18 a promise worded in such a way as to apply
only to Peter, and defining his special position.[212] In that case the

[207]This also appears in Matt. 24.9, where τῶν ἐθνῶν is inserted: the Church
is the Israel whom the Gentiles hate (G. Harder in *Theologia viatorum* 4, 1952,
80).
[208]It hardly goes back to Jesus. See 2b.
[209]It is clear from the context (see 18.19 ff.) that this promise concerns all
Church members, and not, say, only the disciples as special office-bearers
distinct from the others (cf. also Reid, *The Biblical Doctrine of the Ministry* 15).
[210]Elsewhere Matthew also uses the plural οὐρανοί instead of the singular.
But above all the saying about the keys of the kingdom of heaven (a typical
Matthean expression) has grown. Farrer, *Ap. Min.* 181, decides the other
way, but only because, without any support from the text, he assumes that
18.17 f. refers to the Church directed by the apostles as a body under the presi-
dency of Peter.
[211]So Bultmann, *Synopt. Tradition* 150 f., where representatives of the opposite view are also mentioned.
[212]On this cf. Cullmann, *Peter* 206 ff.

same must be true of v. 19. This is very interesting for two reasons. It is, indeed, a matter of dispute whether the binding and loosing means the pronouncing of the ban and the releasing from it, or the laying down of what is allowed and what is forbidden in the sense of the rabbinic interpretation of the law;[213] probably neither can be separated from the other.[214] In any case, Peter's apostolic authority can be seen in his exposition of the law. Right interpretation and application of the law is the key to the kingdom of heaven. But this contains the second point: Jesus' exposition of the law did not for its part become a law that is finished and closed—it has to be carried out afresh in the fundamental apostolic teaching. That is what lays the foundations of the Church, and in that consists the unique importance of Peter. The question is, however, whether Peter has a successor to whom such a unique position was transferred;[215] and here 18.18 answers clearly: the apostle has, in fact, successors, namely the whole Church.[216] As the apostolic Church it succeeds to the authority to teach, though in such a way that it must always listen to what Peter says. Thus it is Matthew too who incorporates in Jesus' mission charge to the twelve quite general precepts that concern every believer (10.32, 42), and so makes it clear that he regards the demands and bestowal of authority on the apostles as valid for all the believers of his time.[217]

g. That the right understanding of the law and the right obedience to it are vital is also shown by the existence, in the Matthean church, of Christian scribes who are characteristic of at

---

[213]Str-B I 738 ff.; IV 293 ff.

[214]So too v. Campenhausen, *Kirchliches Amt* 138.

[215]On the whole question see also F. M. Braun, *Neues Licht auf die Kirche* 76–88: the promise concerns Peter, and is not to be levelled out by simply being made to apply to everyone; nor on the other hand is it to be extended to successors.

[216]It is understandable that for Kuss, as a Roman Catholic writer, the only reason why the popes were not mentioned as successors is that the end was still expected to come soon, and that the correct interpretation only took shape gradually during the period up to Leo I (*TQ* 135, 1955, 49 f.). This, however, is an admission that there is nothing of that to be found, at any rate in the New Testament. For the basic question see 1d, e.

[217]Of course this process already begins with the adoption of the speech in Mark, and of its tradition in Q; only it is not so plain there that it is meant for all church members, and not only for 'missionaries'.

least a certain period of development.[218] That, however, at once raises the question whether there was a settled hierarchy of authorities for the exposition of the law and the management of the Church. Jesus' sayings, as they are collected in, shall we say, the Sermon on the Mount, certainly take first place; and it is also clear that the Church goes back to Peter for the mediation and interpretation of that message. Jesus' words and works, mediated by Peter, are therefore the final court of appeal. But because in fact this leads to inconspicuousness, to suffering and death, and to allowing oneself to be imposed on, the only hierarchy is the paradoxical one that the highest is the one who renders most service (23.11; 20.26 f.), and that the 'little ones' are the most important members of the Church (18.1 ff.). The Church may certainly have in it scholars who know the Scriptures extremely well; it may have leaders who take over responsibility for the others very competently.[219] But undoubtedly there nowhere appears in the conduct of affairs according to 18.15–18 any office-bearer, and all graduated titles are forbidden to the Church (23.8–10). There are, indeed, people who in fact take over and exercise a certain authority. But the fundamental difference here between the Church and the Qumran community is that neither clerical ordination nor novitiate nor selection and investiture confers any special status or privilege.[220] Nor, therefore, can there be found any indication that Jesus' promise to Peter (16.18 f.) could be continued in a kind of Christian ordination.[221] The whole Church is called on to listen to Jesus' exposition of the law, mediated by Peter, to follow the way of Jesus through lowliness, and to carry out the binding and loosing that will one day be confirmed in heaven.

[218]23.24: πρὸς ὑμᾶς! And indeed, Jesus is the one who sends, and no longer the 'Wisdom' as in Luke 11.49. 23.8–10 also assumes that the title was at least readily used in the primitive Church. Finally the expression 'their scribes' (Matt. 7.29) assumes the existence of other scribes who are Christian, and one of them is referred to in 13.52.

[219]18.12–14 might refer to such people, although this is not stated and is not certain.

[220]See n. 640, on our passage especially 1QS 6. 1, and on that Betz *ZNW* 48, 1957, 75. The Matthean church is at most on the way to being established (Grässer, *Parusieverzögerung* 200).

[221]And Jesus no more ordains Peter than he ordains any of the other disciples.

h. Both the promise and the danger of this idea of the Church are apparent. The Church has succeeded, despite the breach with Judaism, in regarding itself as Israel, and so in not abandoning the Old Testament. The continuity of God's actions is firmly maintained. The law is not a first step that is now done with, but remains in Jesus' new interpretation. But the new element is not denied. This Church has succeeded in carrying right into its organization its faith in the importance of insignificant people and the refusal of all honours and titles; it thinks in terms of the plan of salvation which finds its fulfilment in Jesus and his Church. True, it does not yet reflect on whether and how far the period after Jesus' death and exaltation is also history. For the Church it is the period of obedience to the law as interpreted by Jesus. Jesus' coming and the period of the Church are still to a certain extent seen together as the fulfilment of God's plan up till then.[222]

But the dangers must not be forgotten either. Here too Jesus is certainly more than a teacher; it is his lowliness that makes it possible for the Church to follow him; and his exaltation makes him the one who is always present. And yet it has not so far been thought out in what way the Church's position in relation to the old Israel is fundamentally new. There, as here, there were the righteous and the unrighteous. The popular movement that ended in the pharisaism of Jesus' time also began as a new interpretation of the law in the face of all the rigidity of the official religion. Above all, how can it be maintained that Jesus is the fulfilment of God's whole purpose in history if time and history are still going on? How is the presence of the risen Lord in his Church to be grasped without being put on the same footing as the presence of any rabbi who also lives on, after his death, in the tradition of his teaching? Is there no threat here of an ecclesiastical conception in which, as in the case of the Pharisees, the elect are separated from the lost simply by a better interpretation of the law and a more earnest obedience? It is clear that this was not

---

[222]The quotations showing the fulfilment of the Old Testament are certainly made to refer to Jesus. But the fact that the Church is called ἐκκλησία shows that it represents the fulfilment of Israel (see 3b). In the same way it is in the Church that the law's demands find their fulfilment in relation to the plan of salvation too.

how the Matthean church regarded itself, and that there was a
great deal in it to counter any such danger; but it has not yet been
thought out theologically why any such wrong development is
impossible from the theological conception that is at the very root
of this Church.

5

LUKE'S CHURCH

a. Even for Paul the time between Easter and the parousia is determined by the course of the gospel, and is therefore characterized as a period of history, though a very short one. But among the New Testament witnesses Luke is the first in whom we can see any real reflection about a history that is now beginning to extend over a considerable time.[223] Thus what already stands out in Matthew is here reflected much more clearly. For Luke it is not merely that Jesus, as an interpreter of the law, for example, lives on in the obedience of the Church—there is for him a real Church history filling out the time between Easter and the parousia. This means, not only that a Church that remains the same produces a history proceeding from it, but also that it is itself subjected to history. In what sense is this true?

b. We start from the Lucan terminology. Here 'Israel' habitually denotes the Jewish nation, and 'Gentiles' the non-Jewish (though not necessarily the non-Christian) nations. Thus the old conception in Matt. 8.11 f., according to which those chosen by God from the nations are added to Israel, can be taken over by Luke.[224] The early Catholic point of view, which refuses to allow the name of Israel to Judaism and regards the Church as the only true Israel, is therefore not yet reached.[225] This is also true in the main for the use of the term 'people' (λαός). It can indeed denote in general a body of people; but even in this sense Luke confines it to Jews.[226] It often denoted Israel in contrast to the Gentiles,[227] so

[223]Conzelmann, *Luke* 149 ff.
[224]Luke 13.28 f. (though subject to the addition of 30); Acts 2.39, where *Luke* is certainly thinking of the Gentiles.
[225]N. A. Dahl, *NTS* 4, 1957/8, 324, 327.
[226]*Ibid.* 324 f. Thus it does not appear in the whole account of the journeys in Luke 9.51–18.14, because there Jesus is going through Samaria. Only 6.17 remains uncertain; but there too Luke is probably thinking of the Jewish population of Tyre and Sidon.
[227]Acts 4.8, 10; 10.2 (but cf. 22); 13.17, 24; 21.28; 28.17; especially 26.17, 23; on the other hand cf. 8.6 etc.

that this honourable Old Testament title is not taken over from Israel to the Church either. There are only two exceptions: in the middle of Acts, which marks the beginning of a new period of Church history, the 'people' is mentioned that God has chosen out of the 'Gentiles' through Peter's mission (15.14). The same is true of the 'people' that God calls in Corinth (18.10).[228] Both cases deal with God's act of choosing, which corresponds to what happened with the ancient 'people' of God. Now there may be behind this a tradition that took up thoughts from Zech. 2.11, so that what was originally thought of was the band of people whom God brings out from among the non-Jews and adds to his people Israel.[229] But in any case Luke himself was no longer conscious of this. He obviously understood the idea of 'people' in these two passages, not in the full sense of God's people, but in the more general sense of a band of people whom God chooses for himself. Yet we can perceive there a consciousness that does not yet take shape in the terminology—the consciousness that there is a new people, a *tertium genus*,[230] which represents a new factor in relation to Jews and Gentiles, neither λαός nor ἔθνος.[231]

c. This is shown more clearly in the general design of Acts, and in occasional expressions, than in the terminology. Luke is certainly very anxious to underline the continuity of God's course of action, proceeding from Israel, indeed from Jerusalem. God clearly takes up the thread of the way that he took from the time of Abraham on. So far Luke thinks throughout in terms of God's plan of salvation. Israel's piety and righteousness provide the setting in which God's revelation makes its appearance; and it is on them that God bases the new phase of his plan right at the beginning of the Gospel,[232] in the temple at Jerusalem.[233]

[228]In 11.24 ὄχλος stands for the band of people chosen from the Gentiles; and in Luke 19.37; Acts 4.32; 5.14; 6.2, 5 πλῆθος stands for the Church.
[229]N. A. Dahl, *NTS* 4, 326 f.
[230]Aristides, *Apol.* 2.1 (cf. A. v. Harnack, *The Mission and Expansion of Christianity*, ET², 1908, I 240 ff.; R. Knopf in *Die apostolischen Väter*, ed. H. Lietzmann, 1920, 93 f.). Cf. 'new people', *Barn.* 5.7; 7.5.
[231]Q contains the saying that 'God is able from these stones to raise up children to Abraham' (Matt. 3.9 = Luke 3.8); but here the call to repentance is addressed to Israel, and the suggestion is—as probably with Jesus too—that the Gentiles would be incorporated in Israel.
[232]Luke 1.6; 2.22–24, 27, 39, 41 f.; cf. also 7.5; 23.56; Acts 10.22 etc.
[233]Luke 1.8 ff.; 2.22 ff., 37, 41 ff.

It is over 'the house of Jacob' that Jesus will reign, and for Israel that he is sent, although at the same time he will be 'a light for revelation to the Gentiles'.[234] In the synagogue service the prophetic words are spoken which sum up all Jesus' activities (Luke 4.15 ff.). While already in Matthew the 'Son of David' has replaced the 'kingdom of David' in the shouts of hosanna, in Luke's preliminary stories Jesus' descent from David, and the Davidic succession, are consciously emphasized.[235] Still more apparent in Acts is the concern to represent the Church as the rightful successor of the old Israel. Occasionally there appears as the distinctive mark of the Church simply the belief in the resurrection of the dead, which is guaranteed by the first precedent, the one set by Jesus (4.2). Thus any non-Sadducee whose heart is not completely hardened would surely become a Christian.[236]

d. But that does not alter the fact that God takes his Church along a way that in its course changes its character. That change is conditioned by Israel's hardness of heart. The first period after Easter is characterized by the choice that is still open. True, it is already becoming apparent that God will pour out his Spirit on 'all flesh', on his 'menservants and maidservants', so that 'whoever calls on the name of the Lord shall be saved.'[237] But this first period is closed by the persecution of Stephen and his circle, which Acts characterizes as a persecution of the whole Church.[238] It is then that the transition to the Samaritans—occasioned by Israel's rejection of Jesus[239]—is clearly marked in Acts 8.14–17.

---

[234]Luke 1.32 f.; 2.32; also 24.21. Cf. 13.16; 19.9: salvation is for the children of Abraham.

[235]Matt. 21.9, 15 (differently in Luke); Luke 1.27, 32, 69; 2.4, 11. But apart from the preliminary stories the title (which is of ill repute in Rome) is used only in the material taken over from Mark. Cf. 3.31.

[236]Paul can describe himself as a Pharisee, and on occasion put forward only the general belief in the resurrection of the dead as a subject for discussion between him and the Jews without mentioning Jesus, or without seeing in him anything more than an example of this (Acts 23.6; 24.14 f., 21; 26.6–8; cf. 26.22 f., 27; 28.10). Cf. Haenchen, *Die Apostelgeschichte* 177 f.; 186 f.

[237]Acts 2.17–21. The 'Lord' is now, of course, Jesus. The reference to Zion and Jerusalem at the end is omitted, and the addition of μου in v. 18 suggests the thought that what really matters is obedience to God's call, as is expressly laid down in 10.34 f. Cf. Haenchen, *ZTK* 51, 1954, 161.

[238]See n. 126.

[239]Even in the Gospel, the story in Luke 7.1–10, which was originally a call to Israel to repentance, takes on quite a different character as soon as it

The move into the Gentile world proper is still more strongly emphasized. In 8.26–40 the state of the Ethiopian remains obscure, so that the new period of history may be introduced by God's command to Peter (10.1 ff.).[240] Here the argument in 11.2 f. proves that it really is a question of moving out of the sphere of 'the circumcision' into the Gentile world; God himself has annulled the distinction between Jews and non-Jews.[241]

With Peter, however, it was a matter of individuals, so it was really Paul who opened the new period. Luke, indeed, expressly marks him off from the twelve. He is not less than they, but as God's witness to the Gentiles he has a different character. Once more, therefore, we find a fundamentally new start noted in 13.1–3 and then in 15.1 ff.[242] But still, the offer is made first to the Jews, and it is only their refusal that opens the way to the Gentiles.[243] Finally the uproar of the Jerusalem Jews against Paul opens the last period, in which the gospel goes out from Jerusalem, which still remains the centre,[244] to Rome and so out into the world (23.11). But here too the way is not finally free till after the Jewish community in Rome has once more explicitly said 'No' to Paul's message (28.25–28). With that the book closes.[245]

e. Luke therefore tells how the Church develops out of a pious group in Israel into that *tertium genus* that is now to be distinguished from Jews and Gentiles. Jews and Gentiles are already in evidence in Acts 4.27, united in the struggle against

---

begins to be told no longer to Jews but to Christians from the Gentile world. There then exists the danger of seeing in it only other people's guilt. That would be very much the case if the wording of Luke 13.26 f., which identifies the rejected people with Jesus' historical contemporaries, were not the original but the modified form in relation to Matt. 7.22 f.(as might be possible in view of Luke 6.46). 19.14, 27 is obviously intended for the unbelieving Jews. 19.41 ff.; 21.20 ff.; and 23.28 ff. give the destruction of Jerusalem a place of its own in the Gospel.

[240]For the same reason the narrative of 8.1 ff. is not continued till 11.19 ff.
[241]10.9 ff., 28, 34 f., 45; 11.17.
[242]It is only after God's action that the question of circumcision is again raised by malevolent opponents who try to hold up God's course (15.1).
[243]13.46 ff.; 18.6; 28.25 ff.
[244]1.4; 8.14; 11.22; but cf. also 20.16, 22; 21.4, 12 f. and the corresponding emphasis in Luke 9.31, 51; 13.33 f.; 17.11; 19.11.
[245]The sub-apostolic period in which false doctrine breaks in is even more a time *sui generis* (Haenchen, *Die Apostelgeschichte*, 91).

God's anointed, and in 14.5 against his messengers. Both are
hearers of the message, and both must repent.[246] Thus in 19.17
'Jews and Greeks' are distinguished from the Church, and
according to 26.17 Paul is likewise chosen from 'the people' and
from the Gentiles. If the Gentiles' hearts have to be cleansed by
faith, neither could Israel fulfil the law, and the only way of
salvation open to both is through the grace of Jesus (15.9–11;
13.38 f.). The fact that Luke can here make Paul's doctrine of the
law so innocuous shows that for him the Church is something
new; and so he no longer has to wrestle, as Paul does, with the
question why it is not the old Israel, but only the Church, that is
Abraham's posterity actually fulfilling God's intention and God's
law.

It is typical in this connection that Luke is very cautious about
transferring the old titles of Israel to the new Church. This confirms the view just outlined. The notions 'Israel' and 'people'
have already been discussed above; apart from these the only
title used to denote the Church is the 'saints' [of God]' in Acts
9.13, 32, 41; 26.10. The word 'church' itself is frequently used,
but only in 20.28 is it used within a traditional formula in the
Pauline form 'church of God' corresponding to the Old Testament term. Besides that, the word ἐκκλησία can be used in quite a
neutral sense to denote any assembly or even a mob (19.32, 39).
Instead of it there appear new terms, not yet established by
tradition, for this 'third species', in particular the generally applied
expression 'the disciples',[247] then also 'brethren' or 'believers',
'those who call on the name of the Lord', and finally, though only
in the mouths of people of other faiths, the name 'Christians' (11.26).

f. For Luke this new people, neither Jewish nor Gentile, but
already known to God from the beginning (Acts 15.18), is
already preformed in a remarkable way. Israel's opposition becomes clear even during Jesus' earthly life;[248] and here it is for

[246]Acts 18.4; 19.10; 20.21; 26.23. In Luke 2.32 Jesus already appears as a
light for Israel and the Gentiles.
[247]On this cf. Haenchen 217 n. 2. The μαθηταί are already separated from
the λαός in Luke 6.17; this is underlined by the change of the Marcan
presentation, and in Acts 19.9 Paul separates them from the non-believing
Jews.
[248]In the characteristic first sermon in Luke 4.25 ff. it is pointed out that
even in the Old Testament God had found the Gentiles obedient while
Israel had been found wanting. Cf. also 8.21; 10.30 ff.; 11.28.

Luke the 'Galileans' who to some extent 'occupy' Jerusalem and take the place of the population that has fallen away from God and has therefore no longer any rightful claim to Jerusalem.[249] In Acts their place[250] is taken by the 'God-fearers'. In the speeches made before these there is no such call to repentance as is made to the Jews and Gentiles.[251] They are expressly picked out from the inhabitants of Jerusalem;[252] they are the forerunners of the new people.[253]

But they are no more than that—there is no suggestion that the Church might consist only of Galileans or 'God-fearers'. The avoidance of any clear-cut nomenclature, or of any with a sacerdotal flavour, shows how concerned Luke is to keep this circle, which is no longer tied to any particular nation, open to everyone who is willing to be obedient.

g. Thus we can find in Luke no rigidly drawn outline of the idea of a Church, although conversion, faith in Jesus,[254] and baptism[255] are now assumed as a matter of course for entry into the Church, and the Holy Spirit is God's confirmation of it. There is no trace here of the cautious attitude of the Matthean church, which knows that human eyes cannot decide who belongs to the elect and who does not.[256] The Holy Spirit sees through the hypocrites and creates a pure Church for himself.[257] On the

[249]Conzelmann 38, especially n. 1, 202.
[250]They are specially mentioned in Acts 2.7; 13.31.
[251]E. Schweizer, 'Zu den Reden der Ag.', *TZ* 13, 1957, 7, 11.
[252]13.26 f. Is there any connection here with the fact that Luke (Acts 15.5 in contrast to 15.1) explicitly places in Jerusalem the resistance to the spreading of the Church out into the Gentile world?
[253]Cf. 10.2; 17.4; 18.7. Are these also meant in 15.21?
[254]11.17; 13.8. οἱ πιστεύσαντες becomes in fact a designation of the Church: 2.44; 4.32; 5.14; 18.27.
[255]2.38 etc.
[256]According to the Lucan account, Judas does indeed take part in the Last Supper, but only to be unmasked afterwards. Apart from that, the disciples are everywhere exculpated, and their flight is not related here. Luke omits Mark 4.13; 8.16–21, 33; 14.50. Peter's denial is related, but it is preceded by 22.32.
[257]Acts 5.1–11, 13; 8.18–24. The contrast between the sons of this world and the sons of light is also relevant here (Luke 16.8; cf. the 'elect' in 18.7) while the picture of the small flock that is attacked, and of the sheep sent among wolves (Luke 12.32; 10.3; Acts 20.28 f.), expresses both things— the strict separation from the world, and also the difficulty of recognizing this world (the 'wolves') as such.

other hand the Lucan company of the 'disciples' remains a 'way'[258] open to everyone who will take it. The Spirit opens the Church's frontiers to people of whom the Church itself would never have thought. The Lucan church is a part of the plan of salvation in so far as Luke not only accepts the assumption, which the New Testament takes for granted, that the Church is the continuation of the Old Testament Israel, but also recognizes that the period after Easter is a part of God's plan, in the course of which the Church, because of the mission to Israel and the refusal that it produced, becomes more and more clearly that 'third' company for which he does not yet use, or want to use, any definite title. In Luke too the way that the Church takes here is very much determined by its suffering. Persecution opens its way to the Gentiles (Acts 8.1–4; 11.19 f.) and to Rome (20.22 f.; 21.11–14; 26.31 f.; 27 f.). It is an inevitable part of the Church's 'way' (14.22).

h. This realization too expresses itself in the Church's order, as is shown first of all in the Lucan idea of apostleship, which must be clearly distinguished from Paul's as well as from what the twelve were, both during Jesus' earthly life and in the earliest days of the Church.[259] For Luke, the apostle is neither the eschatological ruler in the coming kingdom, nor the person called by the risen Lord to be a messenger. He is the eyewitness of Jesus' earthly life and work, and only as such is he called on to witness (Acts 1.21 f.).[260] Here the reflection about the period after Easter, and the Lucan solution, are clearly shown. Jesus' presence in his Church is at first (though not solely) regarded as analogous to the presence of a historical person who is made alive to later

---

[258]It seems that the noteworthy designation 'the way' goes back to its use in Isa. 40.3, and it is also to be found in Qumran (S. V. McCasland, *JBL* 77, 1958, 222 ff.). But in passages such as Acts 9.2; 22.4 it almost becomes a designation of Christianity as a new religion (Grässer 212; cf. W. Michaelis, *TWNT* V 93 ff.).

[259]This can be seen from the fact that ἀπόστολος appears much more often in Luke than in Mark or Matthew, where it still clearly implies a functional idea (cf. Reid, *The Biblical Doctrine of the Ministry*, 7).

[260]However fundamentally correct O. Linton is in remarking (*Buch. v. d. Kirche* 133 f.) that no final difference exists between personal relation to Christ on earth and relation to him through the Holy Spirit, it is not correct that for *Luke* Acts 1.21 f. and 9.1 ff. were on the same plane. Paul is not for him an 'apostle' (except in the traditional terminology—see Acts 14.4, 14—in which Barnabas too is called an apostle).

generations by witnesses who saw and heard him. For that very reason, however, the apostles can have no successors. That is emphasized by the choice of Matthias—the call of the earthly Jesus is replaced by the lot which the Lord (Jesus?) himself decides; in no other case is it used.[261] But here too his status as an eyewitness is the first condition. To this is added Jesus' call and his intercourse with the twelve after Easter 'through the Holy Spirit' (Acts 1.2 f.). This alone separates them from other eyewitnesses.[262]

But Luke's insight into the historicity of the Church is also reflected in his picture of Church order. We can recognize three lines of thought: (1) Church order changes in accordance with the stage of its development; (2) it makes apparent the continuity with Judaism; and (3) at the same time it brings out the newness of what God has created.

i. It is characteristic of the first period that the twelve are the Church's only teachers and leaders. The 'midpoint of time' is Jesus himself, and the picture that the eyewitnesses give of it really has to suffice for the life of the Church.[263] When Luke, presumably going against the historical facts,[264] makes the twelve a directing body, it shows that for him their originally eschatological significance has become unimportant. Perhaps, however, there is behind it another tradition which draws a parallel between the beginning of the Church and the beginning of Israel.[265] The Church's growth, and with it the evidence of human inadequacies, are according to Luke the cause of a first reordering. When, once more against the historical course of events,[266] he makes the seven into servants subordinated to the apostles, he shows his interest in the Church as something developing historically; the coexistence of two organizations has become the successive exis-

[261]Completion of their number by lot agrees with the idea of the twelve as having eschatological significance (C. H. Dodd, *According to the Scriptures*, 1952, 58 n. 1; E. Stauffer, *TLZ* 77, 1952, 201 ff.; J. Renié, *RB* 55, 1948, 43 ff.).
[262]They are explicitly stated to be laymen (4.13).
[263]Conzelmann, *Luke* 186 f.
[264]See 3n, and n. 155.
[265]On this cf. Stauffer, 201 ff. The analogy, then, was not consciously present in the mind of the Church at that time, or in the mind of Luke himself, who in fact never refers to any such thing. It might be, however, that during the time between the primitive Church in Jerusalem and Luke the originally purely eschatological function of the twelve was seen in the light of Jewish councils of twelve.
[266]See 3 o.

tence of two stages of historical development within a single unified Church. The number seven may go back originally to the analogy of the Jewish local rulers;[267] Luke himself scarcely felt that, as his account makes them something like deacons.[268]

In 11.30 the elders suddenly emerge. In Jerusalem they form, together with the apostles (15.2, 4, 6, 22 f.[269]; 16.4), the directorate of the Church, and for Luke they are obviously connected with the period when the Church spread out into the world.[270] Here again we can see continuity with the Jewish order. Luke mentions them, but he shows no sort of interest in the origin of their ministry, let alone their appointment by the apostles. According to 14.23 Paul and his companions appoint some such people in a newly established Gentile Christian church,[271] and according to 20.28 the Holy Spirit installs them as 'bishops'. But Luke lays no great stress on this idea either—it appears only on this one occasion, and even here the term denotes their functions, and is not an official title; it is interpreted by a reference to the 'feeding' of God's flock.[272] The connection of these two expressions is already traditional, and probably goes back to Jewish models, perhaps the Qumran group.[273] Again Luke can take up a tradition of that kind, which shows a certain continuity with Jewish order, and yet attach no importance at all to it.

k. Thus, even if Luke can accept a whole series of traditions that point to a connection with Jewish forms of service, his main

---

[267]Str-B II 641; Josephus, *Ant.* IV 8.14 (214), 38 (287).

[268]See n. 126, and on the literature v. Campenhausen, *Kirchliches Amt* 83, n. 1.

[269]They are shown here together with the apostles as 'brethren' of the Church, and not as fellow office-holders with the apostles (W. Michaelis, *Das Ältestenamt*, 1953, 28 f., 35).

[270]On the view that the seventy in Luke 10.1 were not elders, cf. Michaelis 22 ff. That they emerged in non-Jewish congregations in Asia Minor (H. H. Wendt, *Die Apostelgeschichte*, 1913, on 14.23) is in view of the Jewish parallel very unlikely, although the Gentile models may have had an influence later. Cf. also A. Ehrhardt, *The Apostolic Succession*, 1953, 27.

[271]As Paul knows no elders in his letters, this account does not correspond to the historical facts.

[272]Moreover in 1.20 ἐπισκοπή in the quotation from Psalms is made to relate directly to Judas' service, and is equated with ἀποστολή and διακονία (1.17, 25).

[273]The evidence is collated by W. Nauck, *ZNW* 48, 1957, 201 ff. That, of course, tells us nothing certain about the origin of this ministry, but only about the linguistic history of the title 'bishop'. See 24g, i, including n. 764.

interest is in the statements that express the Church's newness even in its order. That may be illustrated negatively by the fact that the priests who have become believers (Acts 6.7) play no sort of special part.[274] But he makes prophets in particular play a large part, and determine the Church's most important decisions.[275] For him they are the Church's teachers.[276] The Gentile Christian church's collection for Jerusalem proceeds from their instructions; and so it is not regarded in any way as an ecclesiastical temple tax or 'Peter's pence', but as a free gift inspired by the Spirit.[277] That shows that Luke cares a great deal about God's way of salvation—a way that leads from Jerusalem out into the world—but not about stressing any ecclesiastical subordination of the Gentile Christian church to a metropolitan church at Jerusalem.

Whatever else we find only shows that Luke, of course, assumes ordered churches.[278] But still any disciple can baptize, and the laying on of hands and the imparting of the Spirit is not the privilege of a special class of people;[279] and where the widows appear (Acts 9.39, 41) there is nothing to suggest that they represent a closed group called to some special service.

l. This almost casual mention of special office-bearers in the Church, and the absence of definite titles, show that the order of these forms of service is not fundamental to the Lucan church. It can therefore assume very diverse forms, monarchical, oligarchic, and democratic elements standing side by side.[280] But orders

[274]See 3m.

[275]Acts 11.27 ff.; 13.1 ff.; 15.32; 21.4, 9, 10 ff.; probably also 20.23.

[276]If in Acts 13.1 the two ideas are not identical, they are at least closely related; cf. J. V. Bartlet, *Church-life and Church-order*, 1943, 19.

[277]Acts 11.27–30. Luke knows of the collection, which is so important to Paul; but he mentions it only quite casually (Acts 24.17; *TWNT* VI 412 = *Spirit of God* 53).

[278]This is perhaps shown by his development of the tradition that came to his hand in Luke 10.7 (μισθοῦ) and 22.26 (on this see Schürmann, *Jesu Abschiedsrede*, 74 ff.).

[279]Acts 9.17 f. On the other hand it should be noticed that as a rule the apostles, like Paul, do not baptize (Acts 10.48; cf. 19.5/6; I Cor. 1.17). Günter Klein, *Die zwölf Apostel, Ursprung und Gehalt einer Idee*, 1961, 175, sees that Luke is not interested in a static hierarchy of offices; but he thinks that he stresses the temporal succession of offices. Authorization by the twelve is the necessary condition for Paul's mission, and authorization by Paul is the condition for eldership in the congregations of Asia Minor.

[280]So Reicke, *Glaube und Leben der Urgemeinde* 25 f. But I estimate more cautiously that this is evidence for Luke's time.

that are at first taken over without having any particular importance can become important in the course of historical development—so, for instance, the elders in relation to the false teachers
who make their way into the Church later (Acts 20.28–31). Luke
is really interested only where a new situation necessitates a new
and hitherto unknown form of service (6.1 ff.; 13.1 ff.). In neither
case is any title given. What Luke feels to be essential, therefore,
is not to point out the origin of a constitutive office of the Church,
but to write an account of a Church that is prepared to be shown
new and unaccustomed ways and also to take them; and then individual church members must be separated for those special tasks.

What is vital, however, is the way in which this is done. It is
always stressed that God has long since marked out those whom
he has appointed for such service; they are 'men . . . full of the
Spirit and of wisdom' (Acts 6.3, 5), 'leading men among the
brethren, prophets' (15.22, 32), who are chosen for it—indeed,
the Holy Spirit himself appoints them (13.2; 20.28). The initiative
for this can be taken in quite different ways. Sometimes it is a
growing dissatisfaction that moves the twelve to act (6.1 f.); sometimes it is the considered judgment of common sense (15.22–33),
and sometimes the Spirit's direct instructions to a small circle of
people who have gathered for prayer and fasting (13.2).

m. It is not easy to determine the part played by the Church
as a whole in this. True, it appears almost everywhere (as early as
1.15 and 2.1). It approves the twelve's proposal, puts up and
chooses candidates (6.3–5). It sends out and receives messengers
(11.22; 14.26 f.; 15.3 f., 40). It even calls the apostle to account
(11.1 ff.).[281] It also approves the decisions of the Council at Jerusalem (15.22; also 25 ?). But in this last case Luke seems to want to
underline the authority of the apostles and elders (15.6, 23; 16.4),
making the bulk of the Church merely approve in silence (15.12).
In the laying on of hands, too, it is never clear whether the act is
performed by the Church as a whole, or by either the apostles or
prophets.[282]

Now Luke is fond of leaving the text in this kind of obscurity

[281]This action is not confined to the 'narrow-minded' members of the
primitive Church (A. Wikenhauser, *Die Apostelgeschichte*, 1951, 101).

[282]In Acts 6.6 it would grammatically have to be the whole Church; and the
same is suggested in 13.3, where we read of another time of fasting and
praying; cf. 1.23–26, where it is no clearer which is the subject. In Qumran,

where he does not want to distort the facts, but does want to suggest to the reader a definite impression.[283] So we may suppose (though it can be no more than a supposition) that he knows about the lack of settled order in which such developments took place in the early days, but that he wants the reader to feel that there is a slight analogy with the practice of ordination.[284] For Luke, indeed, it is no more than that; for in 6.1–6 he is writing about what he regards as a subordinate ministry, and the absence of a title shows, too, that he is thinking of a single case in a special situation, not of the introduction of a general diaconate. Nor, of course, is there any prior term of apprenticeship, and it is not laid down who may practise the laying on of hands.[285] In 13.1–3, however, people who are already prophets and teachers are deputed to a new service, not to a new office; and Paul is here a recipient, not a giver, of the laying on of hands.

---

in spite of the strongly developed hierarchy, permission to speak seems to have been conferred by the assembly as a whole (together with the superintendent, or even in opposition to him: 1QS 6.11–13; cf. Ralph Marcus, *JBL* 75, 1956, 302). On Acts 13.1–3 cf. also R. Bultmann's conjecture (in *New Testament Essays*, ed. A. J. B. Higgins, 1959, 77) that this may originate in the We-source, so that, by deleting the 'we', Luke obscured the fact that the Church had heard the Spirit's voice and had sent the apostles forth.

[283] Anyone who does not know the other Gospels must suppose from Luke 23.25 (worded differently from his tradition in Mark 15.15) that it was the Jews who crucified Jesus. It is not till 23.36 that some Roman soldiers appear, 'coming up'! Before that we hear only of the Jewish authorities' mockery. The facts are not wrongly stated, and the well instructed reader knows that only the Romans can crucify; but the great mass of his readers must get a different impression. In Acts 6.1–6 the title 'deacon' is lacking, perhaps because Luke knows that this ministry did not originate till later (in Gentile Christian circles?). But the reader must see deacons there. Does Luke perhaps also suggest in Acts 18.22a a visit by Paul to Jerusalem, although he only possesses reports of a journey to Caesarea and Antioch?

[284] Against this it may be said that for Luke the initial period is *sui generis* (Conzelmann, *Luke* 209 ff.), so that the twelve cannot be simply identified with some office-bearers or other of a later time. But even apart from that, it may be asserted that not even in Luke does the bestowal of spiritual gifts (A. M. Ramsey, *The Gospel and the Catholic Church*, 1936, 70) begin to come within the sole competence of the twelve (and Paul). Cf. Acts 9.17 f.; 10.44; 19.2 f. Moreover, for Luke Paul does not belong to the twelve.

[285] The distinction between the laying on of hands and the leaning on of hands (D. Daube, *The New Testament and Rabbinic Judaism*, 1956, 224 ff. and 237; J. Jeremias, *ZNW* 48, 1957, 129 f.) may not be of any importance for Luke (or for the New Testament generally), as it cannot be made in Greek, and he certainly does not know it from the rabbinic laws. See 25c.

n. The special nature of this conception of the Church is clear. As in Matthew, there is no break in the connection with the Old Testament and Israel; but as Luke avowedly thinks on the lines of historical development, he can stress at the same time both the continuity and the newness of the Church, without having to assume any breach. Israel has developed further, under God's guidance, into a 'third species' which is neither Jewish nor Gentile. In this change there can be seen the decisive influence of God's action which takes place in Jesus' life and work, in his crucifixion and resurrection. Inasmuch as Luke also sees the period of the Church as a period of historical development, the Church remains open to any necessary change under God's guidance. Thus it can take over old regulations without laying any special weight on them, and can make new ones when circumstances demand them. The question to be asked here is as to the way in which the Church's newness becomes credible; and Luke has a good deal to say about that. Again and again he refers to the Spirit as determining the Church's order. But while Luke thinks in terms of historical development, the goal will really lie in the future. In fact, for him the parousia moved into the distant future, and the present time has become central; but it is regarded as just a period of history between Jesus and the coming kingdom. Jesus' life and work is now a picture of what the coming kingdom will be, and his resurrection a guarantee of the coming resurrection. But the present is also the consequence of previous historical epochs. Anyone who really believed the Old Testament and was consistently a Pharisee would have to join the Church.

Thus even the newness of what was created through Jesus is not stamped radically enough on the Church order. Regulations are taken over, or new ones are made. There are no longer priests, but there are elders. The apostles are regarded as people who, through their eyes and ears, are witnesses of a past period, and their position will always be unique. The greatness of Luke's view lies in his showing more impressively than anyone else that the Church can live only by evangelizing and by following whatever new paths the Spirit indicates.[286] But perhaps that makes it necessary to ask how it differs from a Hellenized Judaism open

[286]This is shown particularly in the way that Luke understands the Spirit: *TWNT* VI 410 (= *Spirit of God* 49 f.).

to the whole world—that is, how far God's action in Jesus Christ meant a new creation not only relatively but absolutely, and how the Church can be a witness to it. However strongly Luke regards conversion, faith, and baptism as unconditional requirements, the figure of Gamaliel is equally typical for him—a figure standing in benevolent neutrality between Judaism and Christianity, and in no way censured.[287] As long as it is a question only of human repentance and conversion, it cannot be made really credible that these cannot exist without God's action in Jesus Christ. What would have to be made even clearer than it is in Luke is that faith is not simply a human achievement depending on repentance. If that became a wall visibly separating the Church from the world, then indeed the form of Jesus' circle of disciples would in one respect be decisively changed.

[287]The change of mood in Acts 5.38 f. (Greek text) probably indicates that the speaker (as represented by Luke) may well know that the truth lies, not in the possibility of 38b, but in the reality of 39a.

6

THE CHURCH OF THE PASTORALS

a. Here too there is reflected the picture of a church that regards itself as living, not through a short interval, but through an extending history. While Paul himself still expected the parousia during his own lifetime,[288] he is represented here, as in Acts 20, as taking thought for the period after his death, and even for the period after the death of those whom he will leave behind in the Church's service.[289] It is a Church that has established itself in the world[290] and is taking over ordinary Hellenistic ethics. Marriage and the bringing up of children become essential; indeed, it is assumed that those who serve the Church have a family of believing children.[291] It is everywhere becoming apparent that the Church already has a fairly long development behind it, that the same thing lies ahead of it, and that it is aware of this. Theologically the Old Testament and the Church's relation to Israel no longer play any part; and it is all the more significant that the Church regards its piety as an unbroken development of Jewish piety.[292] The law, too, is neither the mark of a period closed by

[288]I Thess. 4.15 (*pace* A. Wimmer, *Biblica* 36, 1955, 273 ff.; E. M. B. Green, *ExpT* 69, 285 f., and many other attempts); I Cor. 15.51. And II Cor. 5.1-5 shows no other view. On this cf. R. Bultmann, 'Exegetische Probleme des 2. Kor.', *Symbolae Upsalienses* 9, 1947, 3 ff.; in v. 3, however, I read with W. Schmithals, *Die Gnosis in Korinth*, 1956, 227 f., 'provided that we shall be found clothed, not naked' (as these foolish Hellenist adversaries of Paul think). Thus Paul does not reflect at all whether this happens at the parousia or before. At any rate he does not suppose an intermediate state, but refutes this absurd Hellenistic 'nakedness' which his opponents regard as the ideal. This is rightly stressed by E. E. Ellis in *NTS* 6, 1959/60, 211 ff.; I cannot see, however, that the 'house' of 5.1 could be the corporate body of righteousness, so that nakedness and clothing could be interpreted ethically. Although in Phil. 1.23 Paul considers the possibility of being executed previously, 1.25; 3.20 f. show that the old expectation still remains alive.
[289]II Tim. 2.2; 4.1 ff.
[290]So too Kuss, *TQ* 135, 1955, 163, who does not decide the question of authorship.
[291]Titus 1.6; cf. I Tim. 3.4 f., 12.
[292]'Paul' declares that he has served God with a clear conscience since the

Christ, nor a factor that is finding its fulfilment for the first time
in the Church. It is taken over, but its claims are confined to
'unholy' people (I Tim. 1.8–11). Consequently even the calling
of Paul is understood, not as a break between pharisaic zeal for
the law and the preaching of justification by grace, but as an
'example' for the believers, to show that God's grace is greater
than all conceivable sin (I Tim. 1.15 f.).

Here, therefore, as in Luke[293] (and Matthew) the Christian
Church regards itself as a continuation of the Jewish. Yet the
view of a *history* of salvation is no longer central. The argument
with Judaism is a stage that has been overcome. The sharp
caesura between the preparation for salvation in the Old Testament and its fulfilment in the New Testament has vanished; and
so the Church is no longer strongly characterized, as it is in
Matthew, by the right understanding and practising of the law;
and the conception of the Church is no longer determined by the
question about what special thing separates it from Judaism. But
Luke's view of the historical aspect of salvation is absent. The
Church no longer regards itself as a developing historical factor,
essentially determined by its own history. It feels its own existence
much more strongly as a static one; it has established itself firmly,
and is now concerned to hold on to what has been attained, and
to remain as it is.

b. That is reflected in the terminology. The idea of the 'Church'
occurs three times. A typical expression is 'a people of his own'
(Titus 2.14). This Old Testament phrase is probably a constituent
of the traditional formal language,[294] and shows that the Church
still knows that it is Israel's heir by tradition, though the theological importance of this has little effect. Essentially the Church
sees itself as an important sociological entity, and that is probably
how the idea of a 'people' is already regarded. In particular the
comparison of the Church with the family (I Tim. 3.5, 12; Titus
1.7) points in that direction. Beside these passages we should also

---

time of his forefathers (II Tim. 1.3; cf. on the other hand Gal. 1.13–16;
Phil. 3.4–11!); the same kind of thing is said of Timothy's mother and
grandmother (II Tim. 1.5).

[293]Carrington, *The Early Christian Church* I 270, sees the relation to the
Church that is described in Acts.
[294]See also I Peter 2.9.

regard the term 'house(hold)', used of the Church, first of all in the sense of the family (I Tim. 3.15). But here we see a further characteristic development; this idea already has a history behind it, at the root of which there is probably the equation of the Church with the temple of God.[295] The continuation of the verse adopts this tradition, but not in the dynamic sense as if the thought were of the building of the house (I Peter 2.4 ff.) or of the Holy Spirit's living in it (I Cor. 3.16; cf. Heb. 3.6), but in the static sense— the Church is 'the pillar and bulwark of the truth'.[296]

Thus it becomes an essential feature of the Church to be a guarantor of the 'truth'—that is, of right doctrine; and this, of course, is relevant in all the passages that stress the great importance of right doctrine.[297] Now this is not something completely new—a tradition had existed previously, embodying Jesus' words and deeds; and when the Church preached the Word, it was, of course, always 'doctrine' too. But here it is given quite a new stress. This is connected first of all with the Church's situation as time goes on. False preaching, on the wrong lines, has become a reality; and the Pastoral Letters are heavily engaged against false teachers.[298] Only this does not explain everything, for in the same situation quite different answers would be possible.[299]

c. The answer given here is involved in the view of the Church as a sociological entity that takes its characteristics from its origin. The primary reason for this is that the writer looks back on decades, perhaps even on a century, of development. It is vital that the historical connection with the origin is not lost; and here it is characteristic of the Pastoral Letters that all the stress is on

[295]O. Michel, *TWNT* V 128 ff.; Mark 14.58; I Cor. 3.16; Eph. 2.21; I Peter 2.5; probably also Rev. 11.1; cf. besides Enoch 90.28 ff. also Jub. 1.17, and the equation of *cosmos* and God's temple in Josephus (quoted by O. Michel, *TWNT* IV 891, n. 25; evidence for the substitution of Israel or the Church for *cosmos*: G. Schrenk, *TWNT* V 978.16 ff.; M. Dibelius and H. Greeven, *An die Kolosser, Epheser, an Philemon*, 1953, 79; H. Windisch, *Der II Kor.*, 1924, 191), 1QS 8.5–9; 9.6; 1QH 6.25–27; 4QPs 37 2.16.
[296]It is true that the interpretation depends on the decision about punctuation, according to which either the creed or the Church itself is the 'pillar and bulwark of the truth'. The second, however, is much the more natural.
[297]I Tim. 1.10; 4.1, 6, 13; 5.17; 6.3, 20 f.; II Tim. 2.2 (14, 16, 23); 3.10; 4.3; Titus 1.9, 14; 2.1; 3.9 f.
[298]I Tim. 1.3 ff.; 4.1 ff.; 6.20 f.; II Tim. 1.15 ff.; 2.17 f.; 3.1 ff.; 4.3 f.; Titus 1.10 ff.; 3.10.
[299]See ch. 12 on the Church in the Johannine Letters.

Church Order in the New Testament

'guarding',[300] which is to be ensured by the men who represent the connection with the apostle who has been entrusted with the doctrine[301]—men who faithfully take over his teaching and hand it on unchanged.[302] The matter is therefore clearly one of tradition, not succession; the apostle, and only the apostle, is the guarantor of its transmission—there is no mention of a *traditio viva*. So, too, there is as yet no name for any office that might, as the apostle's successor, develop his tradition.[303] The problem of reinterpretation, of the reformulation that is becoming necessary, is not seen at all. Although the writer himself largely masters this problem, he naïvely assumes that his message is simply the same as Paul's. The false doctrine, however, demands no reformulation of the apostolic doctrine at all, as it consists of nothing but myths and fables that are to be recognized at once as meaningless.[304] To teach rightly, a person only needs to be 'reliable'—that is, he must hand on the message that he has received, without leaving it for new ways of his own choosing.

Here, therefore, the Church lives on what happened in a time that can still be grasped historically. It lives at the same time in reliance on what will happen one day in the future. Speaking psychologically, the parousia has moved away into the distance, and so it plays no great part; but speaking theologically it is the real turning-point. While Jewish piety passes unbroken into Christian, so that the division between the two is felt to be no more than that between two historical epochs, the second of which represents the continuous development of the first, the

[300]I Tim. 6.20; II Tim. 1.14; Titus 1.9.
[301]I Tim. 1.11; II Tim. 1.11.
[302]II Tim. 3.10; the false teachers, on the other hand, 'teach otherwise' (I Tim. 1.3; 6.3), 'wander away' (I Tim. 1.6; 4.1; 6.21; II Tim. 1.15; 4.4; Titus 1.14), and 'make shipwreck' (I Tim. 1.19). Of course, the tradition is still present almost exclusively by word of mouth (H. Schlier, 'Die Ordnung der Kirche nach den Pastoralbriefen' in *Glaube und Geschichte, Festschrift für F. Gogarten*, 1948, 40 f.)—there is as yet no New Testament!
[303]The stress here is quite different from Paul's. With Paul the idea of the tradition is constantly present; but he knows that he himself is a link in the tradition (I Cor. 15.3; 11.23, and on this W. G. Kümmel in H. Lietzmann, *An die Korinther* I/II, 1949, 185; J. Jeremias, *The Eucharistic Words of Jesus*, ET 1955, 102 f.; rather differently in O. Cullmann, *Die Tradition*, 1954, 9 ff.), while in the Pastoral Letters he is clearly the first link (H. Conzelmann in M. Dibelius, *Die Pastoralbriefe*, 1955, 8; v. Campenhausen 169 f.).
[304]II Tim. 3.9; cf. I Tim. 1.4–7; 6.4 f., 20; II Tim. 2.16, 23; Titus 1.14.

parousia will mean an absolute division, which will for the first time bring what the Church really lives for.[305] The longing for the Lord's future appearing is of itself the mark of right faith, while it is characteristic of the false teachers that they speak of the resurrection as having already taken place.[306]

d. So the Church is regarded here as a body that it is vital to understand through the ideas of social order—house and family. It lives in a historical tradition, although the events that have played the greatest part in shaping it are based, not on the causal connection of world history, but on God's miraculous action. For this reason, one of the most striking phenomena is the fact that the Spirit—quite contrary to what we find in Paul—now hardly plays any part. Where he does emerge, he is no longer the one who gives the Church its life today. I Tim. 4.1 appeals to the Spirit in order to show that even the most recent development was already within sight at the time of that historical beginning from which the Church comes. In II Tim. 1.14 he is the power of God, which 'guards' (but does not for instance reformulate or re-interpret) the apostolic doctrine. Only in Titus 3.5 is he presumably seen as the strength of ethical life.

e. Something of the Church's original openness is still kept in the emphatic assertion that God 'desires all men to be saved' (I Tim. 2.4; 4.10). If we take the latter statement literally, that God is the Saviour 'of all men, especially of those who believe', then it is assumed that there is also salvation outside the believing Church. Now it is true that this statement is a polemical phrase used against false teachers who deny the knowledge of salvation to certain classes of people; and so we must perhaps take it to mean that salvation is open to all men on condition that they come to believe.[307] At the same time, we do not find assertions that limit salvation to those who are baptized or who assent to a certain profession of faith; only apostasy from the faith is threatened with judgment. Part of this openness of the Church consists especially in the very widespread adoption of ordinary Hellenistic ethics. In the argument with the false teachers who allot a specially important part to women, the writer can even go so far

[305] I Tim. 6.14 f.; II Tim. 1.12, 18; 4.1 ff.
[306] II Tim. 4.8; Titus 2.13; II Tim. 2.18.
[307] This might be supported by II Tim. 2.10, 19, for example.

as to assert that women will be saved by child-bearing.[308] Even if there is no careful consideration of whether the ordinary ethos of the world could bring salvation, it is none the less very highly valued, and there is a wide opening for it.

f. But beside this there appears a second line of thought, which really conflicts with the first. The experiences undergone, particularly in connection with false doctrine, lead to church discipline. This development is intelligible, but the decisive question is what it is based on. Now there can be no doubt that the Church hopes to win back erring church members, and so it is recommended that only mild action should be taken (II Tim. 2.25). Anything different would be perverse; and I Tim. 5.19 contains another warning against precipitate action. But even in such remarks as these we can no longer see something that still holds good for Matt. 18.15–17, viz. that Church discipline is only the form of pastoral preaching that seeks to speak to an individual in a special situation and save him.[309] Even where there is no thought of the guilty person's being lost, there is a distinct concern to deter others (I Tim. 5.20).[310] Here Church discipline is already moving into another category. It is no longer simply an act of preaching the gospel, but is becoming a means of managing the Church so as to provide for its own purity, the motive for which, of course, is the salvation of its members. This is seen even more clearly in passages where there is any thought of actual exclusion. Here it is hardly expected that the member will be regained, and the Church is explicitly exhorted to keep itself pure by avoiding any contact with such people.[311]

[308]I Tim. 2.15. The AV reads 'if they continue . . .' (plural, as in the Greek); the RSV reads 'if she continues . . .', the latter reading, which is probably correct, introduces a certain restriction.

[309]See 4e and 23e.

[310]Perhaps v. 22 even suggests that the sinner's readmittance should not take place too quickly. See n. 804.

[311]I Tim. 1.20; II Tim. 2.21; Titus 3.10 f. This side is stressed in Bohren, *Das Problem der Kirchenzucht* 61 f. It seems to me that we should have to differentiate more strongly. What is vital is not whether such Church discipline is carried out more strictly or less, but the aim of the action: is the goal of all discipline exclusively the preaching of the gospel of grace, which includes in certain circumstances a definite 'No' to a person (without which it could not be convincingly honest), or is it the keeping of the Church untarnished? That is, does the Church seek the people whom God sends to it (and, if need be, with a refusal that shows them that none but binding obligations will do here), or does it seek its own perfection?

So in facing the world the Church remains open by not simply condemning it in its ethical endeavours, although for the Church itself belief in Jesus' first and second coming, and right doctrine, are of the first importance; but it draws a sharp line between itself and those in its midst who preach, not right doctrine, but their own wisdom.

g. It is also from this point of view that Church order must be understood. It is a matter of keeping to the original message. The origin, however, is still only Paul[312] and 'his' gospel.[313] The problem of reformulating the primitive Church's preaching in the Pauline message has already moved out of sight;[314] and the only thing that now matters is to keep this Pauline doctrine unchanged. Again and again it is stressed how God himself appointed Paul to the apostolic ministry.[315] Timothy and Titus followed him, and are therefore the orthodox bearers of the Word,[316] having been appointed by the laying on of hands.[317] Just as there is apparent here an order of worship largely corresponding to that of the synagogue,[318] so also we see a rite that has analogy in Jewish ordination, and at the same time shows this church's connection with the Palestinian church.[319] Of course, we are bound to see the differences too. This act does not yet bear the character of legal authorization. Timothy is not reminded that he exercises his ministry by right and can appeal to this appointment, nor is the Church expected to acknowledge him because of it. His service is repeatedly, and in direct connection with the mention of ordination,

[312]Not 'the apostles' (with Conzelmann, *Die Pastoralbriefe* 8).
[313]This typical formulation occurs in II Tim. 2.8 (cf. 3.10). The expression is also found in the non-Pauline verse Rom. 16.25; otherwise only in Rom. 2.16, where, however—apart from a variant of the text—it is very doubtful whether the sentence has been correctly transmitted (R. Bultmann in *TLZ* 72, 1947, 200 f.; cf. *TR* 18, 1950, 299). But we find 'our gospel' in II Cor. 4.3; I Thess. 1.5?; II Thess. 2.14; cf. Gal. 2.2.
[314]Acts still knows of this, even if it simplifies the development.
[315]I Tim. 1.12 (διακονία); 'apostle', 'preacher', and 'teacher of the Gentiles' are synonymous (I Tim. 2.7; II Tim. 1.11; cf. 4.17; Titus 1.3).
[316]I Tim. 4.6, 16 (cf. Titus 2.7); II Tim. 2.15. Cf. C. Spicq, *Les épîtres pastorales*, 1947, 199: I Tim. 6.14 f. 'is a call for orthodoxy whose vigour is unparalleled in the NT'. If ἐντολή were here the mandate for office (G. Schrenk, *TWNT* II 552.37 ff.), the passage could be applied particularly to the position of Timothy and Titus; but see n. 324.
[317]I Tim. 4.14; II Tim. 1.6; see 25d.
[318]I Tim. 4.13; see n. 874.
[319]Dix, *Ap. Min.* 232.

based on his being a model to the Church and working through
the quality of his conduct.[320] The mediation of the charism
is an essential in the laying on of hands, but the bearer must
always be kindling it afresh. Thus this action again bestows no
new title.[321] Most important of all, it has been performed only
because of signs that revealed Timothy as the one whom God
had appointed (I Tim. 1.18; 4.14).[322] It is not simply knowledge
acquired, or the completion of studies under the scribes, but God's
free will, which he makes known through the mouth of his
prophets,[323] which is the precondition.[324]

No doubt great stress is laid here on the right 'succession of
doctrine'. What Timothy has heard from Paul he is to hand on to
reliable men, who in their turn can teach others.[325] But it is very

[320]I Tim. 4.12 ff.; 5.22; Titus 2.7. Even the apostle himself authenticates
his ministry by giving himself, his very life, as a sacrifice (II Tim. 4.6).
Streeter (*The Primitive Church* 108 ff.) is right in emphasizing that the Pastoral
Letters are more interested in the ethical attitude of the office-bearers than
in the exact demarcation of the various ministries. Thus the position of the
bishops is, according to Streeter, described with conscious ambiguity,
because some churches were already directed by a single bishop and others
by a body of presbyters. In fact the Pastoral Letters introduce no new
ministries, so that a good deal remains obscure. But there is no doubt that
such regulated ministries do exist.
[321]The many different expressions that are applied to Timothy and Titus
presumably show that there is no intention of establishing a clearly defined
office. Timothy, for instance, is διάκονος (I Tim. 4.6), ἐργάτης (II Tim. 2.15),
εὐαγγελιστής (II Tim. 4.5).
[322]Also emphasized by F. Grau, *Der neutestamentliche Begriff* διακονία
(Diss., typescript, Tübingen 1946), par. 6, p. 84 n. 1, p. 88. Spicq, 47 f.,
points out that even in Chrysostom's time such prophetic references were
frequent in the choice of bishops.
[323]Is διὰ προφητείας (I Tim. 4.14) plural = 'on the strength of prophecies',
so that the passage would be substantially identical with 1.18?
[324]E. Käsemann in *NtlStud* 261 ff. claims, like others, to see in I Tim.
6.11–16 a formulary of an ordination charge. But the exhortations in 11 f.
suggest the situation of baptism (*ibid.* 263 f.), and the reasons for the ordination vow are not very convincing; in baptism particularly, too, the candidate
is brought in to join the followers of the suffering Lord, and into opposition
to the hostile world, for dying with Christ is completed in the suffering of
persecution (Rom. 6.3 ff.; II Cor. 4.9–12; I Cor. 15.30 ff.; Rom. 8.36), and
the ἐντολή can just as well be the obligations of baptism as of ordination.
Nor is it obvious that a section that clearly uses formulary material cannot
be a general exhortation. It must therefore remain open whether the passage
refers to baptism or to ordination; the former seems to me the more probable.
[325]II Tim. 2.2; cf. Titus 1.5. Putting the comma in II Tim. 2.2 after ἐμοῦ
(with W. Lock, *The Pastoral Epistles*, 1924, 93, interrogatively) gives a more
easily understood meaning, but is clumsier linguistically.

interesting that in this connection there seems to be no stress on subsequent appointments in the warranted tradition, for in neither passage is there any mention of the laying on of hands or of ordination. Of course, it is possible that the Pastoral Letters already know of such laying on of hands;[326] but in that case it is doubly striking that they do not mention it.

h. Here too, as in Luke, we can trace the Palestinian tradition[327] behind the elders.[328] The word can still also be regarded as merely denoting an old man (I Tim. 5.1; Titus 2.2)—the natural superiority of old age is not yet fully distinguished from the formally appointed elders. But the elders in the more restricted meaning of the term form a clearly defined group, appointed for special service and receiving some consideration for it;[329] presumably, as in Acts 20.28,[330] they are identical with the 'bishops' (Titus 1.5–7). From the fact that here and in I Tim. 3.1 ff. 'bishop' appears only in the singular, it has been supposed that there was a monarchial episcopate;[331] but a more likely explanation may well be that the writer inserted a traditional exhortation for a bishop.[332]

It is not easy to decide exactly what the elders' ministry was.

[326]Spicq, xlv, certainly infers from I Tim. 5.22; II Tim. 1.6; Acts 13.3; 14.23, that the presbyters were themselves ordained and possessed the right of ordination; but the ordination of presbyters in the passive sense could be referred to at the most in I Tim. 5.22 (but see n. 804). In the active sense it is presumably attested by I Tim. 4.14 (n. 812), but together with the apostle.

[327]See n. 270.

[328]I Tim. 4.14; 5.17 ff.; Titus 1.5.

[329]Titus 1.5; I Tim. 5.17 f.; cf. II Tim. 2.6. Michaelis, *Das Ältestenamt* 115 f., deletes the reference to remuneration in I Tim. 5.18 as a gloss; but if it is in the post-Pauline period (which Michaelis does not accept), there is no need to suspect it. Cf. also *Did.* 13.

[330]On this see 5i and 24g.

[331]v. Campenhausen, *Kirchliches Amt* 116 ff. Streeter 114 f. also takes the singular to be generic, but sees in Timothy and Titus idealized portraits of the (already established) monarchical bishop. It is none the less true that no titles are used for them, and that after some time they leave their position and go back to the apostle. An intermediate position is taken by Spicq, xlvi f., 91 ff.: according to him the bishop is put essentially on the same level as the presbyter-priest; but as *primus inter pares* he occupies a special position by virtue of higher authority or of a more precisely defined office. In the five years after Phil. 1.1, therefore (Spicq accepts the Pauline authorship), the hierarchy has developed (on the literature see *ibid.* 96 f.).

[332]Titus 1.6 goes over into the singular while presbyters are still being discussed. We too could put it in the form 'Appoint . . . as pastors, . . . if someone is . . .; for one who has the cure of souls must be . . .' Michaelis too, 52 f., assumes that bishops and elders are identical.

According to I Tim. 5.17 they are overseers, of whom only some
are entrusted with preaching and teaching.[333] Beside them there
are the deacons, and perhaps the deaconesses.[334] The 'good standing' that they can acquire is not a higher office, as for instance
that of a bishop, as one certainly might infer from Jewish and
early Catholic analogies if it were not excluded by the context,[335]
but is their position before God, or perhaps their prestige in the
Church.[336] The widows too are now a special group clearly defined
by being listed separately (I Tim. 5.3 ff.). The only thing that we
hear about their service is that it is one of intercession.[337] This
service, therefore, is so important to the Church that we hear
almost as much about it as about that of the bishops. The custom
is still maintained, too, that all men are free to offer prayer,[338] and
presumably also to teach,[339] at the meeting for worship.

[333]That it is demanded of the 'bishop' that he shall be 'an apt teacher' (I
Tim. 3.2; Titus 1.9) will be an ideal demand that is not fulfilled in every case.
That the elders 'who rule well' were to be differentiated from others who ruled
less well (Michaelis 109 f.) is unlikely. The τιμή is double compared with the
widows.

[334]I Tim. 3.8 ff. As in the case of the bishop nothing is said about his wife,
v. 11 is more probably to be related to female deacons (there is as yet no
feminine form of διάκονος) than to deacons' wives. That is supported by
Rom. 16.1 and Herm. *Vis.* II 4.3 (compared with *Simil.* IX 26.2). Likewise
Lock xx and *ad loc.*; Spicq, xlviii and Conzelmann, *ad loc.* leave the
question open.

[335]3.13; W. Nauck in *ZNW* 48, 1957, 216 ff. The example shows, however,
how easily such an incorrect interpretation is often suggested; for without
the added καὶ πολλὴν παρρησίαν there would be no gainsaying the accumu-
lated evidence of Qumran and the early Catholic Church.

[336]W. Nauck, in *ZNW* 48, 1957, 218 f., maintains rightly that in any case
there is no distinction between clergy and laity. If the word were to be
interpreted quite analogously to Qumran, it would mean at the most that all
the Church members were allotted a definite rank within which they were to
perform their service, and that the deacons were entitled to a specially high
one. But this analogy too is questionable, even if the expression should come
from there. For example, some Swiss Reformed Churches still speak of the
pastor's 'consecration', although they mean something totally different
from the *consecratio* from which the term has been taken over.

[337]The widow is supposed to have performed diaconal services before she
is received as a widow. That may lead one to suppose that she continues to
perform such services; but that is by no means certain, and it is not demanded explicitly here.

[338]I Tim. 2.8. Τόπος denotes, in customary Jewish language, the building
used for divine service (Kümmel, *Kor. I/II*, 166). In view of 1 f. and 11 f.,
there can be no thought of private prayers; and both the reference to raised
hands and the mention only of men tell against them.

[339]In any case it is forbidden only to women (v. 12).

i. The Church is engaged in a severe struggle with *gnosis*, which is on the increase (I Tim. 6.20). Prophets and prophetesses are going from house to house, trying to win church members over to their speculations (I Tim. 5.13; II Tim. 3.6). The Church is threatened with disintegration in which everyone appeals to his own private discernment and goes his own way. In this situation the Church clings to the apostolic word which has been handed down. It also reflects on its own internal order, according to which not all the gifts are given to everyone; and so it erects a dam against perverted speech and action. In the Pastoral Letters we see most sharply defined a development that was present from the beginning. With a partiality called forth by the gnostic menace, the Church is here regarded as a historical entity that exists only as long as it does not deviate from the historical line of its development. The development from Judaism to Christianity therefore takes place with hardly a break; and this implies that the usages of Jewish worship and Jewish Church order are in large measure taken over. That in itself is certainly not wrong. Jesus too lived as a matter of course in and among the Jewish people, and the same is true of the beginnings of the Church. From the beginning, moreover, not everyone has the same gift and task allotted to him. Jesus himself takes one to walk with him and sends another back to his family, has one work as an itinerant preacher and another give away his money. If Jewish regulations, suitably adapted and revised, were taken over when the Church detached itself from the Jewish connection, that was only natural, for the Church had already been living under those regulations as a matter of course.

But at this point the question arises: Do not these regulations acquire in the course of development an importance that they did not originally have? In their origin they were things taken for granted without much reflection; and now they suddenly have to serve as protecting ramparts against imminent dangers. Thus, instead of being a possibility commended by all kinds of practical considerations, they become a necessity without which the Church can no longer be a real Church. Does not this upset everything? Can we still see in the Church's order the things that make it a Church?

k. No doubt the message of Jesus Christ stands in the midst of this Church; this is attested by the important place occupied by Timothy and Titus, and it is also responsible for many of the existing features of Church order—e.g., the importance of the service of intercession. Yet we cannot quite stifle the question: Does the conviction that the Lord lives in the Church today assume a concrete form? Is not the order biased in such a way that everything becomes free from risk, and thereby unworthy of faith? Is not the sequence threatened with inversion, so that it is no longer the case that one who is called by God receives through the Church the opportunity of carrying out his commission, but rather that one who is appointed to a ministry is thereby guaranteed the acquisition of the divine gift for it?[340] And is not salvation seen merely in the repetition of the old message, so that neither the venture (and consequent risk) of interpreting it, nor the experience of God's living Spirit, is now possible? We shall not simply affirm all that, for indeed the fact that prophetic direction first leads to Timothy's ordination is too weighty, and the Church's real, if unconsciously made, transition to a new situation is too clear. But we have reached the outermost point in the New Testament. This one-sidedness was necessary in the fight against the *gnosis*; but it is clear that there are other dangers too, and that the development from the New Testament would take a wrong course if the other side, the witness of the Lord who lives today and of the freedom of the Spirit, were not also allowed to take shape clearly.

[340]Charism is found only in the singular in the case of an ordained person (Grau, par. 6, pp. 80 ff.). If ἄνθρωπος Θεοῦ (I Tim. 6.11) were really meant for the ordained person, it would be very strongly emphasized that the old Jewish conception, according to which only the man specially called by God has the Spirit, has in practice taken the place of the New Testament realization that the Spirit is granted to every believer. This would not be greatly changed by the fact that the latter belief is still in theory held elsewhere. Cf. E. Käsemann, *NtlStud* 268, and n. 324 above.

C. Paul's Conception of the Church, and its Development

7

THE CHURCH IN THE LETTERS OF PAUL

a. For Paul too the Church is Israel—indeed, it must even be said that he was the only one who thought out to its logical conclusion the idea that it is the Church, and not the synagogue, which is now Abraham's posterity chosen by God.[341] Here, although the relative numbers are completely changed, he can keep to Jesus' view that the Gentiles are received into the original company of God's people, who are, almost as if by nature, the possessors of holiness.[342] For him too the Church is taken into a history that begins in the Old Testament with the choice of Abraham and his descendants, and ends with the redemption of Israel.[343] But even in Old Testament history, Israel was not just the nation visible in that history, but the number chosen by God and known only to him, within that nation.[344] From the very beginning, therefore, the nations that do not belong to this people are included in God's plan of salvation, simply because membership is a gift of grace, and is not conferred by merit or by ancestral privilege.[345] It is only from this conception that the thought can be carried through logically that only the Church is Israel in the

[341]Gal. 6.16 (cf. I Cor. 10.18); Phil. 3.3; Gal. 4.28 ff. (stressed in Cerfaux, *The Church in . . . St Paul* 7 f.).

[342]Matt. 8.11; Rom. 11.17 ff., 24; Cerfaux 60–62. Even Eph. 2.11 ff. still sees it in that way (Dix, *Jew and Greek* 61 f.); only the question is how far that language is still alive, and how far it has merely been taken over. In I Cor. 7.14 Paul can even take over the Jewish idea of God's people in a way that he does nowhere else: that God's people live in (almost natural) holiness, and the Gentiles in uncleanness (Dahl, *Das Volk Gottes* 223; H. Braun in *Theologia viatorum* 1, 1948/9, 39 ff.).

[343]Rom. 9.4 ff.; 10.14 ff.; 11.1 ff. Cf. my essay in *NTS* 8.1, Oct. 1961.

[344]Isaac and not Ishmael, and particularly Jacob and not Esau, are chosen, although in the second case there was no sort of difference through birth (Rom. 9.6–13); so too, in Elijah's time, the seven thousand known only to God, and not the whole nation (11.4).

[345]Rom. 9.24 ff.

true sense, while the period of the Old Covenant as the time under the law represents only in a very provisional way what God wills. Thus the whole period of the law, which 'came in' (Rom. 5.20), can appear in Paul's writings in the shape of Ishmael, or his mother Hagar, as if it were only a collateral line, on which God's blessing rests only at second hand[346]—it is only the Church that attains Isaac's full status of sonship.

But this Church of freedom,[347] which is not connected with the people of Israel in the sense of national and hereditary association, is for Paul not merely a late stage in the history of salvation —it is already there with the figure of Abraham. From the very beginning he is the father of the nations, the promise being given him even before circumcision—and that means, for Paul, before he was the father of this particular nation that is distinguished from the rest by the law.[348] The distinctive sign of the Church is therefore in the last resort not its historical classification, either by its representing the fulfilment of a development, or by its being seen as a historically developing entity, but faith—following in Abraham's steps.[349] It is certainly also the fulfilment of Old Testament history and has itself been taken into a history of the course of the gospel; but that is not what really makes it God's Church. For all God's purpose in history before and after Jesus is the demonstration of the freedom of his grace.[350] If the Church is characterized as Israel, it is thereby reminded that it lives only by the history of those manifestations of God's grace. The name also involves for Paul the recollection of God's faithfulness, which still holds contemporary Judaism fast beyond the time of its unbelief and will one day recall it; and so it keeps the Church from all presumptuousness. It is tied to Israel, not because of their historical connection, but because Israel is the final visible sign of the freedom and faithfulness of God's grace.

[346]Rom. 5.20; Gal. 3.17 ff.; 4.22 ff.
[347]Paul therefore never uses λαός to denote the Church, and for Israel he uses it only in quotations (Cerfaux 20 f.). This goes far beyond the development of Judaism, which, although it turned itself more and more emphatically into a religious community, yet remained a λαός.
[348]Rom. 4.9–17; Gal. 3.6–9, 17–19.
[349]Rom. 4.12, 16; Gal. 3.7, 14, 26–29.
[350]Not till the writings of Paul, therefore, does κλητοί denote the Church of Jesus (Cerfaux 176 ff.). While ἅγιοι goes back to the Old Testament, κλητοί corresponds rather to the apocalyptic writings (*ibid.* 118 ff.).

This cannot therefore be misunderstood by supposing that what makes the Church a Church is a mere reliance on a visible, demonstrable connection with this divine purpose in history—Jewish ancestry, the adoption of circumcision and the law, the authentic tradition, and the unbroken development—whether it is traced only as far as Jesus, or back into the Old Testament. What really distinguishes it as a Church in contrast to the world[351] is what now binds believers together with their living Lord—the fact that they are the body of Christ.[352]

b. It is, of course, impossible here to go into all the questions involved in this idea.[353] The difficulty of understanding them lies in the fact that at this point several lines of thought intermingle. One has to start from the Hebrew idea of time.[354] Even if we do not exaggerate the difference between this and the Greek,[355] we have to recognize that the Hebrew verb has no tenses. Thus an idea that can also be conceived in Greek thought is specially close to Hebrew thought: that, in fact, a past event is 'present' to us if we live by it and allow ourselves to be directed by it, while an unimportant event which does not touch us at all can, considered from

[351]Cf. the stressing of its alien status on earth (Phil. 3.20; later Heb. 13.14; cf. 3.7 ff.; R. Bultmann, *CJT* 1, 1955, 79).

[352]The still unadjusted co-existence of the idea of the people of God and that of the body of Christ is stressed by Bultmann, *ibid.* 78, while Dahl 225 ff. underlines their essential unity. Oepke, *Das neue Gottesvolk* 219 ff., understands the idea of the 'body of Christ' in relation to the thought of God's people; but he sees that 'the mountain peaks are shining in the *gnosis*', although that idea represents the 'primary rock'. Still more clearly *TLZ* 79, 1954, 363 ff.

[353]See my article σῶμα to appear in *TWNT*, and a preliminary article in *JBL* 79, 1960, 124 ff. Survey of the various discussions: Michel, *Zeugnis* 44 ff.; J. A. T. Robinson, *The Body*, 1952, 55; on Roman Catholic research, T. Soiron, *Die Kirche als der Leib Christi*, 1951, 9–52. Discussion of this, F. Mussner, *Christus, das All und die Kirche*, 1955. It is certainly not enough to declare that I Cor. 12.12 is mere conciseness, and to explain that Paul does not equate the body of Christ with Christ (128–31, also 123). Nor is G. Martelet's attempt in *Verbum Caro* 12, 1958, 41 f. to interpret the expression from the point of view of Eph. 5.25–33 (wife = body of Christ) adequate. Cf. R. P. Shedd, *Man in Community*, 1958, 161–65; E. Best, *One Body in Christ*, 1955, 169 ff. But neither must we see there a purely formal idea, defining a relation of inferiority (Church = slave of Christ; cf. G. Gloege, *Reich Gottes und die Kirche*, 1929, 291 f.). See nn. 447, 360 below.

[354]On this see T. Boman, *Hebrew Thought Compared with Greek*, ET, 1960, 123 ff., especially 137–47.

[355]Cf. R. Bultmann's discussion in *Gnomon* 27, 1955, 556 f.

an abstract idea of time, take place simultaneously and yet not be 'present' to us. In that sense the body of Jesus of Nazareth,[356] killed on the cross (Rom. 7.4;[357] I Cor. 10.16; 11.27) is present to his Church in the blessing that emanates from it. The 'body of Christ' is therefore first of all the realm of blessing in which the crucified Lord, and the realm of dominion in which the risen Lord, continues to work. We too can speak in this way of something like the 'realm of the Church', which we enter in faith; and it is therefore typical that Paul speaks of the 'body of Christ' only in connection with worship, and in particular with worship at the Lord's Supper;[358] it is there that he will be present to the Church in that way.

Beyond that we are bound to see how heavily the spatial language of Hellenism had long since invaded the originally temporal language of Jewish thought, and increasingly supplanted it.[359]

[356]The unity of the idea of the body of Christ as the body of the cross and as the Church is also stressed by Barth, *Dogmatics* IV/I, ET, 1956, 663 f., 666 f.

[357]It should not be disputed that Paul is thinking here, at least primarily, of what took place on the cross, for the statement is parallel to Rom. 8.2 f., which speaks of Jesus' σάρξ, in which God has carried out his judgment, and thereby dealt with 'the law of sin and death'. The same idea is expressed in Gal. 2.19 f.—the person who is 'crucified with Christ' has died to the law. Cf. also Gal. 4.4 f.: the law is dealt with, because Christ is put under the law (and its curse) in a way that reached its culminating point on the cross, according to 3.13. Cf. for the fundamentals E. Percy, *Der Leib Christi in den paulinischen Homologumena und Antilegomena*, 1942, 25 ff., 43 f.; A. Schlatter, *Gottes Gerechtigkeit*, 1935, *ad loc.*; O. Kuss, *Der Römerbrief*, 1959, *ad loc.*; on the other hand A. Schweitzer, *The Mysticism of Paul the Apostle*, ET[2] 1953, 188 n. 1; C. H. Dodd, *The Epistle of Paul to the Romans*, 1949 = 1932, 101 f.; A. Nygren in *Buch v. d. Kirche* 25; in between, C. K. Barrett, *A Commentary on the Epistle to the Romans*, 1957, *ad loc.*; J. A. T. Robinson, 49; L. Newbigin, *The Household of God*, 1953, 68; with no clear decision, F. Leenhardt, *L'épître de St Paul aux Romains*, 1957, *ad loc.*

[358]Stressed by Michel, *Zeugnis* 45. In the same way, αἷμα Χριστοῦ designates the blood shed at Jesus' death in its significance for the Church, viz., as a means of atonement. We owe especially to O. Cullmann, *Early Christian Worship*, ET (SBT 10) 1953, 26, 33 f., the realization that the body of Christ assumes form in the divine service of the primitive Church.

[359]Typical of this is Gal. 4.25 f., where νῦν and ἄνω are face to face. That is not to deny that from the very beginning each area contained lines of approach towards the other's thought. Yahweh is enthroned 'above' in heaven (e.g., Gen. 11.5; Ex. 24.1, 9), and even in Greece people dream of the coming golden age (although they like to think of it there as a period that recurs in cycles); in Hesiod it is at the beginning of development, and it is not till the later time of the inscriptions of Priene and Halicarnassus and Virgil's Fourth Eclogue that the idea contains a really eschatological note.

There is in Paul's writings, parallel to the formula 'in Christ', the other one, 'in Adam' (I Cor. 15.22). Adam is first, from the temporal point of view, the beginning, the head of the line of generations. His disobedience has affected the whole human race that followed him, however much their own new acts of disobedience involve them in his fate. But Jesus' obedience, once accomplished, determines even more decisively the status of those who receive the gift of God's righteousness.[360] In the same way the Son of man appears as the new patriarch Jacob-Israel in John 1.51 (cf. Gen. 28.12). As such he is the vine, including all his disciples as his branches (John 15.1 ff.). Since Philo (*Confus. ling.* 146–8) identifies God's Son and Logos, who is above all angels, with both Adam and Jacob-Israel, it seems that the same idea of the forefather determining his people could be conceived either in a universal or in a more national way, so that it led to Jesus as either the new Adam or the new Jacob-Israel.

This decisive shaping of the Church by Christ (at first thought of temporally) can also be expressed spatially—it is encompassed by the presence of the crucified and risen Lord; it lives 'in him'.[361] Paul can therefore join to the traditional Lord's Supper formula

[360]Rom. 5.12 ff. Λαμβάνειν can mean the passive reception as well as the active acceptance of this righteousness. To say that the Church should be called the body of Christ because in the suffering Church Christ was still sacrificing his body for the world (Manson, *Ministry and Priesthood* 63 f.) is certainly not, in this form, in accordance with the New Testament. This does, however, rightly recognize that in this idea the Church is seen as the one that shares in Jesus' destiny, in his death and in his resurrection. On this and the following section cf. Schweizer, *Lordship* 45 f., 120, 123 f., and *JBL* 79, 1960, 124 ff.; *TLZ* 86, 1961, 161 ff., 241 ff.; *NTS* 8.1; Best 34 ff.

[361]Cf. Heb. 7.9 f.; also 1 QS 4. 15; I John 5.19 f. The important article by F. Neugebauer, *NTS* 4, 1957/8, 124 ff., shows how in Paul's writings the originally spatial ἐν defines the determining fact of Christ's cross and resurrection (as in the expression 'in the law'), so that time and space combine remarkably. Percy, 43 n. 83, points out that in II Cor. 5.21 the Church becomes the righteousness of God 'in him', because Jesus was made to be sin 'for our sake'. The 'in Christ' therefore defines the validity for the Church today of what took place on the cross. According to I Cor. 1.4, 30 this formula describes the historical event that holds good for the Church of today. Cf. also the change between διὰ and ἐν in Rom. 5.21; 6.23; 7.25; 8.39; I Cor. 15.57 f.; I Thess. 4.14 (cf. IV Macc. 16.25), 16 (Cerfaux 211 f.); further the ἐν(τῷ) Θεῷ (not to be understood mystically) of I Thess. 1.1; 2.2. Behind I Cor. 1.12 too there is probably the idea that Christ lives in his Church as in his body, because he is crucified for it (cf. μεμέρισται ὁ Χριστός and ἐσταυρώθη ὑπὲρ ὑμῶν).

about the 'communion of the body of Christ', which, as the
parallel 'blood of Christ' shows, includes the thought of the crucified body present in blessing, his own interpretation that the
Church is the *one* body.[362] This direct identification is certainly
facilitated by analogous phrases that were already current at that
time.[363] Paul can say similarly in II Cor. 5.14 that because one has
died, 'all have died'. On his principles, the death of 'all' is accomplished in Jesus' death on the cross, just because, as Paul puts it
in the preceding sentence (though not quite logically according to
our way of thinking), the one has died 'for all'.[364]

c. But this saying about the 'body of Christ', which is primarily
a local conception, makes it possible for Paul to regard the Church
in the first place as the one that is at present united with its now
living Lord. Even so, that in no way excludes the presence of
what then took place in the cross and resurrection. But to Paul
it is most important that this presence is no longer to be regarded
as a historical after-effect—such a view would be bound to lead to
misunderstanding, as if Jesus Christ were to be understood
essentially as the originator of a historical movement the effects of
which are still going on. There certainly is a history of the Church
too; it goes from Jerusalem to Illyricum (Rom. 15.19), from
Judaism to the Gentiles and back again to the Jews (Rom.
11.11 ff.); but the Church can be understood in its essence only in
its being 'in Christ'.[365] Even when it is characterized as Abraham's

[362]Beside Percy (in n. 357) cf. also J. Reuss, *Bibl. Zeitschr.*, n.F.2, 1958,
103–27, especially 116 f., and L. S. Thornton in *Ap. Min.* 70–76. He also
emphasizes that the idea of the body of Christ is already implied in the
community of believers whose existence with him Jesus presupposes (55–62).
Cerfaux 283–6, who is more cautious, recognizes that the idea cannot be
explained solely from Old Testament roots.

[363]The Stoic simile, current in various forms, that I Cor. 12.14 ff. adopts
objectively, is certainly pre-Pauline. But I Cor. 12.12 f. and other passages
mean more than this. For their background see Schweizer, *Lordship*, 119 ff.,
and σῶμα in *TWNT*; also *TLZ* 86, 1961, 161 ff.; Best 83 ff.

[364]It is this vicarious 'for all' that brings that death into the present for
the people of today. It is clear from the history of the idea thus understood
that the figurative expression is not to be over-interpreted to mean that
Christ could no more exist without the Church than the Church could without
Christ (on the other hand see Davies, *Normative Pattern of Church Life* 20).
In Paul, therefore, it is even less possible to separate juridical and mystical
thought than Oepke does in *TLZ* 79, 1954, 364 f.; he sees rightly that the
latter has no value of its own as opposed to the former.

[365]It is most unlikely that Paul would have preferred the adjective 'Chris-

posterity, that does not mean a later stage that developed out of the first one, of which we read in the Old Testament. The Church is, indeed the posterity of Abraham only because it has become 'one' (masculine, not neuter) 'in Christ' (Gal. 3.28 f.). Strictly speaking, only Christ himself is this posterity, the fulfilment and the divine aim of all history (Gal. 3.16). It is only for his sake, only 'in him', that the Church belongs to Abraham; and in this oneness with Christ, time is in a way abolished for it. In preaching, in baptism, and in the Lord's Supper there becomes present for it what historically was spoken decades before; and it is there that the fact of its being the body of Christ is manifested.

d. The special nature of the Pauline, compared with the Lucan, idea of the Church is shown in the way that the two understand the Spirit. For Luke the Spirit is still, as in the Old Testament and in Judaism, an additional power of God which enables one who is already believing and obedient to carry out his special historical task. The new factor in the Church is that all its members are endowed with the Spirit, because they all have a responsible place in the historical task of the mission (in the widest sense). For Paul, however, the Spirit is essentially the power of God, which gives faith and causes man to live in faith. In that Spirit the span of time between then and now, the distance between there and here, is annulled, in him the simultaneousness of events in salvation is a reality.[366] He therefore makes the Jewish Christian or Gentile Christian group, which may be defined historically or sociologically in this way or that, an eschatological entity. In Paul, therefore, we do not find the view of an unbroken transition from Judaism to Christianity. He can hold fast to the continuity, indeed the identity, of Israel and the Church only by seeing at work, even in Old Testament Israel, God's free election by grace, which has again and again singled out the true Israel from within the historical nation of Israel.[367]

---

tian' if it had been available (Cerfaux 214). Paul's main concern is to see the special nature of the Church not in its qualities, nor even in its Christianity, but in the fact of its living on God's action, which took place outside it, 'in Christ'.

[366]Cf. *TWNT* VI 422 ff. (= *Spirit of God* 67 ff.).

[367]See 7a. 'God's people' became an eschatological idea even in the Jewish tradition (Dahl 76 ff., especially 83). The prophets too stress the absolute

e. The more strongly the Church's newness and its distinctness from the old world is emphasized,[368] and the more consciously it is looked on as an eschatological entity, the more consciously must it be separated from the world that does not live in such newness. We saw how Jesus' message separated the saved from those under condemnation, and put the Galilean towns under a judgment more severe than that on Sodom and Gomorrah. The rigour of this separation is maintained when Paul cannot, as Matthew does, see the Church as a *corpus mixtum,* but supposes that everyone who has become a member of the body of Christ is saved,[369] while he nowhere indicates that salvation is to be shared by any people outside the Church. In a world that judges the gospel to be 'folly' and 'a stumbling-block', the faith must be preached, to some for life, to others for death, and it must take shape in confession, baptism, and the Lord's Supper.[370] Thus the only way to call on the world is to call on it to believe, to become the Church.

f. But at the same time Paul knows more clearly than almost anyone that such faith is never a human achievement. In the death of one all *have* died (II Cor. 5.14). It is not the believers who are reconciled because of their faith, but the *cosmos* (II Cor. 5.19). Salvation does not depend on man's will or exertion (Rom. 9.16). Jesus' death took place before the Church believed, so that salvation will simply be 'much more' certain for the believer (Rom. 5.8–10). For Paul, therefore, the one who comes from outside, the ἰδιώτης, is the most important; it is by his understanding that the preaching is to be measured, so that a church that developed a secret language unintelligible to the world would cease to be a church (I Cor. 14.16, 23 ff.). How could it be otherwise? No one in the New Testament knows as clearly as

---

newness of the Church of the last days, and in the New Testament the mention of the 'New Covenant' presumably dates from before Paul (I Cor. 11.25; cf. Cerfaux 67 f.).

[368]H. Thyen, *Der Stil der jüdisch-hellenistischen Homilie,* 1955, 119 f., shows this, e.g. in the transformation of the Jewish-Hellenistic form of speech, into which the contrast between 'then' and 'now' is accepted as an entirely new feature.
[369]I Cor. 3.15; 5.5; but cf. also II Cor. 5.10; I Cor. 10.12 beside 13.
[370]I Cor. 1.23 f.; II Cor. 2.16; Rom. 10.9 f.

Paul that the Church shares in Jesus Christ precisely as it allows itself to be drawn, in the enduring of persecution, not into material greatness, but into submersion and death—for the world (Rom. 8.36; I Cor. 15.30 f.; II Cor. 4.8–12; Rom. 12.1; II Cor. 1.4–7; Phil. 1.12–14; I Thess. 2.14).

Thus the dialectic becomes apparent: man outside the Church can come to faith only through being called to enter the Church. At the same time, however, the Church can only be called on to allow itself to be beaten in pieces in suffering for the world; and it can therefore never regard salvation as a security (I Cor. 10.1 ff.). Just as God's promise, which will achieve its object, already covers non-believers (Rom. 11.25 f.), so the threat of judgment is over the Church. Wherever the Church's self-confidence and presumptuousness in relation to those outside swallowed up its faith, it would cease to be a church (Rom. 11.20–24). We are bound to ask whether the time has not come to follow out these lines of thought even more resolutely to their conclusion.

g. Again the Church's understanding of this matter determines its order. Just because the Church not only represents a development of Israel, but actually is Israel, Jerusalem remains important for Paul (Gal. 2.1 ff.; Rom. 15.31). The first apostles' authority is not disputed (Gal. 2.1 ff.[371]), and even the argument with Peter (2.11 ff.) only shows that they are fundamentally one, even though the latter does not, in Paul's opinion, draw the logical conclusions from his faith (cf. also I Cor. 1.12 ff.). But the decisive fact is that Paul does not regard his own authority as less than or different from that of the first apostles, even by a hair's breadth. His authority, however, is based not on tradition, but on a direct meeting with the risen Lord—not on participation in the historical event in Palestine about the year 30, but in an event in which Jesus Christ became present to him outside Palestine and outside the 'midpoint of time'. It is true that Paul does not try to make that event similar to simply any vision;[372] and he seems to regard the series of such revelations (in view of the supposed imminence of

[371]On this cf. Kuss, *TQ* 135, 1955, 155 f.
[372]The vision of II Cor. 12.1 ff. is not the subject of apostolic preaching (any more than that of Stephen in Acts 7.55 f., Leuba, *New Testament Pattern* 105); the revelation before Damascus, on the other hand, lays the foundation of it and thereby of the Church (Gal. 1.1, 11–16).

the parousia) as closed.[373] But this equalization is intensely exciting, for it means that the meeting with the risen Lord, which took place at a distance in time and place from the historical events in the divine plan of salvation, is at least in this case essentially equated with what happened to the historical disciples.

h. Of course Paul does not doubt for a moment that the risen and the earthly Lord are identical; and of course that identity is for him vital and inviolable—it is, indeed, the stumbling-block of the cross, which first called forth his opposition, and which is therefore central from the very beginning of his apostolic ministry.[374] But this same earthly Jesus can, as the risen Lord, meet him, overleaping the historical tradition which in other circumstances has to bridge time and space. The Damascus experience is certainly an exceptional event to Paul, and his preaching would be fruitless if it did not agree with that of the other apostles. All this is a safeguard against what happens in *gnosis*, namely that the historical element disappears and only the idea remains and again becomes fully present to everyone who has knowledge, so that the account of the historical event would be at the most an example and an impulse to the contact that is made by this spark of knowledge.

These two things, therefore, are contained in the Pauline apostolic idea: on the one hand, the Church does not come into being without an apostle, and is still under his authority. This emphasizes that it does not live apart from history, but lives from the preaching that comes to it from outside and has its beginning in a unique event.[375] On the other hand, if Paul stands with equal right beside the others, it emphasizes that where the message is effective the hearer is the equal of the eyewitness of the historical event, because those saving events become present for him. Both are true: the Church lives on that event that took place at a specified time and place, at which God spoke to all peoples and

---

[373]Ἔκτρωμα in I Cor. 15.8 denotes a premature birth, not the exceptional case of one born late. It can therefore hardly be related to the time of his calling, but only to his unworthiness as a persecutor of the Church. Yet ἔσχατον will not be meant only relatively. This, of course, does not exclude the theoretical possibility that it might please God at some time to call further apostles.

[374]This, of course, is not to say that its significance was established from the very first in the full clarity of later expressions.

[375]See 26b, c.

all times; and by so doing it is united with him and taken out of time and place.

i. This dialectic determines the whole of Paul's Church order.[376] As a Church that is still living in time, it consists of many members, none of whom is perfect, so that each depends on the other's service; and there is therefore an abundance of different gifts and tasks. At the same time, however, the Church is a new entity, established solely by God's action and not to be regarded as a historical development. The miracle of this newness is shown by there being no fundamental organization of superior or subordinate ranks, because the gift of the Spirit is adapted to every Church member.[377] Whenever such working of the Spirit actually takes place, superiority and subordination will always follow.[378]

Thus we do not find in Paul's writings the forms of service that we know from the Jewish community. If there were already elders in Jerusalem when Paul was there—or at least, as long as he was still living in Antioch—then Paul's omitting to mention them[379] is in fact a demonstration in which he throws overboard everything that is merely conservative and retrospective, and stresses the vitality of the ever-present Spirit in the Church of the last days.[380] The Church becomes a Church, not by tradition in itself, but by the repeated action of the Spirit, which brings such tradition into the preaching of the apostle, but also into the

[376]On the contrast both with Qumran and with the primitive Church in Jerusalem, cf. S. E. Johnson, *Harvard Theol. Review* 48, 1955, 157–9. Kuss 152 f. sees this based only on Paul's early expectation of the parousia.
[377]It is only in Paul's writings that the χάρισμα concept, which previously occurs only quite seldom, acquires its weighty significance (Grau, par. 1–5, pp. 11 ff.; M. Lauterburg, *Der Begriff des Charisma*, 1898, 41 ff.; O. Michel in *Deutsche Theologie* 1942, 133 f.; Friedrich, 'Geist und Amt' in *Wort und Dienst* 1952, 82; L. H. Charles, *The Charismatic Life in the Apostolic Church*, diss. Edinburgh 1958 [typescript]). But after Paul this meaning is almost entirely lost again: see n. 519.
[378]Thus the prophet who is actually speaking gives way to the other, to whom the Spirit gives the word of authority (I Cor. 14.30).
[379]The argument in Farrer, *Ap. Min.* 152 f., that Paul's silence is only accidental, and that I Corinthians is addressed to elders because Isa. 24.21–23, which mentions elders, has an echo in 6.1 ff., is highly unconvincing. Apart from the fact that any accord with Isa. 24 is most questionable, Old Testament quotations are often used without regard to context. On I Thess. 5.14 ff., cf. n. 394.
[380]H. Greeven in *ZNW* 44, 1952/3, 41, and in *Wort und Dienst* 1959, 111 ff. Otherwise Kaiser 100 nn. 121, 123 in discussion with v. Campenhausen.

interpretation of the teacher, the prophet, and the speaker of tongues. Thus the apostle can at one time be distinguished from all others as the one to whom that message is entrusted by which all later preaching must be judged,[381] and who is therefore the right person to establish the Church. But at another time his service can take its place beside all other forms of service, since his message is not to be preserved and handed on as a possession, for it becomes effective only because the Spirit makes it so.

k. First of all, the freedom of the Spirit can be seen in the Pauline church. Everyone has the Spirit—'Any one who does not have the Spirit of Christ does not belong to him' (Rom. 8.9). Everyone therefore, without exception, is given his ministry,[382] and the diversity of these rests solely on their free assignment by the Spirit himself, who gives what he pleases to everyone (I Cor. 12.11). As tasks given by the Spirit they are all, therefore, fundamentally equal, and superiority and subordination are to be regarded as only incidental.[383] Thus the enumerations of the different kinds of gifts are quite unsystematic, with no sort of hierarchical character.[384] There is only one standard for measuring their relative importance: whether they testify to Jesus as Lord, or not (I Cor. 12.3)[385]—or, to look at it from the other side, whether they edify the Church or not (12.7; 14.1 ff.). Only from that point of view can we realize that ministry of the word is always to the fore, although it is formulated variously and unsystematically, and that in I Cor. 14 Paul regards prophecy as the real gift, to be aspired to by all. But even here I Cor. 13 must not be forgotten:[386]

[381]The fellow-man is therefore not only yardstick by which the message has to be measured. The apostles who have seen the Lord are clearly marked out in I Cor. 15.5–8 from the rest. It is when, from v. 6 onwards, Paul himself speaks, that it becomes plain how he here agrees with the old formula of v.5.

[382]Rom. 12.3; I Cor. 12.7, 11, 18; 14.26; cf. Eph. 4.7, 16; I Peter 4.10.

[383]See n. 378 on I Cor. 14.30.

[384]Rom. 12.3 ff.; I Cor. 12.8 ff., 28 ff. (against Soiron, *Die Kirche als Leib Christi* 185).

[385]It is very unlikely that Paul was thinking here of persecution (O. Cullmann, *The Earliest Christian Confessions*, ET 1949, 27 f.; *Christology* 219 ff.). Persecution is never mentioned in I Corinthians, and after 11.17 the subject is worship. Besides, πνευματικά (or -οί) in 12.1 is certainly not to be interpreted otherwise than in 14.1 (37). Cf. further how in Eph. 4.14; I Tim. 3.15 f. (as the conclusion of directions to bishops and deacons) the importance of the creed is stressed.

[386]The chapter is certainly not to be regarded as a later interpolation (thus

in the last resort the decisive factor is the degree of love that characterizes a ministry. Without it even the most precious gift of grace becomes empty (13.2), and it can be shown in full measure in a gift that is not in itself specially suitable for edifying the Church.

Nor, therefore, is there any blind submission in the Church; it must not and cannot say 'Amen' unless it has really understood (I Cor. 14.16). So, too, Paul knows no one in Corinth to whom he could apply as a leader, to achieve an ordered observance of the Lord's Supper for instance, or of worship; he can appeal only to the Church as a whole. Probably, however, the most important observation about this aspect of Church order is that for Paul an ordination, any explicit appointment on undertaking a form of service, is impossible.[387]

l. But that means no enthusiastic overleaping of facts. The *Corinthians*[388] are clearly in danger of anticipating the resurrection from the dead, and of living here and now as a 'heavenly' church of divinely perfect people.[389] For them the Spirit is the inrush of heavenly power, in which finality is already anticipated. In reply to this, Paul reminds them that the Spirit is only the beginning of what is still to be attained.[390] According to them the effects of the Spirit can be most clearly seen where he appears in the most unusual way, where everything natural, everything that can be grasped by the reason, recedes: in the gift of tongues. But that is exactly what Paul opposes; he pushes it to the last place, not

---

J. Weiss, *Der erste Korintherbrief*, 1910, 309 ff.; J. Héring, *La première épître de St Paul aux Corinthiens*, 1949, 115: originally standing with ch. 8, coming from another letter, or from an independent piece of writing?); for in Rom. 12.3 ff. too the enumeration of the various forms of service merges into the call to ἀγάπη (v. 9), and ends with that (13.8–10).

[387] I Cor. 16.15 f., 17 f.; Phil. 2.29 f.; I Thess. 5.12 prove that such ministries have long been going on in an unconstrained way before they are acknowledged by the Church (without any rite). See 7m.

[388] I Cor. 14. (33–)36 proves that the differences between the churches were not excessively marked (cf. Weiss, *I Kor.*, 342 f.). Rom. 12.3 ff. assumes fundamentally similar conditions in the Roman church which Paul did not direct. Only the danger of misunderstanding seems to have been particularly great in Corinth.

[389] I Cor. 4.8; 15.12 ff. (misunderstood by Paul? Kümmel, *Kor. I/II*, 192 f., and the authors named there).

[390] Rom. 8.23; II Cor. 1.22; 5.5.

because he despises it, but because it is not particularly suited to edifying the Church.[391] Instead he includes among the gifts of grace the performance of such 'natural' ministries as the guidance of the Church, or the care of other people—things that it would never have entered the Corinthians' heads to regard as the effect of the Spirit.[392] So no church member can unite all the gifts in himself, and therefore he is freed from any ambitious chasing after other people's gifts of grace, and may be content to 'think within God's limitations', and to fit in with what God bestows on each one (Rom. 12.3 ff.). A church member who wanted to exercise all gifts would anticipate the kingdom of God, and so would be trying to make himself a little Christ.

This means that everyone there will give place when a gift that he himself lacks is exercised by someone else. Because the Spirit—for Paul as for the Old Testament—is God's Spirit, and therefore faces man without ever becoming his property which he can treat as he likes, he demands obedience. Only the fanatic, therefore, can fail to see that in the Church too there is an order. The great question is simply what sort of obedience and order it is.

m. Here, certainly, we can see the newness of the Church in contrast to the Jewish community. The Spirit's authority is obeyed as it actually comes to be; this leads to an order that conforms itself afterwards to the 'event' of the Spirit; and its only purpose is to make room for the Spirit to carry out his work of edifying the Church with as little hindrance as possible. For that reason, too, such order can be interrupted at once if the Spirit wishes to speak through another person (I Cor. 14.30). All order is an 'afterwards', an attempt to follow what God has already designed. It is not because a person has been chosen as prophet or presbyter that he may exercise this or that ministry, but on the contrary, because God has given him the charism, the possibility is given to him, through the Church order, of exercising it. It

---

[391] I Cor. 12.10, 28; 14.2 ff.

[392] They are therefore mentioned in I Cor. 12.28, but not in 12.20 f., as they are not among the gifts that are coveted and aspired to in Corinth. See 22c. J. Brosch, too, in *Charismen und Ämter in der Urkirche*, 1951, 132 f., puts them among the charismata; but that is because he thinks that only the office resting on apostolic appointment has a special character, in contrast to all free ministries. See n. 698.

does not matter whether such order is expected to last only for an hour, for a few weeks, or without a time limit. In I Cor. 14.26 ff. the worship is arranged for the single period of the assembly so that God's gifts may be unfolded for the Church's benefit with as little hindrance as possible. The prophets are therefore not to speak at the same time, but one after the other; people who speak with tongues are to have their say only when there are interpreters present; and the number of speakers is to be kept within tolerable bounds. In II Cor. 8.18 ff. a companion whose spiritual gifts are already widely known is deputed to represent Paul, so that the charitable gift may really bear fruit; and in I Cor. 16.16 the church is called on to acknowledge those to whom God has given special gifts which they have long since been exercising, so that they can perform their ministry as widely as possible, with no time limit.

n. Such ministry can also be facilitated by the Church's relieving some of its members, either wholly or partly, of any anxiety about their livelihood;[393] but the Church's action is always to be in response to a service that is already being rendered, or to such a person's obvious gifts.[394] But no such acknowledgment by the Church turns the ministry into anything new. Whether a ministry is specially regulated or not depends very largely on outward circumstances. One who exercises the ministry of deacon must be known to the Church, because he has to be called in emergencies; but one who exercises the ministry of intercession need not be generally known, and on that account his ministry has no other character. But we may notice here that on the one hand gifts of grace are developed in service and are acknowledged and regulated subsequently, while on the other hand certain necessary things, such as Paul's journey to Jerusalem, require service to be rendered; so the Church looks out for people to whom that particular gift of grace has been given.[395]

[393]I Cor. 9.4 ff.; I Thess. 2.7; II Thess. 3.9; Gal. 6.6.
[394]See n. 387. That the whole section I Thess. 5.13b–28 consists of directions for the pastoral office of the 'overseers' who remain subordinate to the apostles (Farrer, *Ap. Min.* 154; Dix, *Jew and Greek* 83) is impossible exegesis, for the ἀδελφοί in v. 14 must be the same as those in the quite parallel sentence in v. 12a, and how should vv. 16–18 and 23–25 not apply to all?
[395]Schmithals, *Die Gnosis in Korinth* 11 n. 5, considers that σὺν ἐπισκόποις καὶ διακόνοις (Phil. 1.1) is a later gloss. But as Paul knows the διακονία or the ἀντιλήμψεις, as well as the κυβερνήσεις, as spiritual gifts, it is quite possible that such services were part of the order later too.

o. This twofold view of the Church, as it appears in Paul's writings and also characterizes the order of the Church that he influences, corresponds to its twofold nature as a sociological entity which, standing in history, is determined by time and place, and as an eschatological entity which, being taken out of time and place by its union with the risen Lord, lives in the presence of God's saving act. True, we have to ask whether the looseness of this order, which entrusts so much to the working of God's Spirit, can be maintained in a period when Paul's personal influence has ceased. Or is it inevitable that the Church does not sustain this freedom that subordinates itself to God, and that it either develops the momentum of Church order one-sidedly into a Church with an organized hierarchy, or just as one-sidedly turns the momentum of freedom into a system, till it dissolves in gnostic individualism? But must not an *ecclesia semper reformanda*, well knowing that it can never keep as its own possession the most ideal, perfectly balanced, biblical order, repeatedly learn afresh to let itself be guided by those writings in which the abundance of New Testament understanding is fully absorbed with regard to both sides?

8

THE CHURCH IN THE LETTERS TO
COLOSSIANS AND EPHESIANS

We still have to refer, by way of supplement and as briefly as possible, to writings that are more or less influenced by what Paul said.

a. In essentials Paul's utterances continue to have their effect on the Church. In Colossians there is a new danger, towards which the writer must make his position clear: there has come into being in the Church an angel-worship which takes the powers of nature seriously. A presupposition of this is the Hellenistic view of the *cosmos,* in which man is handed over to the powers that rule the respective spheres—powers that are represented by the inexorable course of the stars, which determine the destiny of mortals. In contrast to them, the risen Christ is preached as 'the head of all rule and authority' (2.10); and so in the Church's faith he takes the place that destiny held in the Hellenistic world.[396] 1.15–17, in a hymn taken over by the writer,[397] bases Christ's supreme power on the fact that he was before all things, and that everything is created in him. Presumably the connecting link with these utterances is Jewish speculations on God's wisdom. Here Christ appears in v. 18 as the head of the body, that is, of his Church,[398] while in v. 20 the reconciliation effected by his death is thought of on a cosmic scale.[399]

[396]Schweizer, *Erniedrigung* 128.

[397]On the analysis cf. finally J. M. Robinson in *JBL* 76, 1957, 270 ff. I think that an original Christian hymn (vv. 15, 16a, c; 18b, 19, 20a) is first enlarged by a middle strophe (vv. 17, 18a), and later adapted to the Colossian situation by the author of the letter (vv. 16b, 18c, 20b, c): *TLZ* 86, 241 ff.

[398]So also 2.19; 1.24 (Mussner, *Christus, das All und die Kirche* 141 f., distinguishes here between the sufferings of witnessing and those of atonement; otherwise Soiron 111; Manson, *Ministry and Priesthood* 29 f., recognizes this distinction, but does not think it particularly relevant; see n. 611, and for further exposition Schweizer, *Erniedrigung* 140, n. 635).

[399]But not in such a way that the Church would include the powers (Cerfaux, *The Church in . . . St Paul* 339–41). Cf. Best, *One Body in Christ* 115 ff.

In whatever way we analyse this passage, this much may be clear, that an assertion that Christ is the head of all powers was connected in a secondary way with an assertion that Christ is the head of the Church—obviously with a concern to assure the Church that for it the powers of nature are finished with, and that it is free under Christ (2.14 f., 20). The result of this is that the recognition of this lordship of Christ over all powers is decisive. Because this mystery was once hidden, but is now revealed, the times divide at this point (1.26); and so the newness of the time is particularly stressed. The Church is already under the rule of the King, transplanted into the realm of the Son (1.13). Heaven and earth are already reconciled (1.20). The Church is already raised with Christ (2.12; 3.1), and has now only some 'members' on earth—that is if, as is really impossible, it is still living in immorality and similar vices (3.5).

b. So in this writing the Church at once receives the attributes of the kingdom of God, and so, too, it is seen much more markedly than in Paul's writings as a sole world-wide Church.[400] We should therefore really expect an idea of the Church similar to that in John's writings; and if 4.5 speaks of 'outsiders', we might see there that sharp separation of the Church from the world. But the expressions that already see the Church as a heavenly and completed entity are clearly and materially corrected by those that refer to the Church as still growing.[401] Indeed the reference to the body of Christ gets its new shade of meaning precisely because it describes, not the static unity of Christ and the Church, but growth proceeding from the head and spreading through the limbs and joints (2.19). But what is particularly stressed by the new distinction between head and body, underlining the pre-eminence of Christ over all powers, is also the fact that Christ and the Church in a way face each other. Even 4.5 is said only within the summons to the missionary task whose universality is unlimited (1.28).

c. That is why the Church's newness is strongly attested here too in its order, but without its disintegrating in spiritual extravagance. What is said about the body of Christ, whose joints and ligaments are no doubt expressly mentioned, presupposes the

[400]Kuss, *TQ* 135, 1955, 157; Cerfaux 196 f.
[401]1.10; 2.19; cf. 1.6; 2.7. Cf. *NTS* 8.1, Oct. 1961.

Pauline variety of gifts, without turning it into a hierarchical gradation. Like Paul himself, Epaphras and Tychicus are only fellow-servants.[402] Paul's apostolic ministry is accomplished above all in his suffering (1.24). Of course, as in Paul's letters, all church members are 'saints'. The dangers that have arisen in Colossae are met on the facts of the case, not by recourse to offices and order.[403]

d. In the letter to the Ephesians, too, the Church knows that Christ has been installed at God's right hand above every principality and power (1.20 f.; cf. 1.10). But this is not nearly as central as in Colossians. Instead, the Church itself has become here an important object of faith; and it is the Church through whose existence the revelation is made known to the principalities and powers in heaven (3.10). Here too the Church's newness is very much stressed; it is raised up with Christ and made to sit with him in the heavenly places (2.6), though in the next verse this is interpreted to mean that this heavenly state can be expressed only in view of the glory that is to come. Here too Christ appears as the head of his body, the Church. In 1.22 this is entirely parallel to the statement that God has put everything under his feet, and it therefore emphasizes his authority over the Church; but the next verse stresses the Church's close connection with Christ— a thing that cannot be said in the same way about the powers.[404] Christ's authority over the Church, however, is particularly stressed in 5.23 with its reference to head and body, though in such a way that vv. 29–32 again underline their unity.[405] Here too the turning-point of time is characterized by the fact that what was previously hidden is now revealed (3.5). The fundamental separation of the Church and the world is more clearly stated, the 'sons of disobedience' being contrasted with the 'children of light' (2.2; 5.6, 8). This contrast is intensified by the fact that, as in the Johannine writings, the Church's election is transferred into an absolute act of God's will before the foundation of the world.[406]

[402]Διάκονος and σύνδουλος (1.7, 25; 4.7, 11 f.); see n. 413.
[403]Kuss 159.
[404]It is not certain whether the thought is of the Church filled by Christ, or of the head (i.e. Christ) as completing the abundance of the body (cf. Dibelius and Greeven on Col., Eph. and Philem., 65).
[405]In 2.15 f. the passage about the one body merely describes the unity between Jews and Gentiles within the body (cf. also 4.4). It is, of course, only through Christ that this can become a reality.
[406]1.4 f., 11; 2.10; 3.11.

e. The Church's life is based on Jesus' giving of himself on the cross (5.25). The reconciliation that is regarded in Colossians as of cosmic scope is regarded here as the bringing in of the Gentiles, who are far from God, to share Israel's citizenship (2.12–14; 3.6). That goes so far that in 2.19 even the Israelites appear as 'saints', whereas elsewhere it is the members of the Church who are so named.[407] As in Colossians, what is said here about the body serves to describe not so much the Church's state as its growth; this is true both for 4.12–16, where the head is both the source and the object of growth, and also for the image of the temple or God's dwelling, where everything grows from Christ the cornerstone, and from the foundation laid by apostles and prophets (2.20–22). This image is closely related to the first one, because in ancient times people were much more inclined than we are to think of a building as a living organism.

f. Again, the Church's order witnesses to the fundamental conception. The fact that Israel and the death on the cross, and also the growth of the Church till it is complete, move more definitely into the centre, has its analogy in the stress laid on the apostles and prophets as the foundation; indeed, they actually appear in 3.5,[408] in contrast to all the usual language, as the 'holy' apostles and prophets to whom the revelation was granted.[409] It is certainly vital here that the (New Testament) prophets too have become a factor of this kind in the plan of salvation. It is therefore not only the meeting with the risen Lord, which occurred only once, and so could still underline the connection with the historical uniqueness of Jesus of Nazareth;[410] it is the gift of the Spirit that entrusted a group of people with the revelation.

---

[407]The concept includes above all those who now believe; but clearly in such a way that they now stand exactly where Israel once stood. We must therefore wonder whether we may with Mussner (*Christus* . . . 105 f.) really regard 'spiritual Israel' as being meant here, and not simply the Israelites by race, who once formed the chosen people without the Gentiles, and who now through Christ form it with them.

[408]If this is not a later gloss. But cf. Ign. *Magn.* 3.1.

[409]No doubt even 2.20 goes beyond what Paul would have said; for in his own writings the apostle, in spite of his special position, is on the same footing as all believers (Dibelius and Greeven 72, and the writers named there).

[410]In any case, that is how Luke understood the unique nature of the apostleship. See 5h.

True, it is a group that forms the foundation, and which is therefore regarded as a complete entity (of the past?).

Thus we may ask ourselves how far in the practical life of the Church what the letter positively assumes—at least in theory—is still realized: namely that the free bestowal of the gifts of grace, in which specifically 'each of us' appears as a recipient, is still the mark of the Church (4.7, 16).[411] At any rate, apostles and prophets can be named (4.11) together with the evangelists, pastors, and teachers, in the same breath and without any recognizable difference;[412] and Paul, like Tychicus, is a 'minister'.[413] The fact of belonging to the body also presupposes mutual service within the Church (4.25; 5.30); and here the Church is by no means the sole consideration, as it lives, not for itself, but for the glory of God, and its mission is, indeed, of cosmic range.[414]

g. The letters are too short for us to be able to determine with certainty the relation between Pauline tradition and elements from a period of later developments; the decision depends on whether we regard the letters as those of Paul or of one of his pupils. But in any case, the fundamentally Pauline approach to the idea of the Church, and the Church order that results from it, is unmistakable. The letters show a definite development from that approach—a development in which the Church is seen more and more markedly as a world-wide unity that attains even cosmic range. This is connected with the fact that the apostle is no longer simply the father of a particular local church, with which he is in constant, personal, and reciprocal contact, but becomes the foundation of an entity that is developing on a world-wide scale.

[411]C. Masson, *L'épître de St Paul aux Ephésiens*, 1953, 188 f., opposes the view that it is a question here of differentiated charismata.

[412]Without support in the text, Masson 192 separates teachers and pastors as officials of the local church from the other ministries; otherwise L. Simon, *Foi et Vie* 55, 1957, 404 n. 39.

[413]3.7; 6.21, where it must not be overlooked that only Paul is called a minister of the gospel, just as he appears in Col. 1.25 as a minister of the Church. The expressions in Colossians, 'fellow servant' and 'fellow worker' (see n. 402), which include Paul with others, have here disappeared.

[414]1.6, 12, 14 (cf. 2.10); 3.10. See 8a, d.

9

THE CHURCH IN THE FIRST LETTER
OF PETER

a. Here too we must be careful not to read too much into the few indications that can be found. It is, however, apparent that Pauline material is combined here with material from the primitive Church, the most typical case being the section in 2.4–10. Behind this is the idea of the 'spiritual house' which presents a parallel to the Pauline view of the body of Christ. This is heavily underlined by the remarkable image of the living stones that are built up on Christ the living stone.[415] But the Old Testament background can be seen first of all in the choice of the image,[416] which contains above all the idea of growth, which we found in Colossians and Ephesians, when the foundation and the stones added to it are referred to. Here in this image the Church is represented as Israel,[417] but in a different way from Paul's—not because there is taking place in it what has already been taking place all along in the people really chosen by God: God's election by grace and the answer of faith in the working of the Holy Spirit. It is because, in contrast to Judaism, it has made the right decision in relation to the stone that was chosen by God and rejected by men, and so it represents the true historical development of Israel.

This does not set up an irreconcilable contrast to the Pauline view—the First Letter of Peter is itself a proof to the contrary, but in this case the idea of God's plan of salvation throughout

[415]Cf. G. Schrenk, *TWNT* IV 195 f. and n. 447 below. Both images, vine and house of God, are combined in the remarkable passage Pseudo-Philo, *Ant. Bibl.* 12.8 f. (Schweizer, *Lordship* 120).

[416]This is absent from the gnostic material. H. Schlier, *Religionsgeschichtliche Untersuchungen zu den Ignatiusbriefen*, 1929, 120; O. Michel, *TWNT* IV 884 ff. A very close parallel is to be found in 1QS 8.5–9; 9.3–6.

[417]Is this the view of an originally independent song of praise constructed from Old Testament quotations (E. G. Selwyn, *The First Epistle of St Peter*, 1946, 268 ff.)? D. Flusser in *Scripta Hierosolymitana* IV, 1958, 229 ff., suggests, with greater probability, literary dependence on 1QS 8.4–10.

history, with which the thought of the pilgrim (2.11) agrees, is in the foreground, whereas the image by which the Church is essentially shaped in accordance with its unity with the present Lord is only a faint echo of this. Thus the Church is seen as a historical rather than as a timeless entity, determined by what took place at the beginning of its existence in Christ. It is the people on its way through a foreign country to the longed-for goal, the 'inheritance which is imperishable . . . in heaven' (1.4). So the image of the building of a house no longer refers, as with Paul, to a single church, but to the world-wide Church, growing from the foundation of Jesus Christ until the last day.

b. This interpretation takes shape in its Church order. It is maintained in 4.10 f., as it is by Paul, that the gift bestowed by God creates the ministry. The fact that now the only distinction of ministries is that between speaking and serving (in the narrower sense)[418] may mean that the complete Pauline list is no longer alive in the Church; but it may also be a shortened summary.[419] 'Each' is called to such service in the Church; and the Pauline knowledge that in the Church everyone is responsible and free for service is also maintained. That, indeed, cannot be otherwise in a Church whose service is seen to be so central in its suffering as it is here (1.6; 2.21–23; 3.14; 4.4, 12–19; 5.9).

Yet the ordered ministries are given greater importance. Although in 5.5, as in the Pastoral Letters, the expression 'elders' is still used only to denote the older generation,[420] there is no doubt that there is already a definitely fixed circle of elders (5.1). The extent to which they are already engaged in an ordered ministry is apparent from the exhortation to perform their ministry 'not by constraint but willingly, not for shameful gain but eagerly'. Nor is the misuse of autocratic power excluded;[421] in fact, there

[418]As well as the special meaning in v. 10, which includes all the ministries performed in the Church, it can therefore denote, as in Pauline usage, the particular 'serving' of practical ministration.

[419]This is suggested by the reference to the 'varied' grace of God.

[420]For the 'younger' cannot denote any group of special office-bearers (F. W. Beare, *The First Epistle of Peter*, 1947, 175; further O. Bauernfeind, *Die Apostelgeschichte*, 1939, 86 f.; E. Preuschen, *Die Apostelgeschichte*, 1912, 29 on Acts 5.6), or all church members except the elders (so Michaelis 125 f.).

[421]Streeter, 134 ff. sees in this a development that is already well on the way to a monarchical episcopate. The author (Aristion of Smyrna?), like the elder of I-III John, would occupy a position approaching that of an archbishop (see n. 480).

seems to be something like circuits allotted to the individual elders.[422] But the honorific title of king and priest is given, not to individuals such as these, but to the Church as a whole, whose priesthood is not a ministry of reconciliation, but of praise and preaching (2.9). So here too there is no distinction between clergy and laity.

[422]Κλῆρος certainly does not yet denote the clergy in contrast to the laity, but hardly the 'places of rank' either (Nauck, *ZNW* 48, 1957, 211 with reference to 1QS). Acts 17.4 speaks of the people who προσεκληρώθησαν to Paul and Silas. In Acts 26.18 κλῆρος is simply the 'place' among the 'saints', not a particular rank; and the same is true of Col. 1.12. Thus I Peter 5.3 probably refers to the flock entrusted to a single presbyter, whether we are to think of particular parts of a church (W. F. Arndt and F. W. Gringrich, *A Greek-English Lexicon of the NT,* 1957, s.v.), or of various local churches (R. Knopf, *Die Briefe Petri und Judä,* 1912, 190). Cf. Kuss 162.

10

THE CHURCH IN THE LETTER TO THE HEBREWS

a. The central conception of the Church here is of God's people on the move;[423] nowhere is there to be found anything analogous to the idea of the body of Christ.[424] In itself Hebrews thinks on the pattern 'abasement/exaltation', as in the hymn of praise quoted by Paul in Phil. 2.6–11. From this we might expect that the idea of the Church would lay all the stress on the Church's existing union with the risen Lord. This might also hold good for the tradition in which the writer stands; the conception of the heavenly high priest who has already penetrated into heaven, made his way into the Holy of Holies, and so unites the earthly Church with the heavenly world, clearly points in that direction. But the writer joins to this conception a marked emphasis on Jesus' unique historical sacrifice on the cross; and the existing union with the Church consists in the heavenly high priest's presenting that very sacrifice with intercession to God for the Church.[425] This means that the question of union with the heavenly world is certainly raised. However, it is answered in such a way that the union is granted through the sacrifice that was made once for all on the cross. Just as we look back to the beginning of that history, so we also look forward to its goal. The hope of the 'things not seen' is strongly emphasized (11.1 ff.); and the anchor that now reaches into the Holy of Holies is the Church's hope.[426] The Church is therefore God's people moving forward

---

[423]E. Käsemann, *Das wandernde Gottesvolk*, 1939.

[424]Although, in view of 3.6, it cannot be maintained that 'God's house' is to be understood only in a heavenly sense and never as a visible church (F. Schierse, *Verheissung und Heilsvollendung*, 1955, 110), the expression, which may simply mean the 'family' (11.7), is already a current idea without the theological content of e.g. I Peter 2.5.

[425]Cf. Schweizer, *Erniedrigung* 67 ff.; *Lordship* 72 f.

[426]6.19; O. Michel, *Der Brief an die Hebräer*, 1949, 158. It would be different if, with Käsemann, *Gottesvolk* 147 n. 3, we regarded the anchor as representing Jesus, who as a forerunner has already gone into the sanctuary; but ἦν clearly goes with ἐλπίς.

from the cross and resurrection to the parousia of Jesus Christ, and thus its historicity is clearly seen.

b. This appears in the importance of the authentic tradition of Jesus' preaching which has come down to the present Church *via* the apostles (2.3).[427] In this the Spirit's presence is taken very seriously. First, it is the presence of corroborating signs (2.4); the 'various miracles and . . . gifts of the Holy Spirit' are 'distributed according to his own will' in the Church (2.4). The Church is enlightened once for all, possesses the heavenly gift of the Spirit, and has now tasted the powers of the age to come (6.4 f.). Thus all its members ought to be teachers, who no longer need to learn (5.12). Yet the reality is seen soberly. This is not quite how things are;[428] and so the Church is called back again and again to faith, to suffering, to faithfulness, reference being made to its own history (10.32 ff.; 12.1 ff., and often). For that reason it is also referred to its leaders.[429] These are not only managing bodies; they also bear the responsibility for the souls in the Church, and obedience is therefore their due, though it must be recognized that that obedience is not just something due to an office as such, but to the care of souls that is actually exercised, and to that faithfulness unto death which arouses the Church to answer and to do likewise. Nowhere so much as in suffering, in the bearing of Christ's shame, is the Church really a Church; nowhere is its service more genuine service for Christ (13.12 f.).

The fact that the ministry of teaching is based, not simply on tradition as in the Pastoral Letters, but on spiritual growth,[430] points in the same direction. It is not instruction or official appointment that makes a man a teacher, but only that inward growth that is inspired by the Holy Spirit; and moreover, there is no parallel whatever here to the Old Testament ordering of the community and of service. Indeed, we can see that the main concern of Hebrews is for the priestly office of the Old Testament

---

[427]6.1 f. also assumes a certain body of catechetical instruction, which it is quite possible may have been largely modelled on Jewish instruction (Michel 145 n. 3).

[428]In this there is a difference between Heb. 5.12 and I John 2.27 (cf. Michel 143).

[429]13.7, 17. Whyever should we suppose that the letter was meant for elders, and that it thinks of the laity here just incidentally (Farrer 156) if at all? Cf. also 5.11 ff.; 10.25.

[430]5.11–6.8 (Michel 140).

to be completely merged in the priestly ministry of Jesus Christ. Like worship—the Lord's Supper is not even mentioned[431]— ordering of offices is, with the Old Testament, cast off like a 'shadow' by the fulfilment.[432] The period of the Church is that of the last days (1.1; 11.40), simply because all priestly action has been performed once for all in Jesus Christ. This can be demonstrated, taught, and handed on; the Church can be called on to live by it in a practical way, and can be told what that means; intercession too can be made. But an act of reconciliation, bringing the estranged person back into touch with God—in short, a priestly action in the strict sense of the term—no longer exists.[433] There is guidance, but not priesthood. The word that is derived from Hellenistic Judaism to denote the leaders of the Church[434] describes a position of authority, but not really an office with precisely stated powers and a clearly defined sphere of duties. Nor do we find any of the other early Christian terms for special ministries.[435] Only Christ himself is described as 'apostle' (3.1). The tradition is passed on by being spoken and heard, and is not ensured by offices developing in a line from Jesus to the bishops *via* the apostles (2.3 f.). Only the witness itself, or God's Spirit that witnesses to it, carries weight with the hearer; and thus the idea of 'ministering' still describes, not some special office, but the activity of all the Church members.[436]

c. From everything that has been said it becomes clear that theologically we have here quite a different line of argument from that of, shall we say, the *First Letter of Clement*. Ministry here

---

[431] 13.10 presumably refers to the heavenly altar. See n. 433.

[432] P. Vielhauer in *Verkündigung und Forschung* 1951/2, 218 f.

[433] The quotation in 9.20 may take its form from the recollection of the Lord's Supper formula (Mark 14.24; cf. Michel 210); but Lev. 8.5 also shows a similar τοῦτο (which is not in Ex. 24.8); cf. H. Windisch, *Der Hebräerbrief*, 1931, 82. But even if the wording went back to Mark 14.24, it says nothing about a sacerdotal character of the Lord's Supper, for the terminology of the Supper has also coloured the language of the stories about feeding; but that does not mean that everything that is said there holds good for the Lord's Supper. Lastly, in the quotation it is a matter of the action of Moses, not of the priests.

[434] Ἡγούμενοι; cf. the evidence in F. Büchsel, *TWNT* II 910, especially Ecclus. 33.19. As the same idea appears in I *Clem*. and Herm. (*TWNT* II 909. 27 ff.), should we also think of Rome as the place of origin of Heb. (and James)? Cf. Streeter 189 ff., especially 199.

[435] Ἐπισκοποῦντες are still all the church members (12.15; Michel 308).

[436] 6.10, and on it Windisch 57.

bears the stamp, not of the Old Testament law, but of the word of the gospel.[437] It is certainly true that the Church is seen more markedly in Hebrews than by Paul as God's people on the move; that there is therefore much more stress here on the recollection of its beginnings and on pointing towards its goal; that tradition and the ministry of the Church leaders also play an important part; and that here the profusion of Pauline ministries is no longer apparent. But what is really vital is not that the experience of decades settles down here and there in established practice, but that there is carried through theologically the conception that all the Old Testament ministries are fulfilled in Jesus Christ, and are therefore abolished for the Church. Just because it is so important for the original message to be passed on to the Church of the present day, it is doubly worth notice that the writer does not yield to the temptation to make sure of keeping it intact by pointing to an official succession; what is pointed to here is simply the witness of the Spirit. So, however dispassionately all the practical needs are seen, it is nevertheless maintained that the Church really needs no teacher, that all its members possess the Spirit, and that Christ is the only all-sufficient bearer of the Spirit. In that sense we may say plainly that Hebrews combats the institutional Church.

[437]Michel 334 f. Moreover the exposition of the law is extremely important in Hebrews; but only Christ, not the Church's office-bearers, can be seen in parallel to the Old Testament as its fulfilment.

D. John's Conception of the Church, and its Development[438]

II

THE CHURCH IN THE GOSPEL OF JOHN

a. John's view of the Church is marked by the idea, which is
stressed more here than in all the other New Testament writings,
that all the decisive events have already taken place. It is true
that even the Fourth Gospel knows of a consummation that lies
in the future;[439] but its gaze is directed not to a history that still
has to be traversed till that point of time is reached—i.e., to the
mission, or to the time of persecution that still has to be endured
—but to the end as an endorsement of what is already in force.
The Last Judgment is already behind the believer, and the parousia
is taking place in the word that is being preached.[440] As with Paul,
we can see a twofold concern: God *has* spoken in Jesus of
Nazareth, whose life and work can be found recorded in a Gospel,
with details of times and places,[441] and not in a timeless dogmatic
treatise. But this Jesus of Nazareth is present to the Church in the
preached word, in baptism, and in the Lord's Supper.[442] In him,
in a way, time is eliminated—he 'is' before Abraham was (8.58).
A man of this earth, he dwells in the bosom of the Father (1.18).
In his obedience, which experiences its final climax on the cross,
his oneness with the Father and also his exaltation are anticipated.[443]

[438]Cf. E. Schweizer, 'The Concept of the Church in the Gospel and Epistles
of St John' in *New Testament Essays in memory of T. W. Manson*, ed. A. J. B.
Higgins, 1959, 230 ff.

[439]*Ibid.* p. 244 n. 15.

[440]3.18 f.; 5.24; 14.18 ff.

[441]Rightly stressed by O. Cullmann (orally).

[442]But I should differ from O. Cullmann, *Early Christian Worship* 58 f., in
seeing the importance of the preaching of the word much more stressed in
John than that of baptism and the Lord's Supper. But each is certainly
mentioned in an important passage (3.5; 6.52 ff.).

[443]3.14; 8.28; 12.32, 34. This is expressed paradoxically in 3.13 by the
statement that the man of this earth has already ascended to heaven. That
would certainly be otherwise if R. Schnackenburg, in *ZNW* 49, 1958, 88 ff.,

As a man of this earth, therefore, he is also one with him who meets the world in the word of his witnesses.[444]

b. We might therefore expect an idea of the Church such as we find in Paul in the image of the body of Christ. The same conception, in quite different terminology and therefore independently of Paul,[445] actually appears in 15.1 ff.[446] Jesus Christ himself is the vine, which includes all the branches in itself, and on which they all live. This gains even sharper outlines when we realize that the image has grown out of Ps. 80.15, where the Son of man is equated with Israel, the vine planted by God.[447] As there appears within the Gospel a separate tradition which is still clearly recognizable and which revolves round the idea of the Son of man,[448] the origin of this statement will likewise have to be looked for in that circle. It is not the nation of Israel, nor even a true remnant in it, that is God's 'true vine'; it all needs to be thought of much more radically. It is Jesus Christ himself—the one who draws his disciples together in himself as branches which without him 'can do nothing' (15.5).

---

were right. According to him 3.13–21 is a meditation of the evangelist that has been fitted into the wrong place.

[444]This becomes particularly clear in 3.11, where Jesus' 'I' suddenly turns into 'we', reappearing as 'I' in the next verse.

[445]And therefore independently of the supposed gnostic myth about the redeemer's gigantic body into which all the redeemed are absorbed.

[446]Cullmann, *op. cit.* 73, points out that behind John 2.12–22 there is objectively the equation: temple = Church = body of Christ.

[447]C. H. Dodd, *The Interpretation of the Fourth Gospel*, 1953, 411 f. He has convinced me, with regard to the view that I expressed in *EGO EIMI*, 1939, 37 ff., that the Old Testament passages must be given considerable weight, though that does not exclude a mythological accretion. This is also supported by the parallel of 10.1 ff., because there too the Old Testament background is still apparent (*ibid.* 358 ff.; cf. J. A. T. Robinson in *ZNW* 46, 1955, 233 ff.). In Pseudo-Philo, *Ant. Bibl.* 12.8, we find that passages like Ps. 80.8–11 are spun out into cosmic ideas, with the vine of Israel reaching up to the throne of God! What is thought of here in an Israelite context appears in Paul in the context of mankind and under another image, the old mankind being in Adam, and the new in Christ 'one (cosmic) body'. On the other hand, the parallel image of the cosmic house or temple (9a), alternating with that of the vine (8, 9b), is again typically Israelite (not gnostic: see n. 416) in its conception (cf. O. Michel, *TWNT* V 123. 42 ff.; 126. 28 ff.; 128–32; on Qumran see n. 131 above, also 1QH 6.15 f.).

[448]S. Schulz, *Untersuchungen zur Menschensohnchristologie im Johannesevangelium*, 1957, 96 ff.

In contrast to Paul's writings, however, the name 'Israel', indeed the designation 'saints' or 'God's people', is no longer associated with Jesus' Church.[449] The comparison with the people of the Old Testament and with Jesus' contemporaries indeed recurs repeatedly, but it does not say that in the 'true vine' a new Israel replaces the old one, as if there were two different periods in the history of salvation, or that John accepted the Pauline view, which separated the community chosen by God, even in Old Testament Israel, from the rest of the people. Israel's election is not denied. But for John God's revelation is confined so exclusively to Jesus Christ that, apart from a few great figures who have 'seen the Father',[450] the whole *cosmos*, including Israel, is seen as being in darkness. It is true that God did call Israel before all others to believe; and so Nathaniel is 'an Israelite indeed' (1.47). Salvation, therefore, is from the Jews (4.22),[451] and Jesus is the King of Israel (1.49; cf. 19.19–22). But this election is seen in the fact that Israel's unbelief is the very type of all unbelief, the rejection of God *par excellence*. In this sense Nicodemus, who understands nothing of what God's revelation really is, is '*the* teacher of Israel' (3.10).

Thus the Jews, as the Israel that has already rejected Jesus, are the representatives of the world in general.[452] On the other hand, the believer of 4.46 ff. is not now, as in the Synoptic tradition, a Gentile representing the contrast with unbelieving Israel (Matt. 8.10). Belief and unbelief have here become plain possibilities for all human beings.[453] In the true vine, therefore, there is not a new period in the history of salvation in contrast to an old one, but rather the Church in contrast to the world, God's realm instead of the devil's, the sphere of light instead of that of darkness. Whoever is cut off from the vine suffers annihilation.

[449]Cf. W. Gutbrod, *TWNT* III 388; Israel is 'almost a supra-temporal entity', but 'in John there is no trace of an extension of the name to the new people of God'.
[450]5.46; 8.56; 12.41.
[451]'Ιουδαῖοι instead of 'Ισραήλ, because the Samaritans naturally regard themselves too as part of Israel? For the rest, see Menoud, *Judaïsme* 19 f.
[452]The world takes their place as soon as—in the farewell discourses—the situation of the earthly Jesus working in Palestine is abandoned.
[453]There is therefore never any mention of the contrast that is specially typical for Israel, viz., between faith and works, grace and law, which is central with Paul (cf. Schweizer, 'The Concept of the Church . . .' 234).

c. It follows from this idea of the Church that in the last resort everyone is joined to Christ in the same way, and that the question of the historical line from Jesus to the present Church becomes irrelevant. The eyewitness certainly does play a part, because John maintains unreservedly that God's revelation was made in the man Jesus of Nazareth (e.g. 19.35). But the question how the gulf between the original witness and the present Church is to be bridged by the tradition is cut short by the fact that the Spirit's witness is regarded as the only decisive one (16.13 etc.). That can be seen in the strange co-existence of the Spirit's witness and the evidence of the eyewitness, where the latter seems to come in almost as an appendage (15.26 f.). It becomes even clearer in the stories which show that no one who has come to believe needs the original witness any longer (4.42). It is shown finally by the general absence of the 'apostle' idea.[454]

d. This certainly does not mean that in John all idea of history as a development going on in time has been lost. When the grain of wheat dies that it may not remain alone but that the ear may sprout from it (12.24), when the shepherd so leads the flock that sheep from other folds come to join them (10.14 ff.; 11.52), there is bound up with this the idea of a certain history of the Church. And it must also be borne in mind that the disciples are hated by the world and are to bear witness in face of it (15.18 ff.). Finally we must remember Jesus' prayer that the Church might be one, so that it might bring the world to faith (17.20 ff.). But it is not accidental that such development is represented by the ideas of natural growth, so that what develops was there from the beginning. For the Church there is no really new step forward,[455] but only a continuance in its origin.

John therefore does not describe the Church, as Paul does (e.g. I Cor. 9.19 ff.), as being in a state of war—the warfare of mission. He mentions neither the calling (Mark 3.13 ff.) nor the sending out (Mark 6.7 ff.) of the twelve. Nor in fact is it at all expected that the world can change, for membership of the Church is seen here as an absolute gift of grace, to be described only as being born of God (1.13). It is the Father who draws to himself whom he will (6.44) and gives him to Jesus (6.37; 17.2);

[454]In 13.16 the word means 'messenger' in the general sense.
[455]See n. 471.

and it is the Son, who as the risen Lord draws his own to him
(12.32; cf. 14.3). That is taken so seriously that it is laid down from
all eternity, not only for the elect, but also for the world. The
former belong to him from the very beginning, while the latter
is 'from below' from the very beginning (8.23). The world cannot
recognize him, simply because it is the world (14.17; 16.3). It
is bound to hate him and his Church (15.18 ff.),[456] and for that
reason there is now no command to love one's enemies (Matt.
5.44 ff.; Rom. 12.14 ff.)—it is always brotherly love to which one
is summoned (15.17–19).[457] 'Greater love has no man than this,
that a man lay down his life for his *friends*' (15.13). The Church's
tribulation consists only in tribulation caused by the hating and
persecuting world, not, as with Paul, in its own 'flesh'. There is
therefore no mention of the Synoptic stories about Peter's sinking
(Matt. 14.30), of the disciple who becomes 'Satan' to Jesus (Mark
8.33; cf. John 6.68 f.), and of the flight of the eleven (Mark
14.50; cf. John 18.8).

e. It is here, therefore, that the sharpness of the division
between the Church and the world is expressed most clearly. In
that sense it may be said that the openness of Jesus' circle of
disciples has vanished; and yet that is not all that is to be said
about it. No one has emphasized as clearly as John that Jesus dies
for the world, not for the Church; and so the sharpness of the
division is at bottom nothing else than what was already there in
Jesus' lifetime, namely the separation accomplished by God
when people rejected Jesus. For John too it is only Jesus who
sees through men (2.24 f.; 6.64); and it is John who emphasizes
so strongly that faith's 'Yes' is always purely and simply a gift,
and can therefore never lead to the arrogance that would enable
the Church to look down on the world. The sharpness of the
division between the Church and the world is thus only the
sharpness with which the Church traces everything without
exception to God's deed, God's election, God's gift, and thanks
him for it all; and so the first way in which it takes practical shape
is that the Church is the community of those who suffer, and

---

[456]In the emphasis on predestination the kinship with the Qumran community is, of course, clear (on this cf. F. Nötscher, *Bibl. Zeitschrift*, n. F. 2,
1958, 131 f.).
[457]D. Faulhaber, *Das Johannes-Evangelium und die Kirche*, 1938, 38 f.

thereby shares Jesus' special position in relation to the world
(12.24–26; 15.18–20; 21.18 f.).

f. Strictly speaking, such predestination excludes all development within the Church; and in a certain sense that is what
happens. From the very beginning the traitor is already what he
will later show himself to be[458] (6.64 f., 70 f.; 17.12[459]). From
the very beginning, too, the disciple's discernment is complete
(1.41, 45), and therefore Peter's confession, which appears here
too, according to tradition, as a caesura at the midpoint of Jesus'
activity, is not the expression of a new discernment, but the
loyalty that remains faithful to one whom it has recognized
(6.66 ff.). Yet even with the disciples there are still misunder-
standings that Jesus has to overcome, and so there is also something like a divine education. Both are united in the fact that
Jesus is for John a living person. 'To be in him', therefore, is
indeed the final salvation; but this is to be regarded as something
living, as 'life'; and thus the disciple who has come to believe
has continually to believe anew.[460] On the other hand, of course,
this is only the constantly fresh realization of what has been there
from the very beginning. So if we may say, at the risk of some
over-emphasis, that in John the Church, like every individual in it,
has from the beginning represented a complete and rounded-off
unity, we must at once add that such a living state must continually be achieved afresh, just as, on the other hand, the world has
indeed been the world from time immemorial, but became the
'world' in the qualified sense only through its rejection of Jesus,
and by that refusal it continually becomes 'the world' afresh.[461]

g. But this brings us to another aspect of this concept of the
Church. The more strongly the direct union of the believer with
Christ is emphasized, the more clearly he is seen as an individual.[462]
We are told in the Synoptic Gospels that whole cities accept or
reject Jesus; and where individuals are called to follow him, their

[458]On predestination in the case of Judas, cf. N. Krieger in *Novum Testa-
mentum* 2, 1957, 73 f.
[459]In John it is Jesus himself who by a kind of 'satanic sacrament' pushes
the traitor into his action (W. Wrede, *Vorträge und Studien*, 1907, 136).
[460]1.51; 2.11; 11.15; 13.19; 14.29; 16.31; cf. 15.2, 8. In 8.12 it is promised
that the follower shall in future walk in the light. Cf. R. H. Lightfoot, *St John's
Gospel*, 1956, on 14.2, and J. H. Bernard, *The Gospel according to St John*, 1928, 55.
[461]Faulhaber 29.
[462]Faulhaber 51 ff., 64 f. Also stressed by Oepke, *Das neue Gottesvolk*, 231.

personality remains quite shadowy.[463] Repeatedly in John the individual person is called, and the question how his resistance is overcome and he is brought to discern the revelation is extremely important (1.35 ff.; 3.1 ff.; 4.7 ff., 46 ff., etc.); and so here only a few specially named disciples are described psychologically. But the image of the vine too, mentioned above, has its own peculiar stamp. Whereas Paul uses the image of the body to show how no member can live for himself alone, but always depends on the others, what is exclusively emphasized in John is the dependence on Jesus himself. The same is true of the image of the grain of wheat out of which the ear grows (12.24),[464] or of the flock under the one shepherd (10.11 ff.). Tendril grows beside tendril, grain beside grain, sheep grazes beside sheep. They are kept together because they are all from the same vine, draw their strength from the same root, and are led by the same shepherd. But they do not serve each other as the arm serves the fingers, or the mouth the stomach; and so in John not only the Old Testament designation of Israel is absent, but also the word 'Church'.

h. The same is true of the relation between the churches. Paul expects one church to serve another with the gifts that have been specially bestowed on it. If Jerusalem has served the Gentile churches with the 'spiritual' gifts of preaching, it has been served by them with the 'fleshly' gifts of the collection (Rom. 15.27). On the other hand, the faith of the Gentiles is to stir up Israel on its part to take the way of faith (Rom. 11.11). If Peter has been given the gift of the apostolate to the Jews, Paul has been given that of the apostolate to the Gentiles (Gal. 2.7 ff.). In John there is no such differentiation, and so one church's need of the others' service is out of the question. Certainly the unity of the Church throughout the world is strongly emphasized here (10.16; 11.52; 17.20 ff.)—only thus can the Church become the revelation of God's glory for the world. But here too one can only pray that what already exists may be outwardly manifested—the oneness of the Church that is already one in Jesus Christ.

[463]It may rather be said that the interest in the individual and in his decision emerges when someone turns away from Jesus (Matt. 18.12 ff., 15 ff.; Luke 15; Mark 10.17 ff.).

[464]On this cf. T. Preiss in *EvTh* 16, 1956, 305 (translation from *Hommage et Reconnaissance, Cahiers théol. de l'actualité prot.*, hors-série 2, 1946). Cf. without an image John 12.32.

i. This view of the Church sets its stamp on its order; we see here the Church's newness in its final and most radical form. Even the various gifts of grace no longer exist; there is only one gift of the Spirit, namely the revelation of the Father in the Son. There are no longer any special ministries.[465] Pentecost goes by with no unusual linguistic miracle (20.22 f.). Again and again the final fact is the individual, standing, under the working of the Spirit, face to face with God. No one can teach him, and no one can correct him; one who is born of the Spirit (not only the Spirit himself) is like the wind, of which no one knows whence it comes or whither it goes.[466] 'Office' exists for John only among God's enemies, with the 'Jews', with Judas (12.6), with Diotrephes (III John 9). The word 'apostle' has disappeared. The twelve have not disappeared—how could they?—but they take a very back seat in relation to the beloved disciple. He points out, however, the believer's intimate union with the Lord—he 'was lying close to the breast of Jesus' (13.23). So in 20.19 ff. it is not even clear whether the ten (not the twelve, nor even the eleven) are present, or whether it is a larger group. They are specifically mentioned as 'disciples', not as 'the twelve', and this shows that they are the representatives of the Church as a whole.[467] But this is true of the farewell discourses generally. It we wanted to confine to office-bearers the promise that was here given to the disciples, we should also have to limit in the same way, for instance, the commands about love and suffering. Thus the individual's direct and complete union with Jesus Christ sets its stamp on the ordering of the Church.

[465]There is a special commission mentioned in a postscript (21.15 ff.); but this too is connected with the exceptional position of the eyewitness, and here too the 'beloved disciple' appears as at least of equal standing.

[466] 3.8. For Ignatius this has become too uncanny: the God-given Spirit (in the bishop) 'knows, in fact, whence it comes and whither it goes' (*Philad.* 7.1). The same gnostically in *Evangelium veritatis* 22.13 ff.; cf. Clement of Alexandria, *Excerpta e Theodoto* 78.2.

[467]C. K. Barrett, *The Gospel according to St John*, 1955, 472 f. It is therefore simply exegetically untrue to declare that the apostolate of the twelve (in any case there are only ten) is thought of here as the centre of the Church (Leuba, *New Testament Pattern* 64). For the idea of 'the disciple whom Jesus loved' as representing the Johannine church in its relation to Jesus, cf. A. Kragerud, *Der Lieblingsjünger im Johannesevangelium*, 1959: he is the symbol of the spiritual ministry of preaching, of the prophetism represented by the Johannine group.

12

THE CHURCH IN THE JOHANNINE LETTERS

a. The features that we have already noticed in the Johannine idea of the Church are also shown here in a more advanced stage.[468] Here too it is clear that whoever recognizes Jesus as truly God thereby has everything (5.20).[469] The sending of the Son is the revelation of God's love from which all love lives (4.9 ff.). It is true, the expectation of the coming completion, which we also find in the Gospel, is again combined here with the Church's doctrine of the parousia (2.28 ff.), Jesus' coming in the flesh is strongly emphasized in opposition to the false teachers who deny it (4.2). Moreover, the phenomenon of false doctrine means opening up the problem of the tradition: what is the Church's present position with regard to its beginning (1.1 ff.; 2.7, 24 etc.)? We may add that the Church has had experience of members who talk of brotherly love without really practising it, that the writer therefore presses some very practical examples on it (3.17 f.), and that here, for the first time in the New Testament, the question of sin after baptism is really taken up (2.1 f.). All this suggests that the Church is seen with more emphasis on its historicity and on its position—determined by all kinds of earthly circumstances involved in living together—between the incarnation and the parousia.

But we must also notice that this is obviously the correction of an originally different interpretation that was forced on the Church, above all by its encounters with false doctrine. Here too, eyewitnesses and witnesses of later generations are on the same plane and 'see' the same Son sent by the Father (1.1 ff.; 4.14).[470]

[468]It does not matter much here whether the writer is the same as the writer of the Gospel (as most think) or not (so C. H. Dodd, *The Johannine Epistles,* 1946; H. Conzelmann in *NtlStud* 201: 'a "Johannine Pastoral Letter" ').
[469]The references are to I John, unless II or III is specified.
[470]The 'we' in 4.11–13 and in 16 ff. certainly refers to all believers; so also therefore in v. 14. In 1.1–3 it must be recognized that we have the wide-

Here too the Church *has* passed out of death into life (3.14). Above all, however, the solution of the problem of the tradition here is that the Spirit living today teaches nothing but what was 'from the beginning'. Wherever anything else emerges, it simply shows the presence of a false spirit; and so the Church can be called on to 'abide', and warned not to 'go ahead'.[471] Only this abiding is not now as clearly as in the Gospel the abiding in the living Christ, but rather the abiding in orthodox doctrine.[472]

b. How strictly the Johannine concept of the Church is kept to is shown in 2.19. The appearance of false teachers within the Church would necessarily abolish the sharp separation between the Church and the world, and the unconditional validity of the divine election that was to be seen in it. Is there then, after all, nothing of the world in the Church? Is there no straying and falling from election? But the old conception is strictly maintained. The emergence of these false teachers only shows that they have never belonged to the Church, and that the world has merely been wearing a mask, and has not attained to a knowledge of Christ; and thus the summons is issued even more urgently than in the Gospel not to love the world, but to separate from it.[473] So here too the talk is only of brotherly love, not of a love that includes those who stand outside the Church. But even the understanding of the possibility of sin after baptism—a possibility that can no longer be disregarded in view of the realities of Church life—does not lead to the renunciation of this concept of the Church. Such sinning is quite clearly regarded in 2.1 f. as an exception, a special case; and 3.4 ff. is the perhaps over-emphasized formulation of the fundamental sinlessness and perfection (and indeed,

---

spread (Rom. 16.25 f.; Col. 1.26; Titus 1.2 f.; cf. Eph. 3.5, 9; II Tim. 1.9 f.; I Peter 1.20) epiphany-pattern (cf. the typical ἐφανερώθη, and on λόγος Titus 1.3). It is, therefore, the 'we' of the eschatological time, who know that God's mystery has become visible, audible, and tangible.

[471]II 9: 'Any one who goes ahead and does not abide in the doctrine of Christ does not have God.'
[472]Conzelmann in *NtlStud* 195 ff.
[473]2.15 ff. If John 16.33 says that Christ has overcome the world, I John 5.4 f. (cf. 2.13 f.) hands this on to the Church. On this idea of the 'world' cf. H. Sasse, *TWNT* III 895.

regarded ethically, of the freedom from all unrighteousness) of
the Church that is born of God.[474]

c. Thus the Johannine Church order is maintained; indeed, we
find here the most radical statement: 'You have been anointed by
the Holy One, and you all know[475] . . . and you have no need
that anyone should teach you; as his anointing teaches you about
everything, and is true, and is no lie . . .' (2.20, 27). Here there
is no longer any kind of special ministry, but only the direct union
with God through the Spirit who comes to every individual;[476]
here there are neither offices nor even different charismata;[477] here
there is only the witness of the Spirit himself.[478] A personality who
is obviously something like a monarchical bishop[479] appears only
as an opponent of God (III 9). The writer certainly calls himself

[474]It is a question what attitude 1.7–10 takes to this. Is not the thought here
of the sins that are confessed at baptism (cf. the perfect tense in v. 10), so
that he then 'cleansed us from all sin' (v. 7) and from thenceforth we no
longer walked in darkness (v. 6)? But 2.1 f. is certainly thinking of the baptized
person, although the sin appears there as an exception. So the present tense
(e.g. 1.9) probably refers to the practice of confession in the Church. But in
that case, do not 1.7–10 and 3.4–10 contradict each other? That is probably
the fault of the opponents who, in a dangerous misinterpretation of the
Johannine passages, on the one hand assert that the pneumatic possesses a
divine character that he cannot lose, so that for him there can be no sin;
and on the other hand claim that precisely on that account he may behave
immorally with an easy mind—in fact, that he must do so, in order to
demonstrate his freedom from the law (so the gnostic opponents in Irenaeus,
Haer. I 6.2).
[475]Or 'you know everything' (so W. Nauck, *Die Tradition und der Charakter
des I Johannesbriefes*, 1957, 95 n. 4).
[476]The Spirit is what the 'anointing' means (*ibid.* 94 f.; cf. 147 ff.).
[477]R. Schnackenburg, *Die Johannesbriefe*, 1953, 216. As there is a warning
against pseudo-prophets, the 'spirits' that are to be tested (4.1–6) are probably
to be interpreted concretely as prophetic utterances; but that by no means
implies that the prophets inside the Church represent a special group
(correctly *ibid.* 190). Evidently every church member is on principle a 'prophet'.
[478]5.5–7 bring in the witness of baptism and the Lord's Supper as signs of
the baptism in Jordan and the death on the cross of the historical Jesus to
supplement the decisive witness of the Spirit (in the word?). Cf. E. Schweizer,
'Das joh. Zeugnis vom Herrenmahl', *EvTh* 12, 1952/3, 344 ff. But it is
very uncertain whether it is possible to reconstruct from this (as Nauck
does in *I Johannesbr.* 147 ff.) an order of the admission of catechumens, in
which the communication of the Spirit, baptism, and the common meal
succeeded each other, as might be expected from the background of the
Qumran community.
[479]Streeter, *The Primitive Church* 85.

'the elder' (no name needing to be added). It is clear that this does not denote either his apostolic rank or his membership of a directing body in a local church; it means that he is regarded by the recipients as a highly esteemed prophet or teacher who still stands 'on this side of any ecclesiastical constitution'.[480] We have already seen that in principle church members have the same status as the eyewitnesses, although the historicity of Jesus is strongly emphasized in countering false doctrine. So the Church is a completely free group, living from the Spirit's 'anointing'; and again it is no accident that its members are addressed as 'beloved', 'children', 'brethren', and not as 'saints', 'God's people', 'Israel'. The word 'church' appears only in III 6, 9 f. It is the company of those whom the monarchical bishop, wishing to eliminate the influence of the 'elder', would like to subject to himself. It is characterized elsewhere as 'the elect lady' (II 1)—that is, in its divine rank, and not in its earthly historical form.[481]

d. The strength and weakness of this concept of the Church, and of the order that corresponds to it, become apparent. The question how the Church can live here and now on what took place in Jesus of Nazareth there and then is solved with impressive and systematic strength. The problem of bridging the temporal and spatial distance between God's saving actions and the Church that reads these letters exists no longer, for in the working of the Spirit the believer is united directly with Jesus Christ; indeed, it may even be said in a certain sense that the fulness of the Son's presence is achieved only in what is declared by the Spirit (John 16.7, 13). This is a protection against any such misunderstanding as that of making faith a mere affirmation of a certain doctrine or of an ethical model or of the Church's historical origin. But here, too, the flight to something better that is still to come on the other side is impossible. The Church is placed in the present, and is fortified against idolizing either the past or the future.

But the one-sidedness of this conception becomes clear too.

[480]G. Bornkamm, πρέσβυς in *TWNT* VI 670 ff.; v. Campenhausen, *Kirchliches Amt* 132. In view of the concept of the Church in the Johannine Letters, it is impossible to see in him (as does Streeter 88 f.) something like an archbishop (cf. n. 421).

[481]It is therefore not enough merely to say, with Kuss, *TQ* 135, 1955, 164 f., that the Church is seen here, not in its organization, but from the inside. There is no organization at all here in our sense.

Even I John shows that the coming of Jesus in the flesh has to be strongly emphasized in face of the false teachers, though its theological basis does not become very plain; and that in the same way the Church's doctrine of the parousia is taken up, though it is not firmly anchored, and is not balanced with the statements about the change that has already taken place. And is the problem of the tradition, as it now emerges, really solved? If this is not simply to issue in the anarchy of the testimonies of the Spirit, it must be stressed that the Spirit calls for nothing else than to 'abide' in what was 'from the beginning'. In that case, however, there is a threat of the opposite danger of rigidity in mere orthodoxy which can no longer take seriously the urgent question of relating the old message to the existing circumstances of the Church. That danger would be inevitable as soon as the living Christ presented by John was replaced by orthodox doctrine; and even if the former is not yet forgotten, something of this development becomes apparent in the Letters.

e. There is another respect in which we may see the strength and weakness of this answer. The Church is seen here with impressive determination as purely and simply the work of God himself; all righteousness through works is here excluded, and so is all misunderstanding of the Church as an association existing on the strength of its members' decisions and performances. The Church is necessarily 'born of God', and the world is 'from its father, the devil'. But again the first Letter shows the danger of the one-sidedness of such an emphasis. Is not the solution of 2.19 simply a surrender in face of the problem of recalling erring members of the Church? Are we not threatened here with the danger of the pious conventicle that either dissolves in pure individualism in which everyone listens only to 'his' witness of the Spirit, or vegetates in mere orthodoxy and in one way or another can only dismiss the world (which does not listen to any such spiritual voice or accept any such dogma) and direct his love towards the brethren only?

That is not yet the case, as the counterweights are still there. It is still clear that the Church is living between the historically unique life and work of Jesus and the coming completion, and that the Spirit leads it to abide in Jesus Christ himself, and so to a faith that is continually finding its basis in him anew and therefore takes a given situation as a summons to do so. So there is growth in faith, as the disciples in the Gospel prove, and as the exhortations of the first Letter assume, without prejudice to the fact that in principle everything is bestowed as a gift from the very beginning. It is still clear, too, that the brotherly love in which the Church lives can always be something new, entering into the brother's actual need at the time. The only way, therefore, in which the Church can live in love is by constantly receiving it anew as a gift from him who has loved not only the Church, but the world too, as indeed John is careful to stress. It is still not forgotten that it is above all by enduring persecution that the Church confirms its existence as the Church. Thus the world is seen at least as the world to which the Church is bound to give its witness. If these safeguards disappeared, the Church would become a gnostic group in which everyone is sufficient to himself and no longer needs his brother. The one-sidedness of this conception was historically necessary in face of the danger of the consolidation of the institutional Church. Where it is accepted, safeguards must be earnestly sought that prevent any such wrong development.

13

THE CHURCH IN THE REVELATION

a. Here we find something quite different from the Church just described[482]—an orientation on the future.[483] How far contemporary events are important, whether they can be seen at all, whether they only serve as ideas and images for other statements, whether they are themselves regarded as constituent parts of history moving on towards its end, is a matter of argument. But it can hardly be disputed that here the Church has to take a certain course till the end. It does so above all in its suffering; it is the woman who is led into the wilderness and attacked by the dragon, but protected by God, and 'on the rest of whose offspring' the enemy's attack is then again launched (12.13 ff.). It needs endurance and faith (13.10); it must endure to the end through the real tribulations that arise from its time and circumstances (ch. 2 f.), and there is a definite period, determined by God, during which it still has to hold out (6.11 and frequently). From this we should expect a conception of the Church that is specially characterized by the idea of God's people on the move. At first this is the case; the image just mentioned of the woman in the wilderness is marked by the idea of Israel moving through the wilderness. In particular, however, it is clear that the Church is seen as Israel, and it has Israel's honourable names: 'kingdom' and 'priests' (1.6). The synagogue wrongly bears the name 'Jews' (2.9; 3.9).

[482]It is clear, in spite of all theological kinship, that Revelation comes from a different author. The striking linguistic arguments would be weakened if we assumed that the Gospel and Letters might be a translation. But the difference in the contents too, particularly the attitude towards the expectation of a future parousia that means the end of this world, is, *pace* Lohmeyer (see next note), at once apparent.

[483]E. Lohmeyer's interpretation, according to which here 'eschatology in pictures of the future represents what is the meaning of faith in the past, present, and future' (*Die Offenbarung des Johannes*, 1926, 188) cannot be maintained in this over-emphasized summary form. It is also clearly limited by what is said previously (186 ff.), which should be stressed even more strongly than in Lohmeyer.

This assumes, of course, that the Church is the heir to these titles; one day it will reach its goal in the heavenly Jerusalem, whose gates bear the names of the twelve tribes (21.12), and 'those who had conquered' again sing, as the eschatological Israel, Moses' song on the sea-shore (15.2 f.). In particular, the Church is identified in 7.1 ff. with the twelve tribes of Israel.[484]

b. This goes beyond anything to be found elsewhere in the New Testament. It is unique that not only the theological concept of Israel, stressing God's choice, but even the national designation 'Jews', is here denied to those who do not believe in Christ. That they are actually described as a synagogue of Satan shows the radical nature of these ideas. The same is true of 11.8, where the earthly Jerusalem is prophetically unmasked as Sodom and Egypt. Here the Church is no longer merely the legitimate development of Israel—it *is* Israel. In all this there is no reflection about pre-Christian Israel,[485] nor is there the Pauline idea of a chosen remnant of Israel within the Jewish nation. We can see here some reason for the timeless interpretation of Revelation.[486] As the Church's identity with Israel is assumed with no suggestion of its being a problem, and no line of development from the pre-

---

[484]This is certainly disputed. Some (W. Bousset, *Die Offenbarung Johannis,* 1906, 287 ff. and the authors mentioned there; Dahl, *Das Volk Gottes* 191) claim to see there only the Jewish Christian part of the Church, or think the chapter is not homogeneous. It seems to me clear, however, that the 144,000 from the twelve tribes and the innumerable multitude from all nations represent one and the same group (Lohmeyer, 67 f.; Oepke 78). It is the nation of the twelve tribes as the people elected by God, as the number known to God, not one of which is lost—the innumerable multitude from every nation when seen from the point of view of its earthly and historical reality. Connected with this is the statement that it is facing the great temptation and is at the same time the victor after the fight; this is essentially the same difference of view.

[485]This certainly might appear briefly in 12.1–4, if Jesus' birth in Bethlehem were referred to here, as is generally assumed. But I still think that a more probable interpretation is the birth, in anticipation of the parousia, of the Messiah in 'heaven', so that the woman is the image of the Christian Church, not only in vv. 5 ff., but from the very beginning (with Michel, *Zeugnis* 77; B. J. Le Frois [according to *RB* 62, 1955, 293 f.]). Whether 1QH 3. 1 ff. represents a parallel—so F. M. Braun (*RB* 62, 29 f.)—or not—thus O. Betz, *NTS* 3, 1956/7, 314 ff.; 5, 1958/9, 67 ff.—is still disputed. (Cf. also G. Hinson, *Rev. de Qumran* 2, 1960, 183–203.) But even in the other case it would only be said that the Church is one and the same before and after Christ's birth.

[486]On this see n. 483.

Christian to the Christian people of God is even considered, so too no thought is expressed about the contemporary line leading from Jesus *via* the apostles to the existing Church, and therefore about the problem of the tradition, of the preservation of the old message in its transition to new conditions. As in the Johannine Gospel and Epistles, the Church is the company of those predestined by God (7.1 ff.; 13.8; cf. 20.15). This alone is vital. God's plan of salvation is treated seriously in that the last, final goal is again called 'Jerusalem'. But has it still really any theological relevance to the historical Jerusalem? It is the heavenly city, whereas the earthly one is Sodom and Egypt. God's Jerusalem is no longer in Palestine; it is wherever there is a believing Church,[487] just as Israel is no longer a Semitic nation, but a company from all nations (5.9 f.; 7.9).

c. But it cannot be denied that there is also a certain timelessness. This does not mean that, for the seer, time is not moving towards an end that is close at hand; it means that as a prophet he is already looking at what will come. So everything to come is already there 'in heaven'; and thus the present Church is at the same time the nation sealed by God for the coming time of trial *and* the company of the redeemed that have emerged from the trial victoriously. The prophet's view makes past, present, and future coalesce into one; and he knows that only that view shows the reality. Reality is what the Church is before God, not what the unenlightened eyes of men can see in it.

d. It is on this basis that the order of this Church is to be understood. It might really be expected that the individuals predestined by God should play a large part, as in John. In part that is what happens; the individual holds on to his faith and stakes his life on it, and thus martyrdom is particularly important as being of the essence of the believer's existence. One single martyr in the Church can be specially mentioned (2.13), and he is given the same title that Jesus himself bears (1.5). In the same way faithful individuals from a Church that is in danger are given prominence (3.4).[488] Yet the thoughts of this book revolve entirely

---

[487]It is probably the Church in general that is represented by the temple in Jerusalem (11.1 f.; A. Feuillet, *NTS* 4, 1957/8, 187 sees in it, as in 7.1 ff.—see n. 484—only the Jewish Christian Church). In 21.9 the heavenly Jerusalem, as the Lamb's wife, takes the Church's place (19.7) without question.

[488]Cf. also Lohmeyer, 188.

round the Church. The Church is addressed. It, and not the individual, is represented in its 'heavenly' existence in the 'angel' —quite a new conception when related like this to a church.[489] If we compare the otherwise closely analogous idea in Valentinus' doctrine of angels, where the 'angel' represents the Christ who comes to the individual, and thus the believer's other self, it is evident how Church-minded Revelation is.[490]

e. But it is a Church without a hierarchy. All church members are kings and priests (1.6; 5.10); all are God's servants (7.3) and 'saints' (5.8 etc.). Membership of the company of the elect is determined only by God's act of grace which is answered by the pure and immaculate who follow the Lamb (14.3 f.). The twelve apostles appear as the foundations of the walls of the now completed Jerusalem (21.14), and in 18.20 beside 'saints' and 'prophets'; but in the present time, apart from the Church chosen by God, there are only false apostles (2.2). It is not the twelve, as in Luke 22.30, but all church members who will one day sit on Christ's throne, so far as they remain faithful (3.21). Thus the reader is merely referred repeatedly to the voice of the risen Lord himself, the 'Spirit' who speaks to the Church (2.1, 7, etc.); in listening to him the Church is bound to unmask the false teachers (2.2).

The only special ministry that can be seen developing in the Church here is that of the prophet; but here too we must ask very carefully whether, for the writer, all are not fundamentally prophets, just as all are 'witnesses'.[491] Such prophecy is described

---

[489]1.20; 2.1 ff. It is clear that this is no monarchical bishop. Throughout the New Testament ἄγγελος denotes either an angel, or in a quite general sense a messenger. The idea of heavenly representation of the Church fits very well into the thought here (*TWNT* VI 448. 27 f. (= *Spirit of God* 105 f.); cf. 669, n. 112). As to his being equated with the leader of the Church, the most that we could suppose is that the latter represents the Church in his person (as is seen by W. H. Brownlee, *NTS* 3, 1956/7, 24 f., e.g., in 1QH 3. 1 ff.). But in that case the designation as 'angel' would not be explained, as this clearly points to a heavenly representation. Cf. Goguel, *L'église primitive* 117.

[490]*TWNT* VI 391. 21 ff.; 449. 4 ff. (= *Spirit of God* 21, 106).

[491]The indications are not entirely clear, but it seems that the writer makes no fundamental difference between prophets and other church members, martyrs and non-martyrs. The expression 'the blood of the saints and the blood of the martyrs' (17.6) cannot possibly separate martyrs from ordinary church members ('saints'); it is therefore an epexegetical 'and'. The same

quite clearly as the coming of the Spirit over man (1.10; 4.2; 17.3; 19.10; 21.10; also 10.8 ff.). Because this has again become a reality, the apocalyptist lives in the present time of salvation and need no longer hide behind a great name of earlier times and use it as a pseudonym, but can speak to the Church simply as 'John' with no further title (1.4, 9; 22.8). But precisely in his capacity of bearer of the Spirit he is only a brother and comrade of all the other church members (1.9). When the 'testimony' repeatedly appears as the ministry expected from the Church, both in general (12.17) and in the case of martyrs in particular (6.9; 12.11), it is explained, in something like a gloss, as 'the spirit of prophecy' (19.10). The whole Church is therefore understood in principle, at least in this passage, as a Church of prophets; so the same thing holds good here for the prophets as for the martyrs: namely, that some of them are called in a special way to the ministry of 'testimony'(i.e. martyrdom) and of 'prophecy'. Thus God is 'the God of the spirits of the prophets'(22.6). There is no other order,[492] for the heavenly elders correspond to the Old Testament council of Yahweh, and can no more be related to earthly office-bearers, or interpreted as analogous to them, than can the four living creatures or the seven torches (4.4–6).[493]

f. So we have here a Church that is clearly seen as a Church in the wilderness, waiting steadfastly amid persecution for the coming redemption. But its real nature is not understood if it is regarded as a historical entity, but only if we see in it the company predestined by God, already standing in the light of the coming glory, and receiving the direct prophetic call of the risen Lord

---

thing will hold good for 16.6; 18.24 ('the blood of prophets and of saints'; cf. 11.18), where saints and prophets stand together. In that case, however, 20.1 ff. is also to be taken to mean that all believers, and not the martyrs only, share in the millennium. That is especially supported by the fact that only the event at the beginning of this period is called 'resurrection'. Although the phrase 'first resurrection' (20.5 f.) really indicates a second one, the bringing to judgment of all the dead after the millennium is not called 'resurrection'; so here it is only the non-believers who are meant.

[492]In a church where many cannot read, to speak of 'he who reads aloud' and 'those who hear' is a matter of course. Of course, it may have already become usual for a certain man or a certain group in the church to carry out this ministry regularly.
[493]Strongly in favour of this: G. Bornkamm, *TWNT* VI 668 ff.

who speaks to it in the Spirit; and thus in the last resort there is but one ministry to which everyone is bound to be called—the ministry of the witness and the prophet.[494] Here, too, we can see something of the abrupt antithesis between Church and world, particularly in the disputes with Judaism. Yet it is not carried through as radically as in I John; for Revelation allows that an entire church may be thrust out by Christ if it sins and does not repent. It is true that there is a certain tension between this statement, which arises from the seriousness of the admonition, and the knowledge of the sealing by God's gracious decree. The tone of the monitory letter to the actual church is not the same as that of the prophetic view that sees the Church as it essentially is before God.

[494]The first definition of this one ministry has in view rather the preaching to those outside, to the 'world'; the second, the preaching to the Church.

14

THE CO-EXISTENCE OF DIFFERENT FORMS

a. If we look back on these different 'Johannine' churches and sum them all up, there arises a problem which ought to be considered, and which is first of all historical: where are these churches actually located? For Revelation the answer is certainly Asia Minor. For I John and the Gospel, tradition points in the same direction. But even if we think rather of Syria,[495] the problem will not diminish; for at about the same time other documents give an entirely different picture.[496] For Asia Minor we can think of I Peter, Acts, and the Pastoral Letters; for Syria, Matthew, and perhaps the *Didache*; and for both, perhaps not very long afterwards, Ignatius. Are we to suppose, therefore, that everything that we read in these Johannine writings is pure fiction that does not correspond to reality? Or does it perhaps show that we have drawn inadmissible conclusions from what we have found in a document that does not specifically deal with the problem of Church order? But that cannot be true, at any rate for the Johannine letters; and it might not be tenable in the case of Revelation either.

In that case, however, we are left with no other answer than that set out particularly by G. Bornkamm[497]—that it is a question,

[495] So for instance, Nauck, *I Johannesbr.* 165.

[496] Bornkamm, *TWNT* VI 669 f. This shows that the evidence of the Church of the early second century in Asia does not clearly prove the existence of a hierarchical order with a monarchical episcopate as something to be taken for granted and therefore going back to old roots (against Menoud, *L'église et les ministères* 9).

[497] *TWNT* VI 670. Michel, *Zeugnis* 73 f., also bears on this. E. Käsemann, 'Ketzer und Zeuge', *ZTK* 48, 1951, 292 ff., sees the ecclesiastical structure rather differently, but was pioneering here. With him, too, the 'institutional' Church, if we are to understand by that the Church to which the future belongs, is given in the person of Diotrephes, while the local church 'elder' whom Diotrephes excommunicates remains a solitary figure who would like to revert to former conditions (but against the assumption of such excommunication cf. Bornkamm, *TWNT* VI 671, n. 121). But whether we think with Käsemann of an elder of a single church, or (as seems to me more probable)

speaking purely phenomenologically, of something like a conventicle church.[498] In that case the elder's opponent in III John does not appear to be a specially unworthy and exceptional person. He represents a line of development that is establishing itself in the institutional Church—the development into a monarchical episcopate, perhaps rather assertive and more pushing than others, but not basically different from others going in the same direction. Revelation certainly contends against fanatical (gnostic?) groups which would dissolve any order; but it also contends against a lukewarmness that remains content with the forms already reached. We do not know the identity of the false 'apostles' of 2.2, who seem to be on a different level from the Nicolaitans who are mentioned later.

b. This means, however—and this conclusion is extremely interesting—that even in the New Testament Church there are side by side at the same time in the same geographical area groups with a quite different form, phenomenologically speaking: the conventicle beside the national church, which is at least on the way to regarding itself more and more as the official Church. The contrast will not be overstressed. Outside III John nothing is to be seen of a conflict between the two groups, and even there it is perhaps more the expression of a tension that culminated when two men met, both of whom represented with exceptional emphasis their own view of the Church. But we cannot escape the plain statement of fact—that churches lived side by side which regarded themselves differently on essential points, and which therefore adopted a very different order.

---

with Bornkamm of the charismatic leader of a conventicle church, we have to make a choice here: if we regard this attempt as one that turned out, through its failure, to be wrong, then we have to regard John's Letters as representing a wrong way. It seems to me that here in a particular situation of danger an element that necessarily forms part of any view of the Church has been stressed in a one-sided way, and that these 'conventicles' were therefore a one-sided but very necessary corrective within the development of the Church as a whole, and that they bore fruit far outside their own boundaries.

[498]Can we thus explain the claim made by the seven churches of Revelation to be *the* primitive Christianity (Lohmeyer, 40)?

E. The Conception of the Church in the Apostolic Fathers

Something must be said under this heading, at least as an addendum,[499] although writings such as I *Clement*, which were presumably written earlier than some of those dealt with above, are more closely related than the latter, as regards their contents, to the post-New Testament development into the early Catholic Church.

15

THE CHURCH IN THE DIDACHE

a. The time and place of origin are very much debated. Syria still seems the likeliest place.[500] As it is unlikely that the document was a Utopian presentation of the early days,[501] it can hardly be dated as late as the second or third century.[502] But it is hardly feasible, either, to put it as early as between 50 and 70;[503] and so we may well favour some time between 90 and 110.[504]

b. The church shows some resemblance to that of Matthew, which may also be supposed to have been in Syria, and with which it has some stratum of Jesus' sayings in common.[505] This

---

[499]A summary treatment is all that is possible without specialist knowledge of patristics.

[500]So most recently A. Adam, *ZKG* 68, 1957, 1 ff. and J. P. Audet, *La Didaché*, 1958, 208 ff. Streeter, *The Primitive Church* 76, 144 (cf. 279 ff.) sees here a continuation of the church structure of Antioch (Acts 13.1–3). R. Glover, in *NTS* 5, 1958/9, 27, argues in favour of Egypt. That would make more comprehensible the difference from Ignatius in Church order (Streeter 140 ff.) and in relation to Paul (but cf. Streeter 150 ff., 162, 176 ff.).

[501]E. Peterson, *Rivista di Archeologia Christiana* 27, 1951, 67 f.; J. A. Robinson, *JTS* 13, 1912, 339–56.

[502]Cf. the exposition of this thesis in Audet 211 ff. The fact that the various ministries do not correspond at all to those of the later Church should make one cautious; for who was still to know in the second or even third century that formerly the monarchical bishop and presbyters beside the bishops did not yet exist?

[503]Apart from a few additions (Audet 187 ff.).

[504]So Adam 1 ff.

[505]This certainly goes back to the common source (Q?). Cf. Glover, 12 ff.

church, too, has a living eschatological expectation which is
described in colours taken from the Jewish tradition (16); and for
it too the observance of the law is central.[506] This is seen to such a
degree as a continuation of Judaism that one wonders whether a
Jewish catechism was not adopted with some introductory pieces
taken from the tradition represented in the Sermon on the Mount,
and with minimal Christian enlargements (1-6).[507] Even when the
Lord's Supper is regarded as a 'sacrifice' (14), this is not so much
a dogmatic statement about its interpretation as a reminder that
the Church sees in it the world-wide sacrifice whose offering is
prophesied in Mal. 1.11, 14, and so in its eucharist too does not
deviate from what Israel was commanded and promised. The
validity of the laws about the offering of the first fruits is likewise
regarded as a matter of course, because the prophets have become
the Church's 'high priests' (13.3 ff.). If the Church calls itself 'the
saints'[508] (4.2), it thereby takes over Israel's title of honour, which
it probably interprets in an ethical sense (10.6[509]).

Here, however the Church's newness is not seen, as it is in
Matthew, in the fact that only Jesus, by his interpretation of the
law and by his walking in lowliness and humility, made such
fulfilment of the law possible for it. How little the *Didache* knows
theologically about what separates the Church from Judaism[510] is
made startlingly clear in 8.1: the latter fasts on Monday and
Thursday, the former on Wednesday and Friday. A new feature
is the clear knowledge of the Lord's coming on the clouds (16),
or, expressed more Hellenistically in a way that is typical of the
stratum represented in the liturgical prayers, 'knowledge, faith,

---

[506]Even the gospel is characterized in its nature as a 'commandment' (11.3).
How important the observance of the law is of itself is shown by 13.3–7.
An offering of first fruits is necessary because of the Old Testament law.
The prophets take the place of the high priests; but even if there are none
there, the commandment has to be fulfilled; and then the poor, as stop-gaps,
take the place of the priests who according to the law are entitled to receive
the first fruits.

[507]J. Schmid, *RAC* I, 1950, 1216 is against this view.

[508]We also find 'thy Church' (referring to God) in the prayers at the Lord's
Supper (9.4; 10.5).

[509]In view of 15.3 we can hardly think there of the Gentiles who are to
repent = be converted to Christianity (so Audet 415).

[510]This is seen as a company of 'hypocrites'! Here too we can see a kinship
with Matthew, who regards the official Judaism of the Pharisees in the same
way.

and immortality' that have come to it through Jesus (9 f.). If, as still seems to me most probable, the 'vine of David' mentioned there means the Church, it is clear, first that the latter applies to itself the Old Testament images for Israel, and secondly that it regards itself as the Church 'revealed' by Jesus. That means that Jesus has caused it to appear as the real and true Church of God. The approach to the conception that is found in John 15.1 ff. is clear. But here the Church is not understood, as it is there, in its unity with Jesus Christ himself; and so its completion is to be expected only in the *eschaton*.[511] In the same image, therefore, quite a different conception of the Church is expressed, its essential nature being seen not in the timeless character of its union with the ever-present Christ, but in its being made an essential part of God's plan throughout history, which leads from the vine of Israel planted with David, by way of Jesus who first caused it to appear in the character that God intended, to the final gathering together of the people who are scattered over the world.

c. As the *Didache* is, in fact, a Church order, we learn relatively a good deal about this. The central position given to the law, which is largely expounded casuistically,[512] is shown in the distinction drawn between the perfect, who fulfil the whole law, and others, who just do what they can (6.2), in the high regard paid to fasting (7.4;[513] 8.1) and to the regular recital of the Lord's Prayer (8.2), and lastly in Church discipline, which is to lead to penitence (15.3; cf. 14.2). In this the Church is already seen as the company, scattered over the world, which, 'gathered from the ends of the earth', finds its real unity only in the kingdom of God (9.4).[514] Not till then will they be redeemed from evil, made perfect in God's love, and sanctified (10.5). There is probably an echo here of something of the Matthean concept of the Church as a mixed

[511]See n. 514.
[512]E.g. 13.5–7. This also becomes clear in the commentary on Jesus' saying 'Give to him who begs from you', where the problem of the unworthy recipient is treated in detail (1.5 f.). The golden rule appears only in a negative form (1.2). Elsewhere too the radical demands of the Sermon on the Mount are based on considerations of utility (1.3: 'and so you will have no enemy'; 1.4: 'for you cannot do so').
[513]On this J. Behm, *TWNT* IV 934. 29 ff.
[514]Cf. Mark 13.27 and the Jewish parallels to it in Vincent Taylor, *St Mark* 518 f.

company of good people and bad, which will be cleansed only in the Last Judgment.

Certainly the Church marks itself off sharply from the Jewish community; and so baptism, which is assumed to be only adult baptism (7.1, 4) acquires great importance. Only the baptized are admitted to the eucharist (9.5). Here, however, as the relatively detailed ordering of the ceremony shows (7), the correct performance of the rite is not yet necessary for salvation. Great freedom as to details is still the rule in the choice of running or stagnant, warm or cold water, and even of baptism by immersion or by sprinkling. The use of the threefold name in baptism is assumed,[515] but there exists, side by side with this, the older form that uses only the name of 'the Lord' (9.5). Set prayers are used for the eucharist.[516] The way in which it was celebrated is anything but clear; but it is most probable that a love-feast, in which those less closely connected with the Church could take part, was followed by the Lord's Supper proper, which may have been celebrated in a special room.[517] The ordinary church service seems to have taken place daily, and the Lord's Supper on Sundays (4.2; 14.1; 16.2).

d. The most interesting fact is the co-existence of bishops and deacons on the one hand, and of apostles, prophets, and teachers on the other; and it is striking that, in spite of the close connection with Judaism, there are no elders. Here too it seems that the latter represent a separate line of development from the one that is characterized by bishops and deacons. In the *Didache* the latter are elected by the Church, and already have to be protected from a certain lack of esteem (15.1 f.). They perform the same ministry as the prophets and teachers (15.1); but they do not pray extempore as the prophets do, but say the prescribed liturgical prayers (10.7).[518] The Pauline insight that all ministry is a gift of God's grace is absent here;[519] and in its place the word 'office' reappears

[515]Here too we can see the kinship with Matthew (28.19).

[516]This term occurs in 9.1, 5.

[517]Cf. Audet 406 ff. (especially 415), 459 ff.

[518]The οὖν in 15.1 perhaps also suggests that they serve particularly at the Lord's Supper (J. A. Kleist, *The Didache* . . . [Ancient Christian Writers], 1948, 164 n. 90).

[519]Χάρισμα is used in a completely general sense only in 1.5 (= δώρημα; Herm. *Mand.* II 4). The same is true of Ign. *Smyrn.* intr.; *Vita Polyc.* 20.2;

for the ministry of the prophets as well as for that of the bishops and deacons.[520] The church (like the Corinthians, though not like Paul) distinguishes between those who can speak 'in the Spirit' and those who cannot; and so the Spirit is interpreted in terms of ecstasy (11.7, 9).[521] Presumably it is even assumed that the prophets combine with their preaching actions that seem to the natural man strange and mysterious.[522] The writer is certainly inclined also to recommend the non-ecstatic ministry of bishops and deacons (15.1); but unlike Paul *vis-à-vis* the Corinthians, he is helpless in face of the conception of the Spirit as ecstasy, and has no other conception to offer. He can only point out in detail how the false prophet may be recognized by his conduct (11.5 ff.), because the Church has already learnt by bitter experience that ecstasy by itself does not make the prophet (11.8).

e. The triad apostles—prophets—teachers is certainly to be found; but it is questionable whether it has more than a chance terminiological significance. Apostles are not the twelve,[523] but men who move from church to church (11.3 ff.). We cannot now say

---

Act. Thom. In I *Clem.* 38.1 at least the general subordination to the others is based on the latter's charism; elsewhere, however, in the New Testament meaning it is only something in the past (Grau, par. 9, pp. 110 ff.). Only in Clement, *Virg.* I 11.10; *Act. Joh.* 106, is there an echo of the Pauline use (Grau, par. 8, pp. 95 ff.). Even Justin hardly knows the charismata from his own experience, and regards their character as essentially miraculous. This is also true for Irenaeus and others who now understand prophecy only as ecstasy (Lauterburg 41 ff.).

[520]Moreover in a typical Old Testament phrase (λειτουργεῖν τὴν λειτουργίαν 15.1; Num. 8.22; 16.9; 18.6 f. of the cult, in the last two passages in the plural). In 15.2 the office-bearers are the τετιμημένοι (cf. Clement of Alexandria, *Strom.* VI 14.107). Streeter 150 ff. sees here the transition from the order of Acts 13.1–3 to that of Ignatius. According to him, the prophet in the Church of the *Didache* already almost occupies the place of a monarchical bishop (13.3; 10.7), and Ignatius himself is also a prophet.

[521]The Spirit indeed makes everyone ready to be well pleasing to God (4.10); but in its narrower meaning 'Spirit' is equated with ecstasy (as in Rev. 4.2; 17.3; 21.10).

[522]11.11. Probably spiritual marriages are meant, in which Christ's relation to the Church is represented. For if we were to think only of symbolic actions (so Audet 452; as a possibility H. Sasse, *TWNT* III 898. 11 ff.), the expression 'earthly mystery of the Church' would be no more probable than the qualification that the real prophet must not call on other people to imitate him (G. Bornkamm, *TWNT* IV 831. 29 ff.).

[523]The question of the line of tradition from Jesus to the existing Church plays no part (cf. Audet 446 f.).

whether, and if so how, they are distinguished from prophets.[524] In 13.1 f. and 15.1 f. there is only the dyad prophets and teachers. An untruthful apostle is not a false apostle, but a false prophet (11.5 f.; cf. 9 f.); and one may therefore ask whether 'apostles' is not merely an additional term for prophets, to emphasize their divine mission.[525]

The teacher probably does not travel, but settles in one place (cf. 13.2 with 1); and so in 11.1 there appears, not the title 'teacher', but only a verbal definition that is probably meant to include all itinerant brethren who preach. The resident teachers, and particularly the prophets, receive payment in kind (13.1 ff.), while an explicit warning is given against such payment to other strangers beyond the usual period of three days (12.3 ff.). The rule that one who preaches the word of the Lord shall be honoured like the Lord, because the Lord is where his lordship is preached (4.1), should probably be related in the first place to one who teaches the catechism; but this is by no means certain, and the passage is too general to be necessarily limited in this way.

f. So here we see a Church which, although it still knows that ministry and guidance are incumbent on and possible to the whole Church (15.3), cannot dispense with the ordered ministry of bishops and deacons; perhaps, too, it already knows catechists. What is more conclusive, however, is that it takes ascetic accomplishments and the gift of ecstasy so seriously that it clearly separates from the ordinary church members the 'perfect' and those who 'speak in the Spirit'. Only those who experience ecstasy are really worthy of honour, the Church's 'high priests', to whom the offerings commanded in the Old Testament are due.[526] But this brings in a new element that is entirely foreign to the whole of the New Testament—the distinction between a higher class and the ordinary church members. Here it is based on an overvaluation of the capacity for ecstasy. From the point of view of the history of religion it is quite intelligible; the Corinthian church probably thought in the same way. But there the attempt was not legitimized, but was overcome by Paul.

[524]Cf. Audet 439 f.; it is simply stated what functions there are, and in that connection there is no thought of a Church based on a hierarchy.
[525]So K. H. Rengstorf, *TWNT* I 433. 21 ff.; ET, *Apostleship* (Bible Key Words 6), 1952, 45. Against him G. Klein, *Die zwölf Apostel* 50 n. 209.
[526]On this see n. 506.

Here we have to distinguish carefully. With Paul a member can be acknowledged by the Church because a ministry was given him by God as a gift of the Spirit and proves fruitful for the building of the Church. In the Pastorals a church member may be honoured and supported as an elder by the Church because a certain order has proved salutary for the Church. But here the 'perfect' person or the one who 'speaks in the Spirit', the ascetic, and the ecstatic, have *ipso facto* a higher status than the others. Here the case is, not that the Church is particularly thankful for a particular ministry that is rendered to it, but that there arises a special class of ascetically or ecstatically gifted people which is marked off from ordinary church members; it carries its quality in itself, apart from whatever function it has in the building of the Church, and it therefore possesses that quality beyond the performance of its ministry. These people are acknowledged and supported, not from purely practical considerations, such as that a special spiritual gift must be allowed to develop as fully as possible in the Church, or that a certain order best serves the right tradition of the apostolic word, but on account of a quality of their own that raises them above the normal level of the Church.

This, however, is something quite new and foreign to the New Testament; it is the distinction between priests and laity, coming up again remarkably transformed after its submersion. For the distinction, so important for Harnack's interpretation, between free charismatic ministries and ordered offices[527] is by no means so conclusive. Whether one overstresses the ecstasy or the office, one has only two variants of the same false distinction—both separate the bearer of the Spirit from the laity that does not possess it, at any rate in the same degree. If this unfortunate way has once been taken, the other position is sure to commend itself quite soon—to characterize the non-charismatic, purely technical ministry as the only one necessary for the building of the Church, by virtue of its being reliable and free from risk.[528] This is already the case in the *First Letter of Clement*.

[527] *Die Lehre der zwölf Apostel.* . . . (TU II 1/2) 1884, 145 ff.; *The Constitution and Law of the Church in the First Two Centuries*, ET 1910, 236 (and on it Linton, *Das Problem der Urkirche* 36 ff.; E. Foerster, R. *Sohms Kritik des Kirchenrechtes*, 1942, 51 f.). Similarly Weiss, *I Kor.* 307 f.; H. Lietzmann, *The Beginnings of the Christian Church*, ET[3], 1953, 142 ff.

[528] Cf. Lietzmann, *ZWT* 55, 1913/14, 132; R. Knopf, *Das nachapostolische Zeitalter*, 1905, 152 ff.

16

THE CHURCH IN THE FIRST LETTER
OF CLEMENT

a. The occasion of this letter, which was probably sent in the year 96[529] from Rome to Corinth, is the removal from office of certain presbyters there (44.3); but there may have been behind that a more far-reaching dispute in which the defenders of an older and freer order opposed the consolidation of the institutional Church.[530] The arguments of the letter only show that the idea of order in general seems very important to the writer; and from that it may be inferred that in all probability on the other side not only are there chance personal antipathies to certain office-bearers, but the question of the progressive regulation of offices is raised as a matter of principle. From a purely historical point of view the counter-movement in Corinth would, of course, have just the same right to be discussed; but as no document from the other side has come down to us, we hear only one party.

b. The designations used of the Church are not illuminating, being taken over from the tradition. Favourite ones are the image of the flock (16.1; 54.2; 57.2; cf. 59.4) and 'the elect' (1.1 and frequently).[531] How little the taking over of traditional titles means is shown by the fact that, although the Church is still called 'the body (of Christ)' (38.1; 46.7), only the parabolic meaning in relation to joint membership and the mutual ordering of the members is relevant (37.5; 46.7), and not the present union with Christ which it characterizes. A new and obviously important

[529]The date is put between 118 and 125 by C. Eggenberger, *Die Quellen der politischen Ethik des I Klemensbriefes*, Diss. Zürich 1951, 181 ff. (with others named there). Otherwise most recently E. Molland, *RGG* I 1837 and those mentioned there (col. 1838); also A. Stuiber, *RAC* III, 1957, 191 f.

[530]Cf. v. Campenhausen, *Kirchliches Amt* 93. These people would therefore be in a position like that of the 'elder' in relation to Diotrephes in III John. For other possibilities see Stuiber, *RAC* III 190 f.

[531]'The Church of God' occurs in the introduction, 'brotherhood' in 2.4. In 1.1 they are called the 'sanctified' (or 'holy') elect.

thing for the writer is the idea that the New Testament Church has issued as 'the 'Holy of Holies' from God's 'people' in the Old Testament, and is therefore a 'holy part' (29.3; 30.1). Elsewhere too we can see how the Church knows that it has developed out of Israel, whose successor it is; it is on the 'journey' (2.1) through history to the parousia which is at hand (23.5), its course decided by the imminent judgment (28.1) and the promised resurrection (24.1).

*c.*What we hear about its order fits in with this concept of the Church. It is true that the letter is sent from a church to a church (intr.), that it is still known that the Holy Spirit is given to all (2.2),[532] and that the 'majority' of the Church still decides what is to be done (54.2). But in fact, this last item is a surprising innovation. In the New Testament there are no majority decisions;[533] and so here too, just as in the setting up in authority of individual office-bearers, secular and civil order comes in and overshadows the testimony given by the Church with its own appropriate order, just as in the *Didache* pagan religious standards succeed in entering. But that can be seen elsewhere too. Our letter, in common with all the writings in which the Church is seen particularly in its historicity, shows that the problem of the tradition is becoming acute. Even the line God—Christ—apostles—bishops and deacons (42.1–4) at first simply means that the latter were appointed by the apostles, not that they are their successors,[534] and still less that there was any guaranteed official succession. Something of the kind might possibly be meant in 44.2, where it is said that the apostles had appointed and installed bishops, so that when the latter died, other well-tried men should take over their office. That would be the case, if the subject of 'died' were 'the apostles', so that the office of the 'well-tried men', the bishops, were that of the apostles. But that cannot be read out of the sentence, especially as the word 'other' clearly distinguishes these

[532]This is also echoed in 38.1 (see n. 519). But we are told of specific gifts of grace only in the case of one specially prominent Old Testament figure— Rahab, on whom not only faith, but also prophecy, was bestowed (12.8).

[533]See 26a. Whether this could always be adhered to in practice is another question, but in any case it is realized that any conflict about vital decisions should be allowed to go on till the Church as a whole can assent to a conclusion.

[534]Goguel, *Min. and Sacr.* 316.

men from those first named, and is therefore to be related to those who follow in the bishops' office.[535] But in any case, the concept 'office' appears here, as in the *Didache*, to denote the ministry of individuals in the Church.[536]

At the same time the Hellenistic terminology of office begins to appear;[537] the demand is clearly for a guaranteed tradition and a guaranteed order. Reference to the order that is to rule in the Church is certainly to be found in Paul's writings too; but here it is no longer merely to serve the building up of the Church, to be the subsequent shaping of whatever the Church learns as it listens to the Spirit. It becomes here an end in itself (cf. 42.2; 65.1), and is therefore buttressed with a whole system of thought. What is now seen is not the Church's peculiar position as one called out of the world and united with its risen Lord (however much it may at the same time remain involved in all earthly circumstances), but only its ordained position as part of the whole of nature. In ch. 20, for instance, a broad presentation of laws of nature, according to which even the heavens revolve, leads to a call for respectful submission to overseers and elders (21.6). In fact, in 37.2 ff. military organization is held up as the pattern of the structure that is valid for the body of Christ, with higher and lower ranks. But the triple linking of obedience to Church overseers with the order resting on obedience in marriage and the family points in the same direction (1.3; 3.3; 21.6). There is an appointed rank for everyone (44.5);[538] and it is no longer the place assigned through the gift of God's grace, occupied in the act of service and open to change according to the bestowal of the Spirit, but an established rank recognized as static; and so one must learn to subordinate oneself (57.2).[539]

d. The most serious thing here is the taking over of the Old Testament order of offices as an unconditionally valid law,[540] the

---

[535]So too Dix, *Ap. Min.* 258 ff.

[536]Λειτουργία, 44.2, 6. See 21a.

[537]W. Brandt, 'Die Wortgruppe λειτουργεῖν im Hebräerbrief und bei Clemens Romanus', *Jahrbücher der Theol. Schule Bethel*, 1930, 155, 163, 173.

[538]Τόπος. Cf. 40.5 = τάγμα 41.1, and on this Nauck, *ZNW* 48, 1957, 213 ff.

[539]Cf. also 60.4, where obedience towards God's supreme and glorious name, and that owed to leaders and rulers on earth, are mentioned in the same breath; probably departments of government are in mind here. The combination of this phrase with 61.1 in some MSS is not original (cf. Knopf, *Ap. Väter*, 145 f.).

[540]The Church is at least obliged to act in a way analogous to this law (A. v. Harnack, *Einführung in die alte Kirchengeschichte*, 1929, 93).

sacrificial system becoming specially important (4.12; 40; 43.2 ff. parallel with 44.1). In general, ideas of sacrifice come into the description of episcopal duties (44.4), and even the distinction between priests and laity is in any case on the verge of going over from the Old Testament community to the New Testament Church (40.5).[541] Indeed, the appointment of bishops and deacons is even turned into a scriptural command by the (probably unintentional) changing of the Old Testament text (42.5).[542] So the penetration of a secular and civil idea of office goes hand in hand with a mainly religious concept, widespread both in the Old Testament and in the pagan world; and again it makes no decisive difference whether it is the fundamental separation of the official from the ordinary subject, or of the priest from the layman, or of the ecstatic from one not moved by the Spirit.

As to details, we learn only that bishops are distinguished from deacons and are also called presbyters or overseers (1.3; 21.6; 44.4 f.; 47.6); so the two lines known as presbyters and bishops have here quite coalesced.[543] It is not clear whether 'overseer' has a still more general meaning, and in particular whether there are already bishops and deacons in Rome, as the letter mentions none there.[544]

[541]How important the Old Testament priests are to the writer is shown by the fact that among Jacob's posterity the priests and Levites, Jesus, kings, rulers, and princes of Israel are enumerated in that order (32.2).
[542]This, the analogy of the Old Testament law, and the belief that the apostles had foreseen the dispute about office and had made general arrangements about it, are the four fictions pregnant for the future (Harnack, *Einführung* 95).
[543]See 15d.
[544]Dix, *Ap. Min.* 255.

17

THE CHURCH IN THE LETTERS OF IGNATIUS

a. The concept of the Church in Ignatius' letters[545] contains numerous lines of thought related to the Pauline-Johannine idea of a Church united with the risen Lord, the body of Christ, the true vine. It is true that there is also thinking on the lines of the history of salvation; the time of the prophets is regarded as the time of prediction (*Philad.* 5.2; 9.2; also Polyc. *Phil.* 6.3); but we may wonder whether in the last resort the difference between 'prophets' and 'gospel' is not merely quantitative (*Smyrn.* 1.2). In any case, the prophets already become (advance) disciples of Christ (*Magn.* 9.2; also 8.2); and the contrast now is not between Israel's time of preparation and the new Israel's time of fulfilment, but between the mutually competing entities of Judaism and Christianity (*Magn.* 10.3; *Philad.* 6.1; cf. *Rom.* 3.3). Essentially, therefore, the Church is shaped by its oneness with 'the flesh and blood of Jesus Christ' (*Magn.* 1.2).[546] It is the local, not the temporal categories that predominate. Thus the image of the body appears; as God himself is a unity, so are the head and the limbs (*Trall.* 11.2). But the unity of Jews and Gentiles too is expressed in the image of the body (*Smyrn.* 1.2). In particular there belongs here the celebrated argument about the Church as a house built by God, the cross representing the lever, and the Holy Spirit the

---

[545] As K. Rozemond points out in *Verbum Caro* 9, 1955, 158 f., Ignatius offers no clear definition of the Church, but rather assumes it in all his thought as the central spiritual factor.

[546] How far Ignatius' thinking is sacramental, or even magical, is a matter of debate. Cf. on the one hand H. W. Bartsch, *Gnostisches Gut und Gemeindetradition bei Ignatius von Antiochien*, 1940, 117–22; H. Köster in ZTK 54, 1957, 61, 68 f.; R. Bultmann in *StudPaul* 47 f.; also J. Behm, *TWNT* III 743. 1 ff.; on the other hand T. Rüsch, *Die Entstehung der Lehre vom heiligen Geist bei Ignatius von Antiochien, Theophilus von Antiochien und Irenäus von Lyon* (Diss. Zürich), 1952, 60–62; C. Maurer, *Ignatius von Antiochien und das Johannesevangelium*, 1949, 88–99.

rope (*Eph.* 9.1).[547] The fact, too, that in the addresses the Church receives the highest titles of honour, and in particular appears as predestined before all time (*Eph.* intr.),[548] shows that it is above all regarded as having been taken by God out of time and the world.[549]

b. But for that very reason, the new element that emerges here as in I *Clement*, becomes doubly clear. From the point of view of Paul and John all the emphasis in Church order must have lain on the Church's present union with the living Lord, that is, on the working of the Spirit, which constantly puts every believer afresh into that unity with Christ. That agrees with what Ignatius feels. Church members are described as bearers of God, of the temple, of Christ, and of what is holy (*Eph.* 9.2); they are told that they are 'full of God' (*Magn.* 14.1), and that the Church is endowed with every gift of the Spirit (*Smyrn.* intr.).[550] Something of the high regard for the free working of the Spirit can also be seen in *Philad.* 7.1 f., where it is a matter of close concern to Ignatius that, without knowing what the situation in the Church was, he was inspired by the Spirit to utter what he then 'cried with a loud voice' in the assembly.[551] In the great emphasis on martyrdom we can see a way of thinking to which God's ever new gift of the Spirit and his guidance by the Spirit on particular occasions are essential. It is only in martyrdom that Ignatius becomes a disciple in the real sense (*Eph.* 1.2; 3.1; *Trall.* 5.2; *Rom.* 4.2)[552] The same thing is shown by the esteem in which the

[547]The image of the body and limbs is recalled by Polyc. *Phil.* 11.4, where 'omnium vestrum corpus salvetis' suggests I *Clem.* 37.5/38.1: σωζέσθω ἡμῶν ὅλον τὸ σῶμα. Beside that there appears the image of the temple as referring to the individual: *Eph.* 15.3 (though in the plural); *Philad.* 7.2. Probably, however, *Magn.* 7.2 should be regarded in the sense of the Church as God's temple.

[548]*Eph.* 8.1 should be regarded similarly, especially if we interpret, 'known to all in all eternity', and do not, with R. Reitzenstein, *Das iranische Erlösungsmysterium*, 1921, 236 n. 2, make it personal: 'known to the archons'.

[549]In Polyc. *Phil.* intr. the same thought is expressed in the epithet 'sojourner', characteristic of the Church in the Jewish tradition.

[550]The same thing, certainly, is said in Ign. *Polyc.* 2.2 of a single person, Bishop Polycarp.

[551]But see n. 466.

[552]With these, however, should be compared the passages in *Magn.* 9.1 f.; 10.1; *Polyc.* 2.1, in which believers generally are called disciples.

ascetic is held (*Smyrn.* 13.1;[553] *Polyc.* 5.2). But it seems that here we are closer to the *Didache* than to Paul,[554] for the measure of esteem is not the ministry that a gift of grace renders towards the building of the Church, but, as in the *Didache*, the 'religious achievement' involved in it. So here too it might lead to a distinction necessarily made between the 'perfect', the special 'bearers of the Spirit', on the one hand and ordinary church members on the other.

c. But what is typical of the Ignatian letters is that ruin awaits the ascetic who is esteemed more highly than the bishop (*Polyc.* 5.2), and that the Spirit's instruction which Ignatius utters at the assembly is 'Keep to the bishop and the presbytery and the deacons' (*Philad* 7.1). The transfer of over-esteem from the ascetic or the ecstatic to the office-bearer is therefore particularly obvious here; and so here too, as in I *Clement*, order[555] as such becomes essential. True, it is no longer the order of nature or of the armed forces that gives the order of the Church its character. Ignatius is not the rationalist, for whom, as for the Stoics, the order of nature becomes an analogy for the divinely spiritual order; he thinks more 'religiously', but that makes no fundamental difference. Now it is the order of salvation, God—Christ—apostles, that is reflected in the Church order; and that religious basis merely gives greater prominence to order as necessary for salvation.[556] Again we see breaking in a line of thought which is foreign to the New Testament. The office[557] is no longer simply the living form taken over as a matter of course from the primitive Church, nor is it the necessary historical link between Jesus of Nazareth and the later Church, ensuring an unchanged tradition.

We can see here that Ignatius' view proceeds rather from the Pauline-Johannine than from the Lucan one; for he thinks of an

---

[553]There is a special class of 'widows', who are apparently not women whose husbands have died, but spinsters who have denied themselves marriage. On the other hand Polyc. *Phil.* seems to distinguish between widows and spinsters (4.3; 5.3; 6.1).

[554]On this cf. Bultmann, *StudPaul* 40.

[555]*Eph.* 6.2: εὐταξία.

[556]In fact, it is the *spiritual* importance bestowed here on the bishop (Rozemond 163) which shows the further development in contrast to the New Testament.

[557]The τόπος (see n. 538 above) is in *Smyrn.* 6.1 the rank in which one is and beyond which one is not to think of going.

office as something finally static, a constituent part of the 'building' which is God's temple, and something that remains constant throughout the centuries. In a way this is also true of the New Testament, where we read that he who receives the disciples receives Christ, and in him God himself (Matt. 10.40). But it is meant there for the one who preaches the word,[558] because in him Christ, and therefore God himself, is constantly present. But in Ignatius this place is taken by the bishop, not indeed in his capacity as preacher, but explicitly the silent bishop too (*Eph.* 6.1 f.), that is, the bishop in his own right, the bishop as an official person, and not now by virtue of his function. It is not now the fact of preaching, or of Jesus Christ's presence, but simply the bishop's position, that has come to represent God (*Polyc.* 6.1; *Eph.* 5.3; *Magn.* 3.1 f.). Therefore the Church must cling to the bishop as it clings to Christ, and as Christ clings to the Father (*Eph.* 5.1; cf. *Magn.* 4; 6.2; *Trall.* 7.1). Nor can his youth be any argument against such obedience.[559] As Christ was subject to God, and the apostles to Christ, so the Church is to be subject to the bishop (*Magn.* 13.2; 7.1). Obedience to Christ is shown in obedience to the bishop (*Trall.* 2.1);[560] to serve him is to serve God, and not to serve him is to become the prey of the devil (*Smyrn.* 9.1). So there is a church only where there is a bishop (*Smyrn.* 8.1); and apart from him there is none (*Trall.* 3.1). Without him nothing must be done at all (*Magn.* 4; 7.1; *Trall.* 2.2; *Philad.* 7.2; *Smyrn.* 8.1 f.); or else one would be standing 'outside the altar space' (*Eph.* 5.2; *Trall.* 7.2).[561] What Paul once said of the apostle in his special position now holds good of the bishop—he is 'not through himself and not through men' (*Philad.* 1.1).[562]

[558]This also holds good for *Did.* 4.1 (15e).

[559]*Magn.* 3.1. In itself this is a right and proper principle; only one asks what is stressed—the gift of grace, which has also been imparted to younger men (so I Tim. 4.12, although with a marked ethical colour), or his official position.

[560]Cf. *Magn.* 2; bishop and presbytery: *Eph.* 2.2; 20.2.

[561]Cf. also *Philad.* 4: 'one eucharist, one altar, one bishop'.

[562]As this is said of this particular bishop, it is not yet asserted that consecration automatically effects that kind of divine appointment; nor must it be overlooked that as yet the bishop possesses no clearly defined rights, and that, as the question of the tradition has not been raised, there is no question of any succession (v. Campenhausen 106 n. 1; 111). The marked stressing of the monarchical office of bishop may suggest that it is not really as firmly established as the writer would wish (Streeter, *The Primitive Church* 173 ff.).

d. Beside the bishop are the presbytery and the deacons (*Philad.*
intr.; 4.1; 7.1; *Smyrn.* 12.2; *Polyc.* 6.1). The co-existence of different spiritual gifts has become a gradation of offices. If in Paul's
writings the most that could be said was that the confession of
the Lord, the usefulness to the Church, and therefore the strength
of the love that seeks not self but others proved to be stronger
in the performance of some ministries than in others, by now a
statically valid gradation is reached, the elder being subordinated
to the bishop (cf. *Trall.* 12.2), and the deacons to the bishop and
presbytery (*Magn.* 2; also *Eph.* 2). So the scale is greatly emphasized by the titles, a careful distinction being made between the
'right reverend' bishop, the 'reverend' elders, and the 'fellow
servants' the deacons (*Magn.* 2; cf. 13.1 and similarly fairly often).
The bishop alone sits in God's place, and the elders sit in place
of the council meeting of the apostles, while the deacons perform
Jesus Christ's service (*Magn.* 6.1).[563] In this it is clear that the bishop
and the presbytery particularly are close to each other (*Eph.* 4.1;
2.2; 20.2; *Magn.* 2; 6.2; 7.1; *Trall.* 2.2; 13.2). But we can already
see the formation of another and more far-reaching gradation. At
least in Ignatius' theory, the bishop is not only the monarchical
director of a church, but also something like a metropolitan.
The Bishop of Antioch is at the same time Bishop of Syria, for
without him the church in the whole of Syria has no bishop
(*Rom.* 9.1; cf. *Magn.* 14; *Trall.* 13.1). On the other side, of course,
it is said that no Lord's Supper is to be celebrated without a
bishop.[564] That is conceivable only if every local church has its
own bishop; but it may mean, as *Rom.* intr. suggests, that the
most important church has the primacy for the whole district, and
that therefore its bishop is on the way to becoming a metropolitan.

e. What has happened here? In contrast to I *Clement*, the question of the historical origin of the existing offices, and therefore

[563] This leads to the remarkable fact that the elders are put in parallel with
the apostles, and the deacons, under them, with Jesus (*Trall.* 3.1; cf. *Smyrn.*
8.1). This is due partly to the author's wish to revalue the deacons' service,
and partly to the already existing comparison between the elders and the
apostles (*Philad.* 5.1). But it betrays the idea that Jesus is 'only' the one who
performs lowly service, whereas the apostles are now the representatives
of an 'office'!
[564] *Smyrn.* 8.1 f. Neither eucharist nor *agape* (are they still the same thing?)
can be celebrated without a bishop, and the same is true of the solemnization
of marriage (*Polyc.* 5.2).

the question of preserving the original tradition intact, are not raised; in fact, those who ask about the scriptural basis are sent about their business. It is enough that Jesus Christ and the faith that he originated require that order (*Philad.* 8.2). Order is therefore regarded neither simply as a servant, nor as the guarantor that the first Christian message will be handed on as faithfully as possible—a task that has already been taken over by the 'Scriptures'. It is a timeless and non-historical religious quantity, just as in I *Clement* the order of nature, according to which the heavens and the seasons revolve, is valid without regard to time and history. The presence of the living Christ has become the timeless entity of the 'Catholic Church'.[565] This, of course, is related to the Ignatian approach to the concept of the Church.[566]

f. The *Didache* proceeds from a high valuation of the free working of the Spirit, but it confuses the Spirit with ecstasy—that is, with human religious endowment and performance. It is therefore driven to over-value the 'religious man', and, as this person is not always available in sufficient numbers, to replace him with the official. I *Clement* proceeds from a conception of the Church as God's people moving through history, so that here order is at first quite rightly regarded as an aid to the preservation of tradition. But the demand for an order that is also a guarantee turns this servant into a master; and so there comes law, which is supposed to be just as inviolable as the immutable order of nature. Ignatius knows a concept of the Church that puts in the centre the present union with the risen Lord. But at the moment when that union ceases to be an event, a continually new action of the living Spirit (which works in the form of ecstasy as well as of sober and rational reflection, by breaking through everything that is usual as well as by admonitions about order), and becomes a guarantee, the transformation of gospel into law has become even clearer.

[565] *Smyrn.* 8.2: ἡ καθολικὴ ἐκκλησία.
[566] This feeling is strengthened by the knowledge of the Church's existence beyond all geographical and national peculiarities; cf. *Eph.* 3.2 (there are bishops as far as the ends of the earth!). On the Ignatian concept of the Church cf. the excursus by W. Bauer, *Die apostolischen Väter* II, 1920, 201 ff., and the book (to which I have not had access) by J. S. Romanides, *The Ecclesiology of St Ignatius of Antioch* (USA, ca. 1957). For a survey of modern literature on Ignatius: G. Maron, *Verkündigung und Forschung* 1956/7 (published 1959), 188 ff.

18

THE CHURCH IN THE *SHEPHERD* OF HERMAS

a. This writing must be treated more by way of supplement, since much in the church that it describes is obviously in a state of flux, and so the results are less clear. It is interesting, however, because it takes us into the Roman church, probably about the time of Ignatius' letters.[567] However deeply the writer is interested in his own local church as a body, he yet looks at the Church repeatedly as a heavenly body that was created before the world, and for whose sake the world originated (*Vis.* II 4.1). Through it, therefore, the Holy Spirit speaks (*Sim.* IX 1.1). It is 'holy' (*Vis.* I 1.6; 3.4; IV 1.3)[568] and comprises the company of the 'elect' (*Vis.* I 3.4; II 1.3; 2.5; 4.2 etc.). This it is as the heavenly body known to God, for on earth the sinners cannot be distinguished from the righteous (*Sim.* III 2; cf. IV, 2);[569] and so it lives here 'in a foreign land' (*Sim.* I 1). Only once does there appear clearly the idea of God's people under the Old Testament image of the vines planted by God (*Sim.* V 5.2; 6.2). But no real relationship to Israel exists any longer. This does not appear in any positive or negative assessment. The idea of the twelve tribes is taken over; but it is taken as a matter of course to refer to the twelve nations of the earth (*Sim.* IX 17.1 f.). On the other hand, the frequent use of the image of the tower (*Vis.* III 12.3; *Sim.* IX 13.1) shows that Hermas' concept of the Church clearly belongs with those that stress, not the Church's historicity, but the fact of its having been elected and taken out of time and history. True, the tower

[567]It was presumably written in Rome between 130 and 150 (J. Hoh in the *Lexikon für Theologie und Kirche* IV, 1932, 988; H. Weinel in *Neutestamentliche Apokryphen*, 1924, 331). Carrington, *The Early Christian Church* I 392, thinks of the work as going on from 100 to 140.

[568]Its members too are called 'saints' (*Vis.* I 1.9; II 2.4 f.). As *Sim.* VIII 3.8 shows ('the saints and the righteous'), the expression also has for the writer an ethical content.

[569]Here Hermas has something in common with Matthew. See 4d.

is still being built (*Vis.* III 8.9). As in I Peter 2.4 f., the stones are imagined here as being alive; they rise and take their place as part of the building (*Sim.* IX 3.3). But this statement is determined in the first place by the fact that in Hermas' time people are still repenting and being baptized, though there is no such differentiating historical view as in Rom. 9–11. Above all, the writer is concerned to press his point that now, shortly before the completion of the building—in view, that is, of the approaching end of the world—the 'stones' can once more repent.

The importance of repentance runs through the whole writing. It is shown, too, in the second interpretation of the image of the 'old woman';[570] the Church, whose spirit has grown old, is renewed by repentance, so that afterwards it can appear as a maiden (*Vis.* III 11.2; 12.2; 13.1 f.). When the penitential purifying has been completed, it will stand there as if hewn out of one stone (*Sim.* IX 18.3 f.). At this point Pauline and post-Pauline passages are also applicable. It is then one body (13.5); indeed, it appears not merely as consisting of one stone (9.7) but as having formed one single stone together with the rock (Christ) (13.5).[571] But the more detailed interpretation shows that the writer is concerned, not with the theological statement about intimate union with Christ, but with the fact that there rules in the Church one mind, one thought, one faith, one love.[572]

b. What is more vital is that here a later stage of the development already noted in the *Didache* becomes evident, 'Christianity' (*Mand.* X 1.4) being given a strong ethical bias. The keeping of the commandments (*Sim.* VI 1.1 and frequently) and the primary importance of repentance (*Vis.* II 2.5; V 7 and frequently) are signs of this; there is a special fondness, too, for describing believers as 'God's servants' (*Vis.* I 2.4 and frequently), while Gentiles and sinners have become almost synonymous terms (*Sim.* IV 4; VIII 9.1, 3). So, too, fasting again emerges as a good work;[573] but above all the martyr is esteemed, for martyrdom blots

[570]The first stresses the idea, already mentioned, of the Church's existence before the creation of the world.
[571]Once there also appears, unemphasized, the traditional image of the bride of Christ (*Vis.* IV 2.1 f.).
[572]This is probably how the writer also interprets the statement about the 'one Spirit' in 13.5 (cf. 'one garment' in 13.7).
[573]*Sim.* V 1.1. It is, indeed, declared in 1.4 that instead of such futile fasting

out all sins (*Sim.* IX 28.3, 5 f.). As in the *Didache*, it is said here explicitly that there is a still greater perfection beyond the fulfilling of the commandments (*Sim.* V 3.3); and here too the ascetic streak is unmistakable, for every action that is combined with a feeling of pleasure is characterized as self-indulgence (*Sim.* VI 5.5).[574]

Hand in hand with this, as in the *Didache*, there goes a specially high esteem for the ecstatic. The 'Spirit' that seizes Hermas is the Spirit that carries one away (*Vis.* I 1.3; II 1.1). A prophet who, when overpowered by the Spirit, is able to answer questions and begins to speak his own thoughts, is a false prophet and no true bearer of the Spirit (*Mand.* XI 3, 5, 16). Thus the problem is bound to present itself again of distinguishing real from false ecstasy (*Mand.* XI).

As in the *Didache*, there is a certain competition apparent here between martyrs and those endowed with the Spirit on the one hand, and office-bearers on the other. Of course, this does not by any means point to a conflict. Both groups are in the Church together, and Hermas, in all modesty, would like to give precedence to the elders; but it is intimated to him that the places of honour belong first to the martyrs, and then to the prophets, although this certainly includes no higher kind of bliss (*Vis.* III 1.8 f.; 2.1).[575]

c. On details it only remains to be said that 'leaders and presidents' are given to the Church (*Vis.* III 9.7). They are called

---

God wants a renunciation of evil; but 3.5 ff. shows that the practice of fasting is to continue in association with it. It is true that the basis of this is to be that the sum saved is to be carefully calculated and allotted to the poor. Fundamentally, therefore, the thought is on the lines of ascetic exercises as good works, although at the same time a purely ceremonial action is felt to be inadequate and in need of neighbourly love as a basis.

[574]'Gerne dien' ich den Freunden, doch tu' ich es leider mit Neigung,
    Und so wurmt es mich oft, dass ich nicht tugendhaft bin'.
(F. Schiller, *Gedichte: Die Philosophen*, ed. Bellermann, I, 1895, p. 180; 'I am glad to serve a friend, but it does not go against the grain; so it vexes me to think that there is no virtue in the action.') But 5.7 qualifies this somewhat.

[575]Cf. also the reference to the places appropriate to merit, *Sim.* VIII 2.5; IX 15.4, where the prophets of God are named after the believers of the first and second generations, but before the apostles and teachers. The jealousy about precedence, censured in *Sim.* VIII 7.4, 6, is presumably to be looked for inside the group of office-bearers.

'overseers' (*Vis.* II 2.6) or 'elders' (*Vis.* II 4.2). The two are identical (*Vis.* II 4.3); and the shepherds of *Sim.* IX 31.5 f. probably mean the same people. Moreover the bishops too are probably not to be distinguished from them, as they never appear beside them in an enumeration (*Vis.* III 5.1). They are always mentioned in the plural, and are rather guardians of the poor as well as being mainly responsible for hospitality to visitors (*Vis.* III 5.1; *Sim.* IX 27.2). In the former passage there are apostles, bishops, teachers, and deacons side by side; but the subsequent words show that the last three contrast with the first as real offices.[576] The special position of the apostles can also be seen in *Sim.* IX 17.1; 16.5.[577] Finally there comes the group of widows and orphans, to whom a certain Grapte preaches; but there is probably no special office involved here. It may be further remarked that it is obviously only deacons, not bishops, who it is thought may in practice carry out their duties badly (cf. *Sim.* IX 26.2 with 27.2).

d. Thus in the *Shepherd* of Hermas a development has once more become apparent that we have already noticed elsewhere, especially in the *Didache*. Here too, as with Ignatius, the problem of the tradition, or indeed of official succession, is by no means completely developed; the Church is, in fact, seen much more clearly in its timeless union with Christ than in its march through history. A certain order of ministries has emerged, and is assumed as a matter of course; but these ministries involve no guarantee, either of the right tradition as in I *Clement*, or of the unity of the Church as in Ignatius. The co-existence of ecstatics and office-bearers shows that, although a certain competition is unavoidable, it implies a line of theological thought that is basically similar, whether it is the former or the latter who are given prominence in relation to the ordinary church members. But in Hermas this is indicated quite cautiously, and the writer is anxious to stress that what is in question here is only a certain place of honour, and not a final distinction.

[576]The corresponding verbs are: to walk according to God's holiness—to supervise—to teach—to serve.
[577]They have taken the gospel to the nations, and even to those who have died before its coming.

19

THE CHURCH IN THE LETTER OF
BARNABAS AND OTHER WRITINGS

We can only refer briefly to a few documents in which, as they show quite a different understanding of the Church and its order, only a few direct statements about them appear.

a. For the *Letter of Barnabas*[578] too—it can almost be taken for granted by this time—the separation of Judaism and Christianity is already an accomplished fact. The former has lost the Covenant, and the latter has gained it (4.7; cf. 13.1–14.5). It is the new people (5.7; cf. 13.1–3, 6[579]). The name 'Israel' is used only for the people of the Old Testament, who are now lost in unbelief (5.8; 11.1) and severed from 'the Church of the saints' (6.16; cf. 7.11; 19.10[580]). Of course, the twelve are seen here, as they are now seen everywhere (with or without Paul?), as the preachers of the basic message (8.3), and it is now only the Old Testament witnesses who are called 'prophets' (1.7 and often). A distinction is also made between those who 'work through the word' and those who 'work with their hands (in works of love) for release from their sins' (19.10).

Much of the total conception of the Church, however, approximates to the Johannine; it is only as 'spiritual men', as a 'perfect temple for God' (4.11) that they are really a Church; God's Spirit is poured out over them; they live in the 'spirits' and with the 'gift of the Spirit' (1.2 f.). This is understood throughout to

[578]An admonition to Gentile Christian Churches (in Egypt? Syria? Asia Minor?), probably from the first half of the second century (J. Schmid, *RAC* I 1217; K. Bihlmeyer in *Die Apostolischen Väter*,[2] 1956, XXII f.; but cf. R. Schütz, *RGG* I 880 f.). Further cf. A. L. Williams, *JTS* 34, 1933, 337–46.
[579]Λαός is used throughout: the Church has taken the place of the Old Testament people that is now rejected.
[580]'Holy' appears here only in the Old Testament quotation and in a formulation that is to be found word for word in the tradition that appears in the *Didache.*

mean that God dwells within every individual in such a way that
he speaks through him, 'prophesies' in the Spirit-prompted
preaching and the Spirit-prompted prayer that overcome the
hearers (16.8–10), in a way analogous to what happened to
the Old Testament prophets (5.6) or Moses (12.2). Thus, too, the
writer's special discernment (of which the Church is worthy!) is
understood as the gift of divine teaching planted in him by God
(9.9); and so the writer firmly claims to speak, not as a teacher, but
merely as the Church's servant (1.8; 4.9; 6.5). Finally, indeed,
they no longer need a teacher, for they are 'taught by God', and
are their 'own lawgivers' (21.4, 6).

So there is a Church living here which, although it knows of
the pattern of the two periods of Old Testament prophecy and
New Testament fulfilment, now at heart regards Israel simply as
the rejected nation that is finished with, whereas the Church
itself possesses God's Covenant. Nor, in fact, is there any trace
of a sequence of events, either leading from the Old Covenant
to the New, or leading from Jesus through the tradition to the
period of the Church as it is now. The only vital thing is the
present union with God who lives through his Spirit within every
individual, so that all are taught by God, and themselves represent
the final authority.

b. A good deal in the so-called *Second Letter of Clement*[581] points
in the same direction. Here too the new 'people' stands in contrast to the Jewish (2.3). There is more emphasis laid on its being
a stranger in this age, and on the longing to leave this world
(5.1; 6.3). The most interesting thing, however, is the timeless
view of the Church, which was created before the sun and moon,[582]
and is the body of Christ,[583] one with him as male and female,

---

[581]A sermon of the middle of the second century (E. Molland, *RGG* I
1938; Bihlmeyer xxx).

[582]Jewish apocalyptic thought makes its way in here: Syr. Bar. 4.3–6;
II (4) Esd. 8.52 (Michel, *Zeugnis* 86, n. 71). Cf. also the influence of Jewish
pseudepigrapha elsewhere, e.g. *Barn.* 16.5 f. (Michel 88).

[583]Paul himself certainly does not think that individuals are primary and
that the body of Christ originates only through their union—Christ himself
is indeed foreordained before all faith. Yet Paul could not speak of the Church
as an entity that pre-existed beside Christ (this is perhaps too little heeded
in A. Fridrichsen's article in *Buch v. d. Kirche* 54). On the relation of individual
and Church cf. H. Koehnlein, *RHPR* 17, 1937, 377; H. Odeberg in *Buch
v. d. Kirche* 73 ff.

spirit and flesh (14.1–4). Although there are elders who 'exhort' and 'preach', the whole Church is called to mutual 'exhortation' and 'instruction' (17.2–5). Here too, therefore, the concept of the Church has its centre in the idea of the closest union with the heavenly Lord, and, united with that, of the Church's timeless and everlasting existence.

c. The *Letter to Diognetus*[584] is interesting only because there appears the concept of the 'new people' over against Greeks and Jews[585] (1; cf. 5.17), and because here the struggle of the Letter to the Hebrews against all ceremonial worship is continued on another plane (3.2 ff.). We must, however, at least refer to the *Odes of Solomon*,[586] in which the images of head and limbs (17.15) and bridegroom and bride (38.11; 42.8 f.) represent the close union of Christ and Church. That community with God or Christ is generally defined in the strongest terms (3.2; 4.9; 8.22; 21.5); it goes so far that the believer himself becomes God's son (3.7; 31.4; 36.3). Thus the believers, in the midst of the dead, are a 'Church of the living',[587] already in paradise (11.16) and in community with all the angels (4.7 f.). There is repeated reference to the Spirit who lives in the believer and speaks through him (6.2; 14.8; 16.5; 28.7; 32.1; 33.8; 36.1), and the believer begins his preaching with the prophetic utterance (9.1).

Of course, much more on similar lines could be found in Montanus and in gnostic writings; but with these we come to a still later period; and what has been said may be enough to illustrate that at any rate the development did not follow only one single line.

[584]An apology from the late second or third century (C. Andresen, *RGG* II 200: about 200? cf. Bihlmeyer XLIX).
[585]Γένος, no longer λαός.
[586]W. Bauer's edition (Kleine Texte 64, 1933). They probably originated in Syria in the second century. The estimates of date vary from the end of the first century to the beginning of the third.
[587]In Syriac *kenushtā*, which rather denotes a (special) assembly than God's people in its exclusive sense. But this probably goes back to Christian usage as shown for instance in the Sinaitic (not in the Curetonian) Syriac (on this K. L. Schmidt, *TWNT* III 529; ET, *The Church* (Bible Key Words 2), 1950, 47 f.).

PART TWO

THE UNITY OF THE NEW TESTAMENT CHURCH

20

THE TWOFOLD VIEW

a. Jesus' disciples knew that they were part of Israel. They belonged to that nation and shared its history. They had therefore experienced God's acts in Jesus of Nazareth primarily as a part of his dealings with his people for their salvation; and the way that they took with Jesus to meet the coming lordship of God was part of the whole way that God took with his people through history. But they did not form just one of various groups in Israel—it was the true Israel, that had now heard God's call. The fact that Jesus called his disciples to follow him made it clear that his call was more than the call of a prophet; and the same thing was shown in his preaching and his actions. It was God's final call, in which the fulfilment that was at the door reached the hearer; for in view of Jesus' claim it was impossible to postpone the decision any longer, as if there were still a historically foreseeable period ahead, in which a choice could still be made. But whoever had heard his call and had come into the company of his disciples had thereby decided for the kingdom of God, and now stood under his law. The signs of the coming kingdom were already there in Jesus' meals with sinners, in the community of the disciples as they journeyed along the roads of Galilee, and in the acts of healing that were performed. When the tax collector was called out of his isolated life and brought into the company of the disciples, when the poor were called blessed, when the sinners were told of the father who received the prodigal son, then the coming kingdom was brought to them.

When Jesus gave them his message through his words and deeds, they found that the kingdom was theirs in the present, saving, and demanding, and not merely the goal at the end of a march that was still before them. Thus the twelve were already those who would one day rule Israel in the kingdom of God. If, therefore, the disciple had wanted to wander off into blissful and ecstatic idleness, he would have had to be told that that liberating call from God was a call to discipleship with its tasks, to Jesus' company as he went about, and so to a new beginning of history. If, on the other hand, he had wanted to lose himself in a fanaticism that tried to build a kingdom by his own strength, or in the temptation to see only his own inadequacy, then he would have had to be told that the kingdom of God had already come to him in Jesus' words and deeds.

b. The same twofold aspect can be recognized in the primitive Church, which likewise regards itself as necessarily belonging to Israel. It is probably more strongly conscious that it thereby shares the history of God's people than were the disciples during Jesus' earthly life. For God obviously gave a further period of time in which all Israel could decide; there is still a road to travel. The message about Jesus, the risen Lord, must be proclaimed, and Israel must be called to repentance. And yet at the same time the primitive Church knows that it has already been raised out of all time and history. The risen Lord has already appeared to it as one who has been exalted to God's right hand; he is present with it when it partakes of the Lord's Supper in the exultation of the last days;[588] in it God's purpose for Israel is fulfilled. When it looks at the missionary task that has been set it, it has a road before it on which the risen Lord will be with it, strengthening it with his Spirit in the time of persecution. If it looks at the meeting that it has already had with the risen Lord, at his constantly renewed presence in the Lord's Supper, and at the Holy Spirit who has been poured out over it and who makes his activity known through signs, then it knows that it is living in the fulfilment of all promises.

It is this twofold view[589] that, in general, shapes the Church of

---

[588]Cullmann, *Early Christian Worship* 29 f.
[589]Leuba has stressed this duality very strongly. It seems to me, however, that its basis is less Christological (Leuba, *New Testament Pattern* 9 ff.) than

the New Testament. The accent may be now on this side, now on that. The Church, however, never regards itself in the New Testament as a gnostic company living only on its present assimilation to God,[590] having indeed to listen to the messenger's call that comes from outside, but not depending on any past or future action of God. Nor does the Church in the New Testament regard itself simply as a Jewish sect that sees the life and work of Jesus only as one period in the history of salvation, fundamentally similar to other periods, as, for instance, those of the great prophets, with the history of salvation flowing on with no essential change.

c. The two lines, however, are clearly distinguishable from each other. One is characterized quite early by credal formulae in which the Church looks back to the vital events of the cross and the resurrection; and on occasion, especially later on, there can be linked with these a forward look towards the parousia.[591] The other is shown by formulations in which the Church looks 'upwards' to the Lord who has now risen, and who is present with the Church, and who takes the place of the destiny, the blind fate, into whose hands the man of that time felt that he was delivered. This line is characterized by the incarnation and exaltation.[592] The two lines do not simply fall apart. If the one

---

eschatological, and that it is much more differentiated than he thinks. Apart from the Pastorals on the one hand and John on the other, I see Paul much more in the centre of New Testament testimony than he does.

[590]The terms for Greek associations (ἔρανος, θίασος, κοινόν, σύλλογος, σύνοδος) are absent (cf. K. L. Schmidt, *TWNT* III 516-20 = *The Church* 24-31; Weiss, *I Kor.* xx ff.; F. Poland, *Geschichte des griechischen Vereinswesens*, 1909, 332). But Greek political organization had no influence either; the ἐκκλησία of the New Testament is essentially due to the LXX (K. L. Schmidt, *TWNT* III 517 against Peterson, *ibid.* n. 27 = [*The Church* 25 and n. 2]).

[591]It is remarkable that the parousia hardly ever appears in such compositions. Where it does appear, it is in conjunction with some kind of thought about the whole plan of salvation. In I Cor. 15.3-5 the cross and resurrection are central; in I Thess. 1.10 the resurrection and parousia are joined together, probably in a free formulation by Paul which leaned only on what was traditional; Acts 10.37-43 is already developed further.

[592]On both lines cf. Schweizer, *Erniedrigung* ch. 14; *Lordship* ch. 11. The second line is typified by the hymns in which the Church looks up to its Lord who is present in worship: I Tim. 3.16, where there is such strong concentration on the union of the two previously sundered spheres of heaven and earth, which has now taken place, that the temporal sequence is quite

expressly states the validity of God's saving actions 'for us', the other never forgets that Jesus' exaltation to God's right hand was based on his incarnation, in which he had humbled himself in human form. Neither of the two traditions, therefore, is to be thought of without the other; but it is typical that the parousia as a future event joins on principally to the first group of formulae, while the eternal heavenly existence of Jesus before he took human form is to be found only in the other. The first development is related to a way of thinking that regards the Church as being above all on its way from the resurrection to the parousia; the second, to an interpretation that sees the Church under its Lord who exists from everlasting to everlasting in heaven, about whom it knows through the revelation conveyed by his incarnation and exaltation.[593]

d. This twofold view also determines the concept and the order of the Church. On the first view the Church's historicity is strongly emphasized. It is seen as a continuation of Israel, and its way through time to the parousia is particularly important, so that here the problem of tradition and of the settlement made with the historical circumstances and dangers becomes central. It is not forgotten that all Church order is determined afresh by Jesus, but the continuity with Israel's order is maintained. As typical representatives of this view we have recognized, for instance, Luke, and at a later stage the Pastoral Letters. On the other view the Church's newness is emphasized. It is the company belonging to the risen Lord, in its faith and life necessarily taken out of time and history; by its oneness with the heavenly Lord it already shares in the world of eternity, and thereby it is a witness in the world like a light in darkness. Thus the testimony of this fundamental newness, of this otherness over against the world, here

disregarded; but also Phil. 2.6–11, where the subjection of all the powers is perhaps originally thought of as having already taken place (cf. I Peter 3.22). That this view already has its roots in the early Jewish-Christian Church is shown by Rom. 1.4 (already corrected by Paul with the preceding υἱοῦ αὐτοῦ in v. 3).

[593]This is also shown by Dahl, *Das Volk Gottes* 270 ff. It is never denied in the New Testament that the Church, like Israel, was called into life by a historical event. But the *presence* of that event, in which God's totally different world broke in, is quite different from the effects of a historical fact on the course of later history.

becomes especially prominent. The miracle of the Holy Spirit's presence must be given the fullest possible scope. It is not forgotten that all this cannot be separated from the historical appearance of Jesus of Nazareth, and the question of the apostolic witness also arises here. But the newness in relation to pre-Christian Israel is also strikingly shown in the fact that the Church's order leaves as wide scope as possible to the free working of the Spirit. John presents himself to us as the typical representative of this view.

e. Dangers threaten along both lines. If on the one hand there appears the temptation of Ebionitism, in which the Church regards itself simply as a historical earthly entity, entering into competition with other philosophical groups, and deals with its problems according to the laws of this world, so on the other hand there is the temptation of docetism, in which the Church disintegrates into a company of perfect people[594] who are already living in heaven, who no longer need each other and have already written off the unbelieving world.

But even where no such extreme position is reached, there is the possibility of wrong development. It may lie in the over-valuation of the ecstatic. Along the first line, the result would be an interpretation of the history of salvation with a strong chiliastic twist. In that case one who held such a view would expect the history of the Church to be continuous as far as his own time, in which the climax of prophecy would be reached and would bring with it the end. Along the second line there would be a Church to which the living union with the risen Lord throughout all time by virtue of the Holy Spirit meant everything, but which understood that Spirit only as ecstasy, and so saw the 'prophets', and perhaps the ascetics, as the real bearers of the Church.

A wrong development can also lie in the over-valuation of office and order. Along the first line a justifiable wish to keep the Church to the original preaching of the apostles would be joined to a demand for safeguards. The Church would then no longer be concerned simply with the faithful transmission of the word in whose strength it put all its trust, but with a guarantee that the

[594]For an important limitation in relation to unqualified assertions about the continuance of the incarnation in the Church, cf. Newbigin, *The Household of God* 79–83.

office-bearer, and in doubtful cases he alone, possessed the correct message and interpretation as applied to specific questions.

But this would show up most clearly if the second line were followed, for it would now mean that union with the risen Lord in the Spirit would no longer be granted to all the Church members, but only to the office-bearers, perhaps in hierarchical gradation. With that the office-bearer (as previously the *homo religiosus*) would become the guarantor of present union between the Church and its heavenly Lord, and the mediator of the rising prayers or sacrifices and of the grace poured down from on high. There would then be a keeper of the keys; the retaining of sins or the releasing from them would now be assigned, not to the preacher of the word as such, but to the office-bearer destined for the purpose. In that case the distinction between priest and laity would again be complete. We found approaches to this kind of development particularly in I *Clement* and in the Letters of Ignatius.

f. It cannot be a matter of balancing these two New Testament concerns as equally as possible and of setting one off against the other, although we have before us in Paul the witness who listens very keenly to both sides, and in doing so has set his stamp on the understanding and the order of the Church that he founded. When, in face of the menace of gnostic fanaticism, there was a danger that the gospel would disintegrate into something timeless and unhistorical, and the Church into a sum total of religious individualists, the Church's historicity, tradition, and order had to be stressed; and that was done in the Pastorals. But with the threat of an institutional Church, in which a monarchical bishop wanted to rule everything, the self-sufficiency of the Church as it stood under the living activity of the Holy Spirit had to be stressed; and this was done in the Johannine churches. As in a mediaeval town the market square can be regarded as the centre, so might Paul be in the witness of the New Testament. But according to the direction from which the enemy attacks, the eastern wall, or the town gate in the west, suddenly becomes the centre. Thus the New Testament canon covers a wide field, within which there is lively debate; and the unity of the New Testament Church consists in its having sustained this debate without breaking up. It did not idealize this diversity or speak of the splendid abundance of formative possibilities. It did not apply the idea of the 'body of Christ' to the whole Church in such a way that every individual church could appeal to its own special charism, regard itself as only one member, and so justify itself in its own particular function.[595] That variety, indeed, gave the Church trouble, and it was not spared hard and distressing arguments. However, it did not evade them, but found its unity confirmed by simply taking the brotherhood of the Church seriously enough to come to terms with it and with the question that it raised. That alone could safeguard it from perpetuating an answer that had been given to meet a particular situation, and from turning it into a rigid credal formula that remains unchanged even in quite different circumstances. It therefore persistently tried, as far as was at all possible, to eliminate such differences. But that does not exclude the distinctive special testimony of the Johannine church or of the church of the Pastorals (when such testimony was necessary in face of some particular danger) in favour of an intermediate theology, ecclesiology, and order. The New Testament Church sustained these very sharply defined groups in the one Church.[596] Only where the Church simply wanted to preserve

[595]Thus, for instance, one church might represent one-sidedly the concern of teaching, another that of social aid, and a third that of the liturgy. This may also be said against Craig, *The One Church in the Light of the NT* 121, who extends the image to the *ecumene*. There certainly is an approach to such thinking in the New Testament linking of the idea of Christ's body to the thought pattern 'in Adam/in Christ', and still more in passages such as Col. 1.18, 24; Eph. 1.23; 2.15 f. Yet it must be maintained that the single church never appears as a member of an inclusive body, and that according to Eph. 4.7, wherever the mutual service of the members is spoken of, the reference is not to churches but to individuals. Newbigin 70 emphasizes that the one 'body of Christ' (as distinct from the many 'bodies of Christians') always becomes particularized in the local church. Cf. n. 717 below.

[596]For the historical necessity and limits of such one-sidedness, cf. the excellent book by W. Marxsen, *Der Frühkatholismus im Neuen Testament*, 1959. In Acts αἵρεσις means in a neutral sense a school, in Paul's writings a separation due to quarrelsomeness (Gal. 5.20; I Cor. 11.18 f.). It is not till II Peter 2.1 that the meaning is determined, as in the parallel course of the rabbinic use of the word, principally by the question of right or wrong doctrine (otherwise H. Schlier, *TWNT* I 181 f.). Wherever in the New Testament there is conflict with groups that are regarded as having ceased to belong to the Church, it is with those that, instead of being content with the grace of God that was given once in Christ, proclaim that something additional is necessary for salvation, e.g., circumcision (Gal. 5.2 ff.), or the worship of angels (Col. 2.18), or gnostic speculations (I Tim. 6.20). The position of the

itself, where it no longer regarded itself as a Church on its way, needing to be repeatedly asked by God whether it was really preaching the old message aright here and now, would it turn into a rigid denominational church, feeling that it no longer needed the others.

Johannine churches in relation to the Church as a whole remains obscure; but even III John 9 assumes that a friendly relationship is the rule. See 14a, b.

21

OFFICE

a. One of the most surprising consistencies of the New Testament witnesses is seen in word-statistics. The Greek language has a wealth of ideas of 'office'.[597] ἀρχή denotes office in the sense of precedence, being at the head, ruling;[598] the term is used in the New Testament only for Jewish and Gentile authorities,[599] and in a wider sense for Christ himself.[600] The same is true of the designation of a person as ἄρχων, ruler.[601] Both terms can also denote demonic powers.[602] τιμή is office in the sense of a position of dignity.[603] In the New Testament the only passage where it is used with this meaning is Heb. 5.4; it refers there to the high priest's official dignity which is Christ's due. τέλος defines the complete power of office, and is nowhere found in this sense in the New Testament.[604] The most suitable would be λειτουργία, which means in Greek life the more or less voluntary services undertaken by the citizen for the community, and by the worshipper for the gods,[605] and in the Septuagint (about 100 times) the ceremonial

[597]Cf. on this Friedrich, 'Geist und Amt', *Wort und Dienst* 1952, 68 ff.

[598]In Greek this often has an undertone of legality: G. Delling, *TWNT* I 479.19. The LXX uses the word in a secular sense (Gen. 40.13, 20 f.; 41.13: Pharaoh's court official) and also in a religious sense (I Chron. 26.10: Levitical doorkeeper; IV Macc. 4.17: high priest).

[599]Luke 12.11; 20.20; Titus 3.1.

[600]Col. 1.18.

[601]Roman and Jewish officials: Delling, *TWNT* I 487. 27 ff.; of Christ, Rev. 1.5. Cf. likewise ἄρχειν, Mark 10.42; Rom. 15.12.

[602]Rom. 8.38; I Cor. 15.24; Eph. 1.21; 3.10; 6.12; Col. 1.16; 2.10, 15; Jude 6; Mark 3.22; John 12.31; 14.30; 16.11; Eph. 2.2.

[603]For evidence as to Greek usage: Arndt & Gingrich, τιμή 2d; F. Passow, *Handwörterbuch der griechischen Sprache*, 1841, τιμή II 3a, b; for the LXX cf. Dan. 2.37; 7.14 (Th. 4.33; 5.18, 20); also Ex. 28.2, 40 (36); Ps. 48.13, 21?; 98.4?

[604]For evidence as to Greek usage: Passow τέλος 2d. Οἱ ἐν τέλει = 'those who are perfect in their power' are the authorities!

[605]In the *polis* of ancient times the two cannot be separated. For evidence: H. Strathmann, *TWNT* IV 223.10 ff. Thus it can also be used for ceremonial services in the mystery religions. But in contrast to διακονεῖν it is preferably applied to public official service: H. W. Beyer, *TWNT* II 81.15 f.; C. Spicq, *L'épître aux Hébreux* II (1953) 22; but cf. Strathmann, 224.10 ff.

service performed by the priest.[606] The same is true of the verb, which also defines the service offered to God by the layman,[607] whereas the description of a person as a λειτουργός, apart from the religious meaning, is also used in the Old Testament in a purely secular sense.[608] The surprising result of an investigation of the New Testament is that this word-group occurs quite frequently. It denotes, however: (1) the service rendered by the Roman governmental authorities (Rom. 13.6); (2) the Old Testament or Jewish priestly service (Luke 1.23; Heb. 9.21; 10.11); (3) the service rendered by Jesus Christ himself (Heb. 8.2, 6); and (4) the service of the whole Church.[609]

There is only one exception to this: in Rom. 15.16 Paul is called a λειτουργός. Now this personal designation is certainly not typical, for it is used in Greek literature, as in the Septuagint, predominantly in a secular sense; but the sequel clearly describes the apostolic action as priestly, and so it may be supposed that Paul is using cultic language.[610] Of course, this priestly action of the apostle does not mean that he is believed to mediate God's grace or revelation to men,[611] but that he brings to God the nations'

[606]This is so precise that in Num. 16.9, contrary to what is usual elsewhere, 'ābad is rendered by λειτουργεῖν, and šērēt by λατρεύειν, because the former relates to Yahweh and the latter to the Church. In the same way Ecclus. 4.14, where in Hebrew there is the same verb šērēt both times, is translated οἱ λατρεύοντες αὐτῇ (wisdom) λειτουργήσουσιν ἁγίῳ (God); cf. Strathmann, 226.21 ff. Similarly for Josephus and Philo, *ibid.* 229.15 ff.

[607]E.g. Ecclus. 4.14 in the preceding note.

[608]In Greek literature as in the LXX: Strathmann, 236.29 ff. Similarly for λειτουργικός, *ibid.* 238.28 ff.; Spicq, *Hébr.* II 22.

[609]Rom. 15.27; II Cor. 9.12; Phil. 2.25, 30 speak of the collection! Phil. 2.17 probably refers to the Church's faith as expressed in its total life (but see next note). In Acts 13.2 the subject is not the whole Church, but a circle within it; but it is clear that what is referred to is not an official action, but an exercise of personal piety by a group of teachers and prophets. Cf. also T. F. Torrance, *Royal Priesthood*, 1955, which emphasizes that the Church shares in Jesus Christ's office.

[610]The same thing might hold good for Phil. 2.17 (see previous note), if we took πίστεως as an objective genitive, and Paul as the one who brings the Church's faith as an offering for God, though the passive σπένδομαι makes that very improbable. Compared to the great offering brought by the Church's faith, the giving of Paul's life is the complementary smaller libation that is poured out over it. That interpretation would be all the more probable if we connected ἐπί with χαίρω. On Rom. 15.16 cf. *NTS* 8.1, Oct. 1961.

[611]It is therefore not a matter here of a ministry of reconciliation. This is also true of Col. 1.24 (see n. 398), which is probably to be interpreted in the sense of II Cor. 1.4–11; 4.10–15; 12.9 f.; I Cor. 9.27; cf. also *NTS* 2, 1955/6, 93.

offering of praise in their faith and obedience. It is not his action, but the Church's faith, that is the offering of praise. What is striking, however, is not that the ceremonial idea is applied once in the New Testament to the action of an individual (an apostle, moreover, about whose peculiar position the Church knows quite well), but that it is consistently avoided elsewhere.[612]

b. What we have just seen is verified in the word-group that includes priest, priesthood, and priestly action. In Judaism, as in paganism, there are priests.[613] In the New Testament priesthood belongs to Jesus Christ alone.[614] It is true that the whole Church shares in it, but that does not apply to an individual or group that would then be distinguishable from the other, non-priestly, church members.[615] Finally, the same thing holds good for the much wider term λατρεία,[616] which in the Septuagint clearly defines the people's relation to God, as opposed to that of the priests, which is called λειτουργία.[617] It appears in the New Testament three times for the ceremonial service of Israel, and once for the non-ceremonial service of the whole community.[618]

c. As a general term for what we call 'office', namely the service

---

[612]It will therefore simply not do to say that in the New Testament there is no longer any distinction between priest and laity, but that there is a distinction between office-bearer and believer (Menoud, *Eglise* 39)—if any more is meant by that than what is said in 24k, l.

[613]In the New Testament Jewish priests are often called ἱερεύς, and the same word is used of a Gentile priest in Acts 14.13.

[614]Heb. 5.6; 8.4; 10.21; likewise 2.17 etc.

[615]I Peter 2.5, 9; Rev. 1.6; 5.10; 20.6. On Rom. 15.16 see 21a.

[616]In Greek literature it can denote any physical service, less often a ceremonial one; in the LXX, where it appears about ninety times, it defines a religious, in fact (apart from Ecclus. 4.14: n. 606) a ceremonial action (Strathmann, *TWNT* IV 59.1 ff.).

[617]*Ibid.* 61.18 ff.

[618]In Rom. 9.4; Heb. 9.1, 6; Rom. 12.1; John 16.2 the word means the service that the persecutors of God's Church think they are rendering. The word is used for the idolatry of the Gentiles (Rom. 1.25) and of the generation in the wilderness (Acts 7.42), for the worship offered by Israel (Luke 1.74; Acts 26.7), by Anna (Luke 2.37), by the Israelite priests (Heb. 8.5; 9.9; 10.2; 13.10), then for the whole life of the Christian Church (Phil. 3.3; Heb. 9.14; 12.28; Rev. 7.15; 22.3) or of Paul (Rom. 1.9), especially where continuity with Jewish piety is to be stressed (Acts 24.14; 27.23; II Tim. 1.3). It is used particularly for the service of prayer: Strathmann, *TWNT* IV 63.25 ff. All this suggests that the New Testament Church is not to be regarded as essentially ceremonial and sacramental (against Fridrichsen in *Buch v. d. Kirche* 61 ff.; Sjöberg *ibid.* 94 ff.); but see 27a, c, d.

of individuals within the Church, there is, with a few exceptions,[619] only one word: διακονία. Thus the New Testament throughout and uniformly[620] chooses a word that is entirely unbiblical and non-religious and never includes association with a particular dignity or position. In the Greek Old Testament the word occurs only once, in a purely secular sense.[621] The verb, which does not occur at all in the LXX, denotes in Philo and Josephus waiting at table and serving in general; in Josephus it refers to the action of a priest three times, twice in the middle voice (unusual in primitive Christian literature[622]) and once in the active.[623] In all three passages, however, the meaning is determined by the context. In Josephus the noun may mean quite generally the service of God, once also service at the sacrifice,[624] and likewise the mutual service of the Essenes.[625] διάκονος means the servant of the prophet, and Josephus himself as the mediator of divine prophecy to the Roman general.[626] In the development of Greek the basic meaning, 'to serve at table', was extended to include the more comprehensive idea of 'serving'. It nearly always denotes

---

[619]On occasion there appear οἰκονομία (I Cor. 9.17; Col. 1.25; Eph. 3.2?; I Tim. 1.4?), οἰκονόμος (I Cor. 4.1; Titus 1.7; I Peter 4.10; cf. Friedrich 72 f.). This term too stresses dependence of the one who serves on the Lord himself rather than his authority over others. It is a different matter with the designation of definite ministries such as ἀποστολή, ἐπισκοπή; on this see 24a, g.

[620]The word-group occurs with this meaning in the Synoptic Gospels and in Acts, in Paul (as also in Colossians, Ephesians, and the Pastorals), and in I Peter. John has it only in 12.26 in traditional material that appears similarly in the Synoptic Gospels, not defining any one kind service as distinct from others (also in 2.5, 9; 12.2 in a purely secular sense). In Heb. 6.10 and Rev. 2.19 it is obviously related to the Church's general conduct.

[621]I Macc. 11.58; in Esth. 6.3, 5 it appears in some MSS. The less typical διάκονος is purely secular: Prov. 10.4; Esth. 1.10; 2.2; 6.3, 5; IV Macc. 9.17 (= na'ar and šērēt pi'el).

[622]Arndt and Gingrich s. v. give no instances; Passow names Lucian, Athenaeus, and Diogenes Laertius.

[623]Middle *Ant.* 7.365; 10.72; active *Ant.* 3.155 (sacrificial service); elsewhere the word means service at table, or obedience (passages in Beyer, *TWNT* II 83.1 ff.); in 10.177 it is said of prophets; in 18. 280 neutrally ('what serves the law's ἀρετή').

[624]Of Samuel quite generally in *Ant.* 5. 344, 349; of David's temple offering, 7.378; of sacrificial service, 8.101, and in a wider meaning probably also 10.57.

[625]*Ant.* 18.21. Stauffer refers to this in *TLZ* 77, 1952, 202. But the idea has no religious meaning here, as it only states that they hold no slaves.

[626]*Ant.* 8.354; 9.54; *Bell.* 4.626.

something of inferior value, but in Hellenism it may also define the wise man's attitude towards God (not towards his fellowmen).[627] The New Testament's choice of this word is all the more striking in that the basic meaning 'to serve at table' is still current throughout, as is the general meaning 'to serve'. Even the recently discovered writings of the Qumran group hardly give any more help. Of course, the 'serving' by all believers in relation to God may be spoken of here,[628] and it may be said that this is done 'in accordance with their authority'.[629] They may also speak of definite 'ministries' to which a person attains because of his age, his merit, and his discernment, and which involve a certain superiority of position over others.[630] But with that we have not, as far as the usage of the word διακονία is concerned, gone beyond the Old Testament, where, of course, serving and ministry are similarly spoken of.[631] The corresponding Hebrew words, however, are rendered throughout the Septuagint by λατρεία or λειτουργία, not by διακονία.[632] This rendering can hardly

[627] Beyer, *TWNT* II 81 f.

[628] *Šērēt* refers to the ceremonial service in the sanctuary, 1QM 2.1–3, to the liturgical service (with a blessing by the priest), 1QSb 4.23; to people who stand on God's side, 1QH 15.24; fragm. 2.14; (8.5); very generally, *Damasc.* 2.4 [2.2]; to angels, 1QH 5.21 (1QM 17.6 should probably read *mišrat*); to Gentile kings, 1QM 12.14; 13.13; 19.16. '*Ābad* denotes the ceremonial adoration of God and of idols, 1QpHab. 12.13; 13.2 f.; 16.18; 17.14; 1QSa 1.13; 1QSb 5.28; *Damasc.* 5.4; 20.21 [7.5; 9.44 B]. On the references to passages in this and the next two notes, see n. 94.

[629] 1QH 12.23 *šērēt*.

[630] We find '*ǎbōdāh* in 1QSa 1.13 ff.; cf. 1QM 2.9, 16 (ceremonial); 1QS 5.14 (general); *Damasc.* 10.19 f.; 11.23; 14.16; 20.7 [13.5 f.; 14.3; 18.5; 9.33 B]; instances other than these are entirely general (1QS 3.26; 1QH 1.12, 16; 1Q36 15.4) or with a religious tone (1QpHab. 7.11; 1QS 4.9; 1QH 6. 19 and antithetically 1QpHab 10.11; 1QS 4.10; 1QM 13.5; 1QH 1.27), of God's work 1QH 2.33, 36. For rabbinical instances cf. O. Michel, *Der Brief an die Römer*, 1955, 327 n. 6.

[631] Cf. as the nearest parallel an instance like Num. 8.24 f.: '*ǎbōdāh* = λειτουργία. It is very improbable that the New Testament διάκονος can be traced back to *ḥāṣan*, the attendant in the synagogue (J. Klausner, *Von Jesus zu Paulus*, 1950, 273), because there is no evidence of any such connection and because the deacon in the New Testament is quite a different figure. We should rather agree with K. Stendahl, *The School of St Matthew*, 1954, 32 f., in thinking of ὑπηρέτης as corresponding to it. But the Hebrew term, like the Greek, is a very wide one with no specific character.

[632] *Šērēt* generally corresponds to the root λειτουργ-, '*ābad* to both roots, and in secular usage there is also δουλ- (Strathmann, *TWNT* IV 59 f., 226 f.). Only in Esther is *šērēt* rendered by the root διακον- in a completely secular use (see n. 621).

be a whim of the translators into the Septuagint, for other writings show little difference in this respect.[633] Thus there remain only the few hints of a new development of the Greek usage in the papyri, where official ministrants in the temple, as well as the devout in general, appear as 'servants of God',[634] and Josephus' occasional usage already mentioned.

d. In view of the large number of terms available, the evidence of the choice of words is unmistakable. Before there has been any theological reflection all the New Testament witnesses are sure of one decisive fact: official priesthood, which exists to conciliate and mediate between God and the community, is found in Judaism and paganism; but since Jesus Christ there has been only one such office—that of Jesus himself.[635] It is shared by the whole Church,[636] and never by one church member as distinct from others. Here therefore there is without exception the common priesthood,[637] with no laity.[638] Jewish priests presumably joined the Church, but they played no special part in it.[639] Again the Church's completely

---

[633]In *Test. Levi.* 4.2 there are only θεράπων and λειτουργός. From the Ethiopic text of Jub. 31.14 nothing can be inferred as to the Greek form.

[634]This is also true of female ministrants in the temple. The διάκονοι may form a body presided over by a priest. On the other hand, διακονία does not appear in the papyri before the sixth century AD (J. H. Moulton and G. Milligan, *The Vocabulary of the Greek Testament,* 1929, 149). The Roman official language (A. Deissmann, *Light from the Ancient East,* ET [rev. ed.] 1927, 376) is hardly important for the early period.

[635]So too Dix, *Ap. Min.* 299 f.

[636]Cf. W. D. Davies in *Religion in Life* 21, 265; Barth, *Dogmatics* IV/2, 692 ff., especially 694 f.

[637]I Peter 2.9. Cf. for the whole subject Brandt, 'Die Wortgruppe λειτουργεῖν . . .', 147 ff. For certain tendencies in this direction at Qumran cf. Betz, *ZNW* 48, 1957, 67; but see also n. 640.

[638]See 16d; Menoud, *Eglise* 21 f. The term is not used depreciatingly till the fourth century AD. Cf. Knopf, *Ap. Väter* 114; O. Kern, 'Λαοί' in *Archiv für Religionswissenschaft* 30, 1933, 205 ff.; v. Campenhausen, *Kirchliches Amt* 96. Brosch, *Charismen und Ämter* 162, maintains that even the early Church recognized the difference between clerical and lay people, though not to such a marked degree as later. Spicq, *Epîtres pastorales,* asserts it at least for the Pastorals. Surprisingly, however, he speaks of the elders simply as 'priests' (XLV ff.), although in XLIV he shows extremely clearly that the New Testament knows only one priest (why with the addition of κατ᾽ ἐξοχήν?), Jesus Christ, and that all believers share in his priesthood.

[639]Acts 6.7 (see 3m). From the fact that (nonconforming?) Jewish priests enter the Church it cannot be inferred (with J. Schmitt in *RevSR* 29, 1955, 250 ff.) that they play a special part as in Qumran. The surprising thing is that there is not the slightest reference to it in our texts.

different character in contrast to the Qumran community is clear.[640]

e. This does not mean that the New Testament overlooks the fact that the form of this ministry varies,[641] the differences being reduced to a minimum only in the Johannine writings.[642] Before, however, we look at the diversity of ministries,[643] the character peculiar to each ministry in the New Testament has to be described. The very choice of the word, which still clearly involves the idea of humble activity, proves that the Church wishes to denote the attitude of one who is at the service of God and his fellow-men, not a position carrying with it rights and powers.[644] This new understanding is the continuing testimony to God's action in Jesus of Nazareth. The fact that it was in lowliness that

[640]Cf. L. Rost, *TLZ* 82, 1957, 669 f.; Nötscher 140. The most important sources of evidence are 1QS 2.20 f.; 6.3 ff.; 9.7 (cf. 8.5 f.); 1QSa 1.2, 23 f.; 2.3, 13; 1QSb 3.23 f.; 1QM 13.1; *Damasc.* 14.3 ff. [17.1 ff.] .The priest makes reconciliation (1QM 2.4 f.); he alone may bless (1QS 6.5 f.), and is even higher than the 'Messiah' (1QSa 2.14). For the designation of the laity in contrast to the priests as *rab* or *rōb* see H. W. Huppenbauer, *TZ* 13, 1957, 136 f. and the authorities given there. On the similarities and differences in the composition of the communities between Qumran and the early Church cf. e.g. O. Cullmann, *JBL* 74, 1955, 213 ff.; J. Daniélou, *RHPR* 35, 1955, 104 ff.; Nauck, *ZNW* 46, 1955, 276 f. = 48, 1957, 203 ff.; R. Marcus, *JBL* 75, 1956, 298 ff.; Betz, *ZNW* 48, 1957, 67 f.; S. V. McCasland, *JBL* 77, 1958, 228 ff. and n. 98. For the royal Messiah's subordination to the priest cf. K. G. Kuhn, *NTS* 1, 1954/5, 168 ff. This dual leadership is continued in some degree with Bar-cochba, but not in the New Testament (L. E. Tooms, *NTS* 4, 1957/8, 66 f.). For the importance of the hierarchical order in Qumran see n. 644.

[641]This is correct in Fridrichsen's polemic against a pneumatism that would wrench the Spirit away from theology, order, and office (*Buch v. d. Kirche* 57, and Linton, *ibid.* 113 ff., Odeberg *ibid.* 80 f.); only we should need a new interpretation of 'office' in the meaning given.

[642]See 11i, 12c. Yet the eyewitness who has seen the historical Jesus (11c) keeps his importance in the face of docetic threats (I John 1.1–4; cf. the role of the first witness who hands on the message, John 1.40 ff.; 4.28 f.; 15.27); although side by side with that we must not forget I John 4.14; John 1.46 ff.; 4.42; 15.26.

[643]See ch. 24.

[644]The importance of exact gradation of rank in Qumran is shown in 1QM 2.6 (on this cf. K. G. Kuhn, *TLZ* 81, 1956, 25); 1QS 2.23; 5.23–25 (on this cf. Nauck, *ZNW* 48, 1957, 210 ff.); 1QSa 1.16 (also 9.20); 1QSb 4 22 ff.; 4QpIs^d 1.8 (and on this J. M. Allegro, *JBL* 77, 1958, 221 n. 70); also *Damasc.* 2.9; 4.5 [2.8; 6.3]. Nauck, 212 ff., demonstrates slight signs of a continuance of such order in the later part of the New Testament. On Qumran cf. further H. Braun, *Spätjüdische Häretik und frühchristlicher Radikalismus* I, 1957, 18 f., also 74, 105 n. 1, 106 n. 1; Nötscher 170; P. Wernberg-Møller; *The Manual of Discipline*, 1957, 56, n. 49 and 55; further 24i below.

God revealed himself as God implies for the Church that through being itself prepared to be lowly it must become separated from the world, to which indeed all kinds of ceremonial associations with imposing dignitaries belong. 'He who is greatest among you shall be your servant.' This sentence, in its six variants,[645] is based in Luke 22.27, in a very primitive formulation, on Jesus' conduct:[646] 'I am among you as one who serves.' Special ministry takes place in the Church only in special subordination. Acts, as well as Paul, likes to describe all special activities, particularly the preaching of an apostle or some other church member, as that kind of 'ministry' or 'service', and the person who performs it as a 'servant' or 'slave',[647] with God, Christ, or men appearing as those to whom the service is rendered.[648]

It is nowhere forgotten that such renunciation of titles, honours, and offices testifies to the Church's newness in contrast to the old religious or secular order.[649] Of course, this does not mean that the ministry carried out in Jesus' name required no obedience. Ministry and authority are certainly not mutually exclusive opposites, either in the teaching of Jesus himself or in

[645]Matt. 23.11 par. Luke 22.26 (with assimilations to the language of the Church). In the form of Mark 9.35 (echoed in Luke 9.48) the absence of 'among you' or 'of you' is probably original, as is perhaps also the contrast 'first/last' (originally without 'servant'?). In the third variant, Mark 10.43 f. = Matt. 20.26 f., the Semitic 'will be', which appears in other forms too, is certainly older than the formulation in Luke 22.25 f. See too next note here; Schürmann 74 ff.; Schnackenburg in *Synopt. Studien für A. Wikenhauser*, 1953, 184 ff.

[646]This statement is certainly original in contrast to Mark 10.45 (Schürmann 85 ff.). The idea that at the Last Supper Jesus is not the head of the house giving hospitality, but the 'servant', scarcely grew up in the Church. But there is much to suggest that the Lord's Supper was determined by a reference by Jesus to his serving, and by an eschatological outlook; *RGG* I 16 f.; *TLZ* 81, 1956, 218 f.; 83, 1958, 190. But the truth that the foundation of all ministry is Jesus' service does not, of course, depend on the authenticity of this saying. See 27d.

[647]'Ministers of the word' (ὑπηρέτης) Luke 1.2; δοῦλος: Acts 4.29; 16.17; Rom. 1.1 and often; διάκονος: I Cor. 3.5; II Cor. 3.6; 6.4; 11.23; cf. διακονία: Acts 1.17, 25; 6.4; II Cor. 3.8 f.; 6.3.

[648]Both are combined in Col. 1.7 ('a faithful minister of Christ on our [your?] behalf'). The Synoptists emphasize the performance of service to men (but cf. also Matt. 10.24 f.), and Paul of that to the Lord (but cf. also Rom. 16.1; I Cor. 16.15; II Cor. 11.8; Col. 1.25).

[649]Matt. 23.8–10; Mark 10.42 f.; 12.39; Luke 11.43; 14.7 ff.; 16.15; I Cor. 4.7–9; II Cor. 10–12.

his Church.[650] But it is not an obedience that is demanded on the ground of position or dignity, but an obedience that is given because a person is overcome by the ministry that is performed, and in particular by the word that is preached.

f. But it is not only the attitude of the earthly Jesus that determines this nature of all ministry in the New Testament; it is also the fact that the call to service can be understood only as an unmerited gift of grace. That is true of the calling of the disciples according to the Synoptic testimony,[651] as well as of the missions in Acts,[652] but especially of the Pauline writings. Paul knows, not only that all service is the act of God himself,[653] but that an essential part of New Testament ministry is that an unqualified person is called to it 'to show that the transcendent power belongs to God and not to us' (II Cor. 4.7). Thus the term 'grace' actually becomes for him the designation of his apostolic ministry, because for him 'grace' is not a general attitude, or even something that indicates God's nature, but a concrete action directed to him personally, so that conversion must always be understood as a call to serve.[654] The same is true of his disciples;[655] and here the miracle of Paul's having been called by God's grace is even greater.[656] On the other hand, there no longer appears here the phrase that is so typical of Paul, 'the grace given to me'. The plural form that he also uses, 'the grace given to us' (Rom. 12.6), does not now mean the separation for special service, but God's eternal choice that has been revealed in Jesus.[657] For the former phrase is now substituted 'charism', which for Paul includes all ministries;[658] and while he knows that he cannot venture to say a word that Christ himself

[650]F. M. Braun, *Neues Licht auf die Kirche* 179 n. 3.

[651]Luke 5.8–10; Mark 2.14–17; Matt. 10.9.

[652]Acts 14.26; 15.40; 3.12; 14.15.

[653]I Cor. 3.7; 15.9 f.

[654]It is the 'grace toward me' and 'with me', I Cor. 15.10; the 'grace given me', Rom. 15.15; I Cor. 3.10; Gal. 2.9. In Rom. 1.5, too, χάρις is not a general pardoning, but is more closely defined by ἀποστολή. Probably Rom. 12.3 (parallel v. 6) is also to be related to the ministry entrusted to Paul himself.

[655]Col. 1.25; Eph. 3.2, 7; I Tim. 1.12–14; I Peter 4.10.

[656]Paul is the least, not only of all apostles, but of all saints (Eph. 3.8), and the foremost of sinners (I Tim. 1.15).

[657]II Tim. 1.9. In Rom. 12.6 the position between χαρίσματα and διάφορα shows that the call of grace specially directed to the individual is intended for special service.

[658]On this see n. 377.

does not say through him, Timothy is now urged not to neglect the gift that is in him, but to rekindle it.[659] All this shows that the danger of misunderstanding by assuming a special official grace, a misunderstanding that stresses the 'in you' at the expense of the freedom of grace, is much less clearly guarded against than by Paul himself.

On the other hand, it is very strongly emphasized in the Johannine circle that there is no service at all except on the basis of the previous service of Jesus (John 13.36–14.6), that only one who has been pardoned is capable of serving as a witness (21.15–23), and that it is the Spirit himself who performs this service of witness (John 15.26 f.; 16.7–14; I John 2.27). Only it must be asked here whether this truth is not so strongly emphasized that the human witness and his special gift almost vanish behind it. The danger here certainly lies in the overvaluation, not of a grace exclusively bestowed by official election, but rather of a spirit that is misunderstood as ecstasy, in which human limitations are overlooked and an illusory perfection is aimed at.

g. Finally, it becomes apparent that with Paul charism and ministry are regarded essentially as an event, as something that takes place.[660] Both words are parallel to the idea of 'working', 'occurrence' (I Cor. 12.4–6); and what is called 'function' in Rom. 12.4 is called 'grace' in v. 6. Our idea of 'office', on the other hand, suggests particularly something that remains the same, unchanged through the centuries.[661] Certainly there is in the New Testament a faithfulness of God on which one can rely; that is shown by everything that there is to be said about the ordering of ministries.[662] But in the concept of ministry, and still more strongly in the Pauline correlates of 'charism', 'working', 'action' there is the constitutive force of the event. The unchanged permanence of a ministry is the miracle of God's grace that constantly recurs.

[659]Rom. 15.18; I Tim. 4.14; II Tim. 1.6.

[660]Cf. Friedrich 84 f.

[661]I once asked a group of non-theologians to call out, without reflection, the first word that came to mind. I said 'Pfarramt' (the office of clergyman), and the first at once exclaimed 'Stempel' (official stamp). The 'Stempel' on the baptismal certificate issued by the church at X is what remains through the centuries, while the incumbent changes.

[662]See 24, 28e.

22

CHARISMATIC AND NON-CHARISMATIC MINISTRIES?

a. But does not the above hold good only for the really charismatic ministries, side by side with which there are purely administrative duties that have to be carried out as a matter of course, as by any civil government? Something of the kind might be found in the co-existence of priests and elders as representatives of the laity in Judaism.[663] We might see the continuation of the latter in the elders of the New Testament, and of the former in the charismatic ministries of the apostles, prophets, and those who speak with tongues. Thus we have to ask whether any such distinction can be made in the New Testament between ministries that are natural and those that are supernatural and charismatic. After that, we have to consider a further aspect of the problem, namely the question whether, although there is no New Testament term that differentiates between office and ministry, there is not a practical separation of offices like apostolate or presbyterate, and of ministries like prophecy or glossolalia induced by the momentary breath of the Spirit.

b. The first question is asked by Harnack's well-known separation of 'religious' (or 'charismatic') ministries, which relate to the universal Church, from 'administrative' ones, which are local.[664] Harnack starts from the analysis of the Church order presented in the *Didache*.[665] We saw that there is here in fact an approach to such a separation, even if in detail both the triad of

[663]Dix, *Ap. Min.* 233 ff.; Bornkamm, *TWNT* VI 659 ff.
[664]Harnack, TU II 145–9. Here only the first have a special rank in the Church; the others get it only gradually in the measure in which they take over the functions of the first. To this there comes a patriarchal organization (elders) and possibly an aristocratic one (ascetics, martyrs). As to the whole genesis of these distinctions, which rest originally on Hatch's other distinction between episcopal-diaconal and presbyterial order, see Linton, *Das Problem der Urkirche* 36 ff.; Foerster, R. *Sohms Kritik des Kirchenrechtes* 51 f.
[665]*Constitution* 236; see 15 d–f above.

the 'religious' offices and their ecclesiastical character as common
to the whole Church are very questionable. It must be asked,
however, whether this is anything more than a popular distinction
that is paralleled in experiences in Gentile religions. In any case,
the mention of the itinerant prophets is not made in order specially
to emphasize their ministry spiritually;[666] on the contrary, the
author tries, although the matter is not clearly thought out
theologically, to put the ministry of the bishops and deacons as
nearly as possible on the same plane as theirs.[667]

   c. The decisive question, however, is whether any such distinction can be traced back to the New Testament. Harnack
appeals to I Cor. 12.28,[668] where apostles, prophets, and teachers
are put 'first, second, third' at the beginning of the list, while the
other ministries are simply added on in an impersonal, not a
personal, definition. But this enumeration is the conclusion of a
section whose whole object is to contest the spiritual relevance
of any distinction between natural and supernatural ministries.[669]
In this same list there appear the gifts of administration and helping,
while the glossolalia that so impresses the Corinthians by its
'supernaturalness' is put at the very end.[670] In the parallel passages
there is quite a different arrangement. Rom. 12.6 leaves out the
apostolate, and puts the 'administrative' office of deacon before
teaching, while vv. 7 f. add other ministries besides. Even in
I Cor. 12.8 ff. there is quite a different arrangement, in which
the gift of healing, for instance, but also the gift of 'faith' appear
before prophecy, while apostolate and teaching are at the most
included in 'the utterance of wisdom' and 'the utterance of
knowledge'. Furthermore, in Rom. 12.6–8, contrary to I Cor.
12.28–30, prophecy is mentioned impersonally, and the person

---

[666]Cf. Dix, *Ap. Min.* 240–2.

[667]15.1 f. This was pointed out by H. v. Campenhausen in *Theol. Blätter* 20,
1941, 282.

[668]Likewise many others, e.g., Menoud, *Eglise* 40 ff. On this see H. Greeven,
ZNW 44, 1952/3, 1 ff.; in *Wort and Dienst* 1959, 113 ff.; v. Campenhausen,
Kirchliches Amt 65 ff.

[669]The most that may be said is that for Paul the 'supernatural' gifts of
grace are in the nature of a sign of the dawning of the last days; but this no
longer concerns the Church, but at the most the unbelievers: I Cor. 14.21,
25 (cf. Dahl, *Das Volk Gottes* 228; but I should not so interpret I Cor.
2.6 ff.: *TWNT* VI 422 f. = *Spirit of God* 68 f.).

[670]See 7l.

'who exhorts' personally.[671] In I Thess. 5.12 the three terms 'those who labour among you and are over you . . . and admonish you' probably denote the same people;[672] at any rate, Harnack's triad cannot be found there. Again, in Eph. 4.11 the 'administrative' pastors are put with the evangelists before the teachers.[673] For the rest, there remains in the New Testament only the conjunction of prophets and teachers in Acts 13.1; but they belong there to the local church, and their functions do not relate to the universal Church.[674] Nor are they put side by side with the apostles; and Luke presumably regards both terms as two names for the same men. No doubt there were prophets and teachers beside the apostles; and it is quite natural, too, that their ministry proved to be a particularly important one, and that it therefore was the first to occur to the apostle in one passage. But in any case it cannot be shown that the triad was a group to be contrasted with other people, still less that it was an itinerant group in the service of the universal Church.[675]

d. This, however, does not finally settle the question whether or not the New Testament knows a distinction between natural and supernatural, administrative and charismatic ministries. The question can be formulated in brief with Hatch's often quoted objection: 'There is no charism of age'.[676] Here we must differentiate. At first the New Testament Church, in line with the Old Testament, in which the Holy Spirit is not necessary for salvation, but is bestowed on those who are specially called to special tasks,[677]

[671]This was pointed out by O. Scheel in *Theol. Studien und Kritiken* 85, 1912, 434.

[672]W. Koester, *Die Idee der Kirche beim Apostel Paulus*, 1928, 11; A. Wikenhauser, *Die Kirche als der mystische Leib des Christus nach Paulus*, 1937, 79.

[673]Menoud, *Eglise* 44, claims to see here too only the triad apostles, prophets, teachers.

[674]E. Peterson's supposition in *Nuntius Sodalicii Neotest. Upsal.* 1949, 10 (=*Recherches de science rel.* 36, 1949, 577 ff.) that it refers to the prophets that had come from Jerusalem, remains a pure supposition; in any case, Luke does not understand it so (Haenchen, *Die Apostelgeschichte* 343 n. 3). In Acts 11.27 we hear of itinerant prophets, whereas those of 15.27, 32 are sent once to another church, and only with a definite object.

[675]Cf. Linton 78 f.

[676]E. Hatch, *Die Gesellschaftsverfassung der christlichen Kirche im Altertum*, 1883, 230, n. 3; on the other hand G. Kaufmann in *Göttinger Gelehrte Anzeigen*, 1884, 321.

[677]A general bestowal of the Spirit is not expected except for the last days: Baumgärtel, *TWNT* VI 360 ff. (cf. 401. 25 ff. = *Spirit of God* 36).

and with parallels in other religions, saw the manifestation of the
Spirit only in extraordinary forms of expression such as miraculous cures or glossolalia.⁶⁷⁸ We were able to follow this out as far
as the *Didache* and Hermas. There might therefore be an approach
here to a distinction between purely administrative, regulated
ministries and those that are bestowed by the Spirit. As far as
we can see, however, this approach has nowhere been carried
further within the New Testament writings, and only traces of
it can be recognized. On the one hand, the prophets themselves
have presumably created permanent statutes,⁶⁷⁹ and some of the
apostles (Peter at least) have also taken part in the government
of the Church.⁶⁸⁰ On the other hand, the elders in the Jewish
community are not a purely civil administration, because the law
there is a divine law, whose transgression is expiated by excommunication; and so they are taken from the ranks of the ordained
scribes.⁶⁸¹ The Jewish rabbi, for his part, is not a priest or a church
official; his work is spiritual in the deepest sense, although it is
not attributed to any charismatic endowment.⁶⁸²

  e. This will keep us from overvaluing the 'charismatic' in
Harnack's sense. As far as we can now see, it can only be said
that even the primitive Church ordered certain ministries by
means of appointment, while others were carried out more spon-
taneously. But this separation, which will be discussed in ch. 24,
is not that between 'natural' and 'charismatic' ministries, since,
for example, the 'charismatic' missionary service of Paul and
Barnabas belongs to the first category, while the 'natural' services
rendered to them by a companion belong to the second.⁶⁸³
Least of all is such a separation possible in the Pastorals; for the
administrative presbyter-bishops are themselves called on to teach
(I Tim. 3.2; 5.17; II Tim. 2.2; Titus 1.9), and the charism is
mediated by ordination (II Tim. 1.6). In I Peter the many kinds
of charism are revealed in preaching and in the deacon's service;

⁶⁷⁸Cf. H. Gunkel, *Die Wirkungen des heiligen Geistes*, 1888, 2 ff. (cf. *TWNT*
VI 409.27 ff.; 413.13 ff. = *Spirit of God* 49, 54).
⁶⁷⁹See 3 o.
⁶⁸⁰See 3n.
⁶⁸¹Bornkamm, *TWNT* VI 660.1 ff.; 661.25 f. Dix, *Ap. Min.* 233 f., is mistaken—they are not ordained to their *eldership*.
⁶⁸²If the seven had originally been elders (but see 26f), then their 'charismatic' character would be apparent (Acts 6.3, 8–10; 7.55; 8.5 f., 13; 21.8 f.).
⁶⁸³Acts 13.1–3, 5; 19.22 (cf. 16.15).

the elders of James 5.14 f. have the gift of healing, and the 'leaders' of Heb. 13.7, 17 carry out the service of preaching and ministry. In the Johannine writings any such separation seems quite impossible, for the 'elder' standing behind the second and third letters is a 'charismatic' personality.[684] That the Church's thought was not determined by any overvaluation of ecstatic phenomena is also shown by the fact that the obvious temptation to describe Jesus in this respect as a pneumatic has been almost entirely avoided in the tradition that has come down to us.[685]

f. Paul was perhaps the only one to see this question as such, and to think it out theologically; and he explicitly repudiates any separation.[686] For him a 'natural' ministry of an administrative kind is, like leadership in organizing, or brotherly help, just as much charism as is a 'supernatural' ministry such as glossolalia, because the degree of singularity has nothing whatever to do with the question whether in a particular ministry Jesus is confessed as Lord and the Church is built up. Just as there is a 'natural' gift for organization, which could also prove its worth in a Gentile state, so there is also 'natural' ecstasy, such as is also manifested in Gentile worship (I Cor. 12.2).[687] Both can be accepted for service by God's Spirit, and so become charismatic ministries. In fact, Paul even lays stress on the non-ecstatic gifts, because they rather promote the building up of the Church, particularly if, like him, one regards the non-believer, or at least the outsider, as the real yardstick for estimating the value of ministries (I Cor. 14.16, 23 f.). Thus a person's 'natural' personality is not to be effaced; what is preached is indeed God's word, but it is 'God's word from us'.[688] There must therefore be no striving for an 'unfruitful mind';[689] and so the nature of the ministry is now determined by combining

[684]See 12c.
[685]*TWNT* VI 400.16 ff. = *Spirit of God* 33 ff.
[686]See 7k, l.
[687]Cf. also those who had cast out demons in Matt. 7.22. This might be said in criticism of Sohm, *Kirchenrecht* I 224, II 136 ff. If we say—with some justification—that ecclesiastical jurisdiction became a suit of armour that choked the things of the Spirit (J. Klein, *Grundlegung und Grenzen des kanonischen Rechtes*, 1947, 10 ff.), then 'spiritual' must not be confused with ecstatic, any more than 'jurisdiction' with spiritual order.
[688]Λόγος ἀκοῆς παρ' ἡμῶν τοῦ Θεοῦ (I Thess. 2.13). Cf. also II Peter 3. 2: 'the Lord and Saviour's commandment of your apostles.'
[689]I Cor. 14.14; cf. G. Bornkamm, 'Faith and Reason in Paul's Epistles', *NTS* 4, 1957/8, 93 ff.

the indicative, with its statement of the unique working God's grace, with the imperative which brings the witness into full responsibility. Paul expects salvation neither from the ecstasy in which a man weak-mindedly abandons himself to the Spirit's breath, nor from the individual exertions of a man who wants to build the kingdom of God.[690] The fulness of grace is shown in God's taking man, together with his full responsibility, into his service.

Is there, then, no charism of age? There is, but only as far as there is, for instance, a charism of ecstasy, and with the same limitations. That means that both also exist, as a matter of course, outside the action of the Spirit of Jesus Christ, but that he can take both into his service. To walk in faith till one is old is a gift of grace;[691] and so by no means all the old church members are elders,[692] but those 'who are blameless, married only once, whose children are believers' (Titus 1.6). In the sociological group of the older church members, therefore, those who perform a special ministry are referred to more and more clearly as *the* 'older men', just as among the widows *the* 'widows' appear as a special group (I Tim. 5.9 f.).[693]

g. The assertion that the gift of grace is bestowed on *every* church member, and that therefore *every* member is called to service,[694] is constant in the New Testament, just as it is an understood thing that every church member can baptize,[695] or distribute the

[690]Cf. also e.g. Mark 9.24 (and on this A. Rich, 'Glaube und Unglaube in unserer Zeit', *EvTh* 19, 1959, 52 ff.); Luke 17.5 f.; on the union of the Holy Spirit and one's own personality cf. Acts 5.32; 15.28; further 4.8; 6.10; 7.55; 21.4, side by side with 11.28; 20.22 f.; 21.11.

[691]So I *Clem.* 63.3.

[692]Among the priests of Egypt there were avowedly young elders (H. Lietzmann, *ZWT* 55, 1913/14, 118). That is certainly unlikely for the New Testament, as technical and non-technical usage long exist side by side (Bornkamm, *TWNT* VI 654.8 ff.). But it seems as if the *essential* part of the preliminary conditions is not age. There is thus no age limit, the only one imposed being for widows in I Tim. 5.9.

[693]In Greek there is no linguistic difference between 'elders' and 'older men'. W. Freytag, in *Ev. Missionszeitschr.* 1942, 268 f., points to young elders and (financially) poor church leaders in the mission field.

[694]For Jesus, see 2l; for the primitive Church 3m–o; for Matthew 4f, g; for Luke 5k; for the Pastorals 6h; for Paul 7i–m, n. 382; for Colossians and Ephesians 8c, f; for I Peter 9b; for Hebrews 10b, c; for the Johannine writings 11i, 12c, 13e.

[695]The apostles do not as a rule baptize (Acts 10.48; cf. 19.5 beside v. 6a; I Cor. 1.14–17); ordinary church members do (Acts 9.18).

Lord's Supper,[696] and has the right to speak in any assembly of the Church.[697] In that case, however, the other distinction (which takes exactly the opposite direction to Harnack's) of offices from free ministries, as it has been worked out by Anglican exegetes,[698] is untenable for the New Testament, if it means anything more than a purely practical description of different kinds. It is certainly quite true that the prophet has authority only as far and as long as his prophecy goes on. But exactly the same is true of the apostles and of the overseers, superintendents, elders, and whatever else they are called; for only where the apostle's words can really inwardly prevail in the Church do they become its real authority.[699] It is certainly true that the Church acknowledges, or even chooses, as its leaders those people from whom it has repeatedly experienced such authoritative guidance, and who have proved themselves; and so it always meets them in the expectation of receiving divine guidance from them again. But the same is also true of the prophets, even if it may be still clearer in their case than in others' that they do not have such guidance just to dispose of as they like, but that they have to wait for God's answer. Thus the ministry of the prophets became, although not everywhere, yet to a great extent in the New Testament Church, even more determinative than that of the superintendent or bishop.[700]

[696]This ministry never appears as a special gift of grace, nor as an office. In I Cor. 11.17 ff. Paul cannot appeal to anyone who is responsible for the proper conduct of the Lord's Supper.

[697]This is certainly true of Paul (I Cor. 14.30), and even in the Pastoral Letters it may still hold good at least for the men (I Tim. 2.8, 12). It is also suggested by the admonition that the recipients of the letters should set an example to the Church, in their teaching, as in other matters (Titus 2.7, where παρακάλει is a governing verb; cf. I Tim. 4.7, 12, 15 f.; 5.22; 6.14; II Tim. 2.15; 3.10–12; 4.5).

[698]Farrer, *Ap. Min.* 145 n. 1: the prophet is only the junior colleague of the apostles, is subordinated to them, and has authority only as long as his ecstasy lasts (Dix, *ibid.* 237 f., cf. 244, is more cautious). On the Roman Catholic side, Brosch, *Charismen und Ämter* 42 ff., 94 ff. (against Sohm), and similarly Kaiser, *Die Einheit der Kirchengewalt* 154 f., likewise separate the transitory charismata from the permanent hierarchy, while Wikenhauser, *Die Apostelgeschichte* 78, sees that, at least in Paul, office and charism cannot be rigidly separated. Adler, too (*Taufe und Handauflegung* 89) separates the gift bestowed exclusively by the laying on of hands, and associated with a formal office, from that which is charismatic in the stricter sense.

[699]See 26a.

[700]The only possibility of avoiding this conclusion would be to declare, with no shadow of proof, that Paul's letters are addressed to elders (see n. 379 and n. 394).

23

THE PRIESTHOOD OF ALL BELIEVERS

a. It is from here that we have to see the part that the Church plays in the New Testament. The choice of the term 'Church' is worth notice. The much-debated question whether the word meant first of all the universal Church, and only later had its meaning extended to include the local church,[701] or whether it was the other way round,[702] probably need not be asked in that form at all. The word has come through the Septuagint, where it designates all Israel as God's community.[703] But we then have to ask why we find that in the oldest documents of the New Testament—that is, in Paul's letters—the word describes the local church and can appear quite freely in the plural, while no clear application of it to the universal Church appears before the (probably post-Pauline) captivity letters.[704] It might be supposed that we could see in it the influence of Greek, in which the term can denote any gathering of people (Acts 19.32, 39, 41), but that explanation is at any rate not enough by itself. If it is what the primitive Church called itself before Paul, the problem may not have arisen as yet, because at first there was virtually only the one church in Jerusalem, and though after a time cognizance was taken of the newly formed churches, the relation to them was not thought out theologically.

But beyond all that, it can be said that of the (approximately) eighty passages where the word occurs in the Old Testament, only five do not certainly refer to the act of gathering together or to the actual company that has gathered. That means, however, that 'church' is not originally an abstract theological term, but one

[701]Cf. e.g. A. Médebielle in *Dictionnaire de la Bible*, suppl. II, 1934, 660, 668.
[702]Recently J. Y. Campbell, *JTS* 49, 1948, 130 ff., especially 138. Representatives of both views in Schmidt, *TWNT* III 503.19 ff. (= *The Church* 1).
[703]Especially the generation of the wilderness (Cerfaux, *The Church in . . . St Paul* 113 ff.).
[704]Cerfaux 187–98.

that denotes an actual happening.[705] Wherever the Greek Old Testament is read, the old meaning of the word, 'Yahweh's levy', is kept; and that means that the Church must be regarded primarily as an event.[706] The Church is spoken of as something that really 'takes place'. The Church therefore comes into existence primarily where people come together as a church—particularly, of course, in the local churches' meetings for worship, but also, for instance, at the 'Council at Jerusalem'. In these circumstances each of these assemblies knows itself to be *the* Church of God, in its particular form at that time and place.[707] There were different manifestations of the same Church, both chronologically in its successive forms and geographically side by side. The later development that lays the main stress on the universal Church, in Ephesians or Ignatius for instance, is not an entirely new departure as long as it remembers that the universal Church appears in the existing local churches.[708]

b. If we ask about this Church's authority, we have to connect the question with what was found in ch. 21. The only office-bearer in the real sense is Jesus Christ himself, and so there is hardly any description of ministry that is not used, on occasion, of Jesus Christ. He is 'servant' (Phil. 2.7; Matt. 12.18; Acts 3.13, 26; 4.27, 30), 'deacon' (Rom. 15.8; cf. Luke 22.27), 'apostle' (Heb. 3.1; cf. Mark 9.37; Luke 10.16; John 3.34, etc.), 'teacher' (Matt. 23.8; John 13.13; cf. Matt. 7.29), 'bishop and shepherd' (I Peter 2.25; 5.4; Heb. 13.20). Not only does his service form the basis of all ministry (Luke 22.26 f.; Mark 10.43–45; John

---

[705] Dix, *Jew and Greek* 28. He stresses that this was not eliminated even by the Hellenizing of the message, for the faith remains tied to the historical person of Jesus (the Synoptic Gospels were not written till after the Hellenizing period), cf. *ibid.* 4–6, 27 f.

[706] K. Barth, *Dogmatics* IV 2, 623 ff. 696 f.; also in *The Universal Church in God's Design* (Amsterdam Report) 67ff.

[707] This is shown by the choice of the term ἐκκλησία and not συναγωγή (see 3b). Cf. Schmidt, *TWNT* III 504.22 ff. (= *The Church* 2); A. E. J. Rawlinson in *Min. and Sacr.* 291 f.; Farrer 177; P. Bonnard, *Revue de Théol. et de Philos.*, 1958, 268 ff.

[708] By 'local church' is meant only the actual assembled company, not the legally organized congregation of an established church today. In the New Testament, therefore, the 'two or three' of Matt. 18.20 should be included in that term, as well as 'the church in their house' of Rom. 16.5; I Cor. 16.19; Philem. 2. The Church can 'take place' in either of these, as well as in the larger assemblies of all the believers in a place. On this see n. 897.

17.18); but he is also its real and only rightful bearer (Matt. 23.8; John 13.13; Heb. 13.20; I Peter 5.4 beside v. 2). In the Church, then, there is really only one single authority—that of Jesus Christ himself (or, alternatively, of God or the Holy Spirit),[709] only a Christocracy. So far, however, this tells us nothing about the Church's order and authority, because the question is in what way this rule of Christ is carried out in the Church.[710] Does the Lord speak through one single office-bearer, through a governing body, through the church meeting?

c. The question must be finally cleared up later; in the present context it need only be maintained that, as we have seen from the linguistic analysis of the expressions relating to office, the Church as a whole shares in the authority of Jesus Christ.[711] Again the New Testament is unanimous that regard must be had to the whole body of members. The emphases are put in different ways. Once Acts mentions the appointment of elders by the apostles, with no mention of the Church (14.23), and the writers of the letters to the churches in Syria and Cilicia appear as apostles and elders (15.23; 16.4). But in the former case it is a question of newly formed churches, and in the latter the Church's support of the decision is mentioned (15.22), just as the church to which the letter is addressed gathers together to hear it read (15.30).[712] Elsewhere, however, the Church has a vital share in important choices and decisions, and takes the final responsibility.[713]

For Luke the conjunction of apostolic initiative and the fully responsible participation of the Church as a whole (11.1 ff.) is typical; and Paul and John particularly stress the joint responsibility of all the adult Church members. The Church chooses its

[709]Cf. passages such as Mark 3.14, 16; Luke 10.13–16; John 15.26 f.; Acts 1.24; 2.1 ff.; 8.26 ff.; 9.15, 17; 10.20; 13.2, 4; 15.7; 16.6 f.; 20.28; Rom. 15.18; II Cor. 5.19; I John 5.8, 10; Rev. 2.1, 7.
[710]We cannot, with Reicke, *Glaube und Leben der Urgemeinde* 25 f., simply name the theocratic element alongside the monarchical, oligarchic, and democratic.
[711]If Rev. 12.1 means the Christian Church (see n. 485), that stands out very strongly there too.
[712]Farrer 144 thinks that the Church stands by in silence, and that even the elders are present only as an audience at the apostles' deliberations, or perhaps as mere recipients of the apostolic instructions handed to them by apostolic leaders (but why?).
[713]See 5m.

messengers who travel with the apostles to represent it at Jerusalem (II Cor. 8.18 f., 23; I Cor. 16.3). Only to the Church as a whole is the fulness of gifts promised (I Cor. 1.7). The whole Church is called on to perform the ministry of admonition which is assigned to some in particular (I Thess. 5.11–14). All are 'taught by God' (4.9). Above all, an obedience that is given only from regard for the apostle's authority, and not from conviction of the truth of his words, is for Paul worthless.[714] The Church's 'amen' is possible only where it has really understood (I Cor. 14.16). All ministries, therefore, are subject to testing by the Church (I Thess. 5.21).[715] In this way, I John 4.1 assumes that all utterances of the Spirit will be tested by the Church, as indeed here it is only the totality of the believers who appear as bearers of the Spirit (2.20, 27).[716]

d. The fact that every church member is a witness for Jesus Christ, that no status as layman releases him from this, and that no office magnifies it, perhaps becomes clearest where the Church's suffering is spoken of. It is in suffering that the Church is most intensively the Church and gives its testimony most unequivocally. To it everyone is called. When Jesus calls his disciples to follow him, he has them share his own way into lowliness. In just the same way not only Paul and John, but also I Peter and Hebrews continually see the Church's ministry of testimony, its common priesthood, in that sharing in Jesus' way of suffering.[717] The apostle's particularly prominent position is for Paul that of special suffering (even as far as in Col. 1.24). But where service is thus seen as suffering for Christ, all questions of dignity and competence become quite incidental. At the most it can be said that this is a ministry of all believers but that some are

[714]Cf. H. v. Campenhausen in *SAH* 1957, 29 ff.
[715]V. 21a refers to the charismata in vv. 18–20, and is developed positively and negatively in 21b and 22. It is quite arbitrary to relate this to certain particular people who perform ministries (see n. 394).
[716]See 11i and 12c.
[717]On this cf. especially Manson's stimulating presentation in *Ministry and Priesthood* 35–64, and 2a, l; 3g, i; 4d, g; 5g; 7f; 8c; 9b; 10b; 11e; 12e; 13a, d; nn. 320 and 360 above. One of the most amazing testimonies of the willingness of a church to die, i.e. to discontinue being a separate denomination, is 'The Last Will and Testament of the Springfield Presbytery' of 1804 (W. E. Garrison and A. T. de Groot, *The Disciples of Christ*, 1948, 109 f.).

specially called to it by God himself. Paul can give thanks that
he belongs to that company.[718]

e. The question of Church discipline is not entirely clear, as
here too we see the differences that we have noticed between the
New Testament witnesses. In the Johannine circle one who im-
poses discipline as an individual is an enemy of the true Church.[719]
The authority to retain or forgive sins is given explicitly to the
'disciples', not to the 'twelve'.[720] In II John 10 the whole Church
is called on to exercise discipline. In Paul's letters, apostles and
Church work together, and Christ's authority is promised to their
joint action (I Cor. 5.4). In this Paul is obviously striving to establish the Church as the real bearer of responsibility.[721] In Acts it is
not really a matter of Church discipline, but of a miraculous
punishment by Peter (5.1 ff.).[722] Only in the Pastorals, which here
too adopt a special attitude, does Paul appear as the one who hands
a sinner over to Satan for punishment (I Tim. 1.20; cf. II Tim.
4.14); and there Titus is called on to admonish such a person, and
if necessary, to repudiate him (Titus 3.10 f.).

The tone varies, too, on the question of the meaning of such
Church discipline. Jesus' twofold concern, not to form a Church
consisting of a separated remnant, and yet to show the ultimate
gravity of a decision, stands out here too. In Matthew's church,
and in fact, in Paul's too,[723] Church discipline is entirely determined
by a concern to regain the brother, or at least to save him at the
judgment. Side by side with this, however, there emerges in Paul,
and still more in the Pastorals,[724] the idea of keeping the Church
pure. This may be right as long as it remains a sign merely meant

---

[718]See 2m.

[719]III John 9 f.: Diotrephes 'puts them out of the church'. See n. 497.

[720]John 20.22; see 11i.

[721]'Your spirit' precedes 'my [Paul's] spirit'; in vv. 2, 7, 12 the Church is
called on to exercise discipline, and indeed in v. 13 the second person singular in the quotation (Hebrew text and LXX except A) is replaced by the
plural. According to II Thess. 3.14 too the Church has to exercise discipline.
Cf. Gal. 6.1; II Cor. 1.23–2.11; 7.12.

[722]As the parallel 13.9 ff. shows it is a question here neither of Church discipline nor of action on the ground of the apostle's special position, but of the
working of the prophetic spirit which has been bestowed on him and which
sees into men's hearts.

[723]See 4e and 7e (n. 369).

[724]See 6f and on John 12b.

to proclaim that the decision for or against God is demanded with the utmost urgency;[725] it becomes wrong when the Church finds in it its self-justification on the lines of Rom. 11.17 ff.

[725]One might here take up Bohren's suggestion (*Das Problem der Kirchenzucht im NT* 97 ff.) that in order to be authentic the Church would have to decide between forgivable sin and definite apostasy. See 4e, 6f. On the whole problem of general priesthood in the New Testament, cf. E. Best in *Interpretation* 14, 1960, 273 ff.; on the uniqueness of the NT see particularly 276 ff.

24

CHURCH ORDER AS A MANIFESTATION
OF THE SPIRIT

FROM all that has been said up to now it is clear that the New Testament is unanimous that the Church never lives without order. We begin with a summary review of the regulated ministries that we have met in our analysis.

a. The first to be mentioned must be the *apostles*. As we saw, this term has been given very different meanings; and it must be realized that we generally use it in a sense in which it scarcely occurs in the New Testament, namely as denoting the twelve disciples plus Paul. Luke has a clear idea of the word's meaning; but he does not include Paul in it.[726] As eyewitnesses, the twelve are primarily the guarantors of the resurrection. Just as, according to Acts 1.13, they are the sole witnesses of the ascension, so, according to 4.33, they alone preach the resurrection, while the Church speaks 'the word of God' (4.31). Of course, there is a special call to bear this testimony which distinguishes them from others who had also been eyewitnesses (Luke 24.13 ff., 33, 36 ff.). As such they lay the foundation of the Church's preaching generally and are its first leaders; but after the Council at Jerusalem they disappear completely. Both Mark and Matthew use the term 'apostle', independently of each other, only once (in editorial statements) for the twelve who are sent out as messengers to preach and heal. The word still clearly denotes function, and is not simply a title. John[727] and Hebrews do not know the word at all. Paul can use it in a wide sense as denoting function (Rom. 16.7; II Cor. 8.23; Phil. 2.25); but he generally uses it for a definite group of Christ's witnesses who have seen the risen Lord

---

[726]See 5h. G. Klein 213 ff. thinks that the concept of twelve apostles originated in Luke, who, in opposition to the gnostics, wanted to show Paul's dependence on the 'official Church authorities'. Originally the twelve were eschatological rulers, not 'apostles'. For a survey cf. E. M. Kredel, 'Der Apostelbegriff in der neueren Exegese', ZKT 78, 1956, 169 ff.

[727]See n. 454.

(I Cor. 9.1) and been definitely commissioned. Both uses apply to himself as to the first apostle.[728] No one is an apostle for the whole body of Christians, but for the particular church for which the commission is given (I Cor. 9.2; Gal. 2.8; cf. 1.16).[729] This group is larger than the twelve plus Paul (I Cor. 15.7[730]).

The difference between this picture and Luke's is deeply rooted. The Pauline apostolate is an eschatological event.[731] To be sure the difference must not be exaggerated. Paul too looks back on the events in Palestine, above all to Jesus' crucifixion and resurrection; and for Paul too the gospel's historical course from the Jews to the Gentiles, and from there back to the Jews, is extraordinarily important. But with him this too is part of the saving event; what happened in Palestine two or three decades previously is present in the apostolic preaching that introduces the approaching end of the world and the Lord's parousia. Just because Paul cannot yet imagine any significance of the apostolate for a further history of the Church that will now have no living apostles, the Lucan view is foreign to him. The gospel becomes alive, and the past present, in the authoritative testimony of one called by the risen Lord himself, not in the accurate historical recollection of an eyewitness who was present at those events. Luke, however, consciously lives in the sub-apostolic period (Acts 20.29–35). The apostles appear as a body belonging to past history also in Eph. 2.20; 3.5; II Peter 3.2; Jude 17; they are confined in Rev. 21.14, as in Luke, to the twelve. In the Pastorals it is only Paul who plays the part of apostle. Finally, the expression 'the twelve'[732] is found in the Gospels, where in particular the phrase 'Judas, one of the twelve' seems to be rooted in the oldest tradition;[733] elsewhere it is found only in Acts 6.2 and I Cor. 15.5.

[728] See 7g.
[729] A. Fridrichsen, *The Apostle and his Message*, 1947, 8 ff., distinguishes still more sharply: Rom. 2.16; I Cor. 15.1; Gal. 1.11; 2.2 (cf. II Cor. 4.3; I Thess. 1.5; II Thess. 2.14; Rom. 16.25; II Tim. 2.8) show that Paul's preaching, even in so far as it rests on the common tradition, has been given a special form, of which Paul is conscious.
[730] In I Thess. 2.7 are his companions numbered with the apostles too?
[731] Cf. Fridrichsen, *op. cit.* 3 ff.; Munck, *Paul and the Salvation of Mankind* ch. 2, esp. section 3;
[732] Also 'the twelve disciples' and similarly.
[733] Mark 14.10, 20, 43. Matt. 26.14, 47; Luke 22.3, 47; John 6.71 (cf. 20.24: Thomas).

b. The content of the term 'apostle' is thus very varied theologically. Luke and Paul see in it the witness to whom the risen Lord appeared and who was commissioned to preach.[734] Luke emphasizes the eyewitnesses' evidence as guaranteeing the truth of the resurrection (Acts 10.41); he does not include in this category the meeting with Paul near Damascus. The decisive thing for Paul is that he is commissioned by the risen Lord; he is an apostle in relation to the churches that have been allotted to him. As representatives of the normative preaching the apostles appear in Jude 17 = II Peter 3.2 and probably Rev. 21.14. In Eph. 2.20 and 3.5 they are associated with the (New Testament) prophets. Here, therefore, it is neither the eyewitnesses' evidence nor the special commission by the risen Lord that is regarded as the Church's foundation; it is rather the message of the earlier time, whether it was delivered by missionaries whom the Lord sent, or by prophets whom the Spirit moved. For the Pastorals there certainly is a guarantor of the tradition, but only one—Paul. Hebrews, on the other hand, represents as initiators of the tradition all who heard Jesus' preaching. For John, who uses the term 'apostle' only once in a completely general sense, the twelve represent God's selective action which alone makes it possible to remain with Jesus when all are turning away from him. That there really are witnesses who saw and heard is essential for him in view of docetic attempts to make the earthly Jesus evaporate into the idea of a heavenly Christ (John 19.35; 21.24; I John 1.1–4). But such evidence of eye-witnesses is no longer associated with the 'twelve' or the 'apostles', nor is it really normative for preaching beyond its testimony to the fact of Jesus' earthly existence. Where the witness is defined more precisely, he is generally represented by the disciple 'whom Jesus loved'. Peter stands out particularly among the twelve (Matt. 16.17 ff.; Luke 22.32; John 21.15 ff.; Gal. 1.18; 2.7 ff.; I Cor. 1.12; 9.5); and apart from him the sons of Zebedee play a certain part (Mark 1.19 etc.; Gal. 2.9[735]).

[734]In Luke it is clear that the Emmaus disciples and the wider circle of Luke 24.33 are not 'apostles'; in Paul it is at least unlikely that the 'more than five hundred' (I Cor. 15.6) are all counted as 'apostles'; besides, the women to whom the risen Lord appeared (Matt. 28.9 f.) are hardly anywhere regarded as apostles in early Christian times (Craig, *The One Church* . . . 59).

[735]We may assume that in this verse James the Lord's brother is meant

Thus the New Testament is unanimous that the apostle in the narrower sense acquires a unique position because of his meeting with the risen—or exalted—Lord (in whatever different ways that position may be understood), and because of the charge given him. To him (perhaps to others too) there is entrusted the fundamental preaching by which the later preaching is to be measured. We can speak of the apostles' pupils, but not of their successors in office. The apostle exercises no priestly functions.[736]

c. The *prophets* frequently appear together with the apostles (Luke 11.49; I Cor. 12.28 f.; Eph. 2.20; 3.5; 4.11; Rev. 18.20; cf. Matt. 10.40 f.). They are found in Matthew, Luke, Paul, but not in John, nor, except for Ephesians, in the non-Pauline letters. In the latter the Old Testament prophets are seen increasingly as the bearers of the revelation of that period. Their service is everywhere regarded as a direct gift of the Spirit; and the Church no more chooses prophets than it chooses apostles. It can recognize them, and it also has to test them (like the 'superlative apostles' of II Cor. 10–12), and either allow or refuse them a place for prophesying in the meeting for worship (I Cor. 14.29 ff.). According to Paul, everyone should really be a prophet, and presumably Revelation takes a very similar view.[737]

d. The *teacher* also plays an important part. The title in this sense appears only in Acts 13.1; I Cor. 12.28 f.; Eph. 4.11; James 3.1. According to Heb. 5.12 the whole Church ought to be teachers; II Tim. 4.3 talks of false teachers; according to I Tim. 5.17 some of the elders carry out the service of teaching; and the same thing is probably indicated in II Tim. 2.2. Matthew, too, is familiar with it when he talks about the 'wise men and scribes', and about no longer being *called* 'master' or 'rabbi'.[738] Paul also speaks of 'him who teaches' (Rom. 12.7; Gal. 6.6). John, on the other hand, can only declare that the true Church

---

(he is the first to be mentioned), and that James the son of Zebedee is dead (Acts 12.2; otherwise K. Heussi, *TLZ* 77, 1952, 67 ff., especially 69; cf. H. Katzenmeyer, *Internat. Kirchl. Zeitschr.* 42, 1952, 178 ff.; J. Dupont, *RB* 64, 1957, 38; on the other hand B. Häsler, *TLZ* 82, 1957, 393 f. and others). Cf. E. Dinkler, *TR* 27, 1959, 197 f.

[736]Craig 60; on Rom. 15.16 see 21a; on the whole subject 26d, e.
[737]See 7k, and for Revelation 13e.
[738]See n. 218.

no longer needs such teachers (I John 2.27). Probably only Matthew assumes a real tradition or school, and so it is probably only with him that this ministry assumes a previous training.[739]

e. The ministry of the *overseer*, too, is a gift of grace; and the clearest statement of this comes from Paul. In his writings, as in Hebrews, there is no settled title for this. The overseers' ministry is to be recognized by the Church, and this will also be shown by a certain order. It will gradually become the custom for the few people who have long been carrying out this ministry to be the first who speak in the meeting for worship, bring forward proposals, or call to order. Specific tasks will be left to them, and perhaps their ministry may even be facilitated by their being relieved of some anxiety about their livelihood. But in Paul's writings they have as yet no title, nor have they any rights allowing them to act in special spheres that are forbidden to others. Whatever they do is also expected of other church members (I Thess. 5.14 compared with 5.12).

f. The order in the Pastorals, in which the function of 'oversight' is assigned to *elders*, is much further advanced.[740] In adopting this title the Pastorals take up a tradition that is also found in Acts, James, and I Peter.[741] Many features of the ministry of Jewish elders have probably been adopted here.

g. In Acts 20.17, 28, and probably also in Titus 1.5–7 (cf. I Tim. 3.1 ff.), *'bishop'* appears as a functional term for the same service.[742] Presumably there is as yet no monarchical bishop in the New Testament.[743] In I Tim. 3.1 ff. as in Phil. 1.1 the *deacons* seem to be connected with him. As the same is true of the *Didache*,

---

[739]Here Stendahl, *The School of St Matthew* 34, may be right. It seems to me, however, to be typical that we find this only in Matthew, who is closely connected with the Jewish-rabbinical movement. In all other places there seems to be a completely different atmosphere from that of the 'school'. Riesenfeld's hypothesis, *The Gospel Tradition and its Beginnings*, 23 ff., seems to me to contradict everything that we can learn about the development of the tradition and of Church order apart from Matthew.

[740]See 6h.

[741]See 5i and 9b; on II and III John see 12c; on Revelation see 13e. The expression 'elders of the church' occurs in James 5.14 (cf. 'elders of the people' in Matthew, and Michaelis, *Ältestenamt* 132).

[742]Otherwise Farrer 161.

[743]In III John one such (with no mention of the title) is repudiated; on the Pastorals see 6h. According to Kaiser, *Die Einheit der Kirchengewalt* 174, a monarchical episcopate is unnecessary as long as the apostles are alive.

which, like Paul, knows no elders, and likewise for I *Clement* and probably for Hermas too, it appears that the identification of bishop with elder, which also holds good for the two last named, though not for Ignatius,[744] represents a secondary stage of development. Originally the order of elders and that marked by the dual form of bishops and deacons may have had nothing to do with each other, and this is probably connected with the fact that the Jewish elder had no servant attached to him.[745] Deaconesses too are presumably mentioned in Rom. 16.1 and I Tim. 3.11.[746] Early steps towards a diaconate are shown in the ministries, not as yet specially regulated, of Rom. 12.7 (cf. I Peter 4.11), but also in the apostles' 'servants' (Acts 19.22; 13.5) though Paul calls them 'fellow worker' (Rom. 16.21; II Cor. 8.23; Phil. 2.25) or 'brother' (II Cor. 1.1; 2.13; I Thess. 3.2; Philem. 1). It is possible that in a similar way the deacons were originally the bishops' servants.[747] In point of fact, the deacons' later ministry may have influenced Mark 8.19 f.,[748] and particularly Acts 6.1 ff., although the title is not mentioned there.[749]

h. Lastly there should be mentioned the *evangelists* and *pastors* (Eph. 4.11). The first of these terms emerges at a time when the

[744]See 15d; 16c, d; 18c. In Ignatius the presbytery is already inserted between the monarchical bishop and the deacons (17d).

[745]It is therefore probably correct to say that the ministry of deacon originated among Gentile Christians (Lietzmann, *ZWT* 55, 1913/14, 111–13; v. Campenhausen, *Kirchliches Amt* 84) and so does not appear in association with the title of elder (Beyer, *TWNT* II 91.18 ff.). Only it has since become clear that the title ἐπίσκοπος at least has some counterpart in the Judaism of Qumran (see n. 762, but also what is said on this in 24i). It may be that the 'younger' (Acts 5.6; I Peter 5.5; but cf. I Tim. 5.1 f.; Titus 2.6) represent something of a distant parallel to the deacons, and show a certain formal correspondence to the lower ranks in the Qumran community.

[746]See n. 334.

[747]This would be contradicted, if at all, only by Rom. 16.1, *if* the word there denoted a regulated ministry, and not a free activity for the benefit of the Church. A certain analogy is offered by Phil. 2.25, which certainly does not prove that 'apostle' originally described a church's ambassador.

[748]Does Matthew leave out this part of the matter because the apostles are not deacons? For greater detail cf. Schürmann, *Jesu Abschiedsrede . . .* 96.

[749]These would be the only passages to suggest that the ministry of the deacons included serving at the Lord's Supper, or even arose from it (as Dix, *Ap. Min.* 245 ff. supposes). But this, like the reference to *Didache* 15.1 (where the οὖν may connect with ch. 14) is very uncertain, and the basis in the New Testament period for the bishop's part in the eucharist is still more slender.

apostles were seen as a separate group belonging to the early days
(also Acts 21.8; cf. II Tim. 4.5); the second is remarkably close
to the 'bishop'[750] (I Peter 2.25[751]). That is to say that the ministries
of bishop and pastor are one and the same.[752] Finally we still have
to mention the widows of I Tim. 5.3 ff., for whom a definite age
limit is laid down.[753] The 'seven' of Acts 6.1 ff. are probably a
unique group produced by a particular historical situation.[754] In
Paul's view, of course, there would also have to be included the
complete list of ministries that he enumerates, as he makes no
distinction between these and the ministries that are more strictly
regulated by the Church.[755]

i. These ministries have their parallels or their origin partly
in Jewish ministries. This is clearest in the case of the elders,[756]
who are probably a continuation of the rulers of the Jewish
synagogue; though it must not be overlooked that they did not
carry out their ministry by any means from the very beginning
of the Church, but that their introduction represents a later
assimilation to Jewish forms. More emphatically still, the idea
that the elders of Jerusalem are not simply a local body, but that
they correspond roughly to the Jewish Sanhedrin, is a very late
construction.[757] But even here the differences must not be overlooked. The expectation of James 5.14 that the gift of healing is
given to the elders is new.[758] But even where, as in Acts, they are
regarded as the guardians of the apostolic tradition, they are in
any case not ordained scribes as in the Jewish tradition.[759] In the

[750]It is questionable whether 'pastors' and 'teachers' can be equated, even
though the article is used only once (Soiron, *Die Kirche als der Leib Christi*
162); possibly the two services were originally separated and gradually
became united, as a rule, in one person.
[751]Ample early Christian evidence in Nauck, *ZNW* 48, 1957, 201 f.
[752]Cf. Dix, *Ap. Min.* 293–6; also J. J. v. Allmen in G. Dix, *Le ministère dans
l'église ancienne*, 1955, 13, stresses this side in Dix. Thus episcopalianism and
congregationalism can unite in the early Church.
[753]This seems to be the only legally verifiable condition for a ministry in the
New Testament. Elsewhere nothing seems to be presupposed but gifts of
the Spirit (as in the case of the widow of I Tim. 5.3 ff.) which are apparent
only to a spiritual δοκιμάζειν.
[754]See n. 126.
[755]See 7i–m and the synopsis in Weiss, *I Kor.* 299.
[756]Bornkamm, *TWNT* VI 655.3 ff.; Michaelis 13 ff.; Dix, *Ap. Min.* 233 ff.
[757]Bornkamm, 662.21 ff.
[758]*Ibid.* 664.11 ff.
[759]*Ibid.* 660.1 ff.

case of the bishops the connection is much more questionable.[760] In the Old Testament, as in secular Greek, all kinds of overseers are spoken of, although no specific ministry is connected with the term.[761] A much closer parallel is suggested by the 'overseer' of the Qumran community.[762] Not only, however, is the linguistic equation still questionable,[763] but above all it is still far from clear whether the ministries referred to actually correspond in the two communities[764]—whether, that is, we have proof of anything more than that each uses a similar name.[765] In the case of the diaconate, which is closely associated with the episcopal ministry, any connection between synagogue and Church is quite uncertain.[766] On the other hand, the Jewish rabbis obviously continue in Matthew's church as the teachers of the flock; for the rest, we

[760]Cf. also Kaiser 132 ff.

[761]Beyer, *TWNT* II 604.37 ff.; H. W. Beyer and H. Karpp, *RAC* II 395 ff.

[762]Nauck, *ZNW* 48, 1957, 203 f. and the writers named there; Schmitt, *RevSR* 29, 1955, 257 f.

[763]*Damasc.* knows only the *mᵉbaqqēr*. On the other hand in IQS 6.14 there is the *pāqîd* who seems to be identical with the *mᵉbaqqēr 'al hārabbîm* (verse 12), who appears likewise in *Damasc.* 15.8; 19.8; cf. 9.8, 22; 13.6 ff.; 14.8 ff.; 15.8 ff.. Any idea of correspondence between ἐπισκοπή and the *pᵉqûdāh* in Qumran (M. Philonenko, *TZ* 14, 1958, 86 n. 14) comes to grief on the fact that the latter term is never associated with the ministry of the 'overseer', but simply denotes 'visitation'. Josephus calls the Essene 'overseer' ἐπιμελέτης and ἐπίτροπος (*Bell.* 2.134), which also corresponds to the title *mᵉbaqqēr*, while ἐπισκέπτεσθαι translates *pāqad*. R. H. Charles has seen in the 'overseer' of *Damasc.* the model of the Christian bishop (cf. W. H. Brownlee, *The Dead Sea Manual of Discipline*, 1951, 25 n. 24; against this J. Strugnell, *JBL* 77, 1958, 110 f.; on the Qumran passages see n. 94 above). But the most obvious translation that occurs to one is no doubt ἐπιμελέτης (Daniélou, *RHPR* 35, 1955, 111).

[764]Even if the monarchical nature of the overseer is less marked in the Qumran text than in *Damasc.* (Reicke, *TZ* 10, 1954, 111; H. Braun, *Spätjüdische Häretik* I 105, n. 1), a different picture is shown by the New Testament with its many 'bishops' in an obviously small Church which developed only quite late into a monarchical episcopate. In any case, in Qumran the overseer stands within a strongly constructed hierarchy, and has no 'deacons' beside him. Moreover, he is the leader there of a group of 'scribes' (Huppenbauer, *TZ* 13, 1957, 136 f.).

[765]So Goguel, *L'église primitive* 119–22, who shows how generally the term was used in the LXX and among the Greeks. Dix too, *Ap. Min.* 252, thinks only of parallel development, not of dependence. Cf. E. J. Palmer in *Min. and Sacr.* 368 ff.; J. Jeremias, *Jerusalem zur Zeit Jesu* II B, 1937, 132 ff.; K. Goetz, *ZNW* 30, 1931, 89 ff.

[766]Goguel too is sceptical, *op. cit.* 122; see n. 631 above. Dix, *Ap. Min.* 232 f., sees the seven of Acts 6.1 ff. as successors of the Jewish guardians of the poor, although he recognizes the differences.

can probably only say that in the New Testament too instruction is regarded as an important task and is entrusted to specified people.[767] It is quite uncertain how far Church leaders have anything to do with Jewish overseers.[768]

Looking at it theologically, the most important question is probably whether the apostle of the primitive Christian Church is to be understood against the background of the Jewish official 'envoy'. [769]In any case, any direct connection is very doubtful.[770] In Judaism, missionaries are never described as 'envoys', nor is that term ever given to prophets or teachers. When on occasion priests or elect men of ancient times are represented as the 'envoys' of God himself,[771] both the age and the factual content of those assertions are very uncertain,[772] and in any case the expression 'God's envoy' does not occur. Least of all can the 'envoy' hand on his authority to other people so that any succession of office could be derived from it.[773] It is rather for the title 'pillars' (Gal. 2.9) that a parallel is to be found in Qumran.[774] Thus rather more analogies can be quoted today from Jewish sources than could be even a quarter of a century ago.[775] It would indeed be quite incredible that the early Church's surroundings should not have affected it at all. But the verdict is not essentially changed: speaking generally, the Church emphasized its different nature with surprising freedom by creating new ministries and transforming old ones.

[767]But there is no longer any suggestion here of pupillage under a rabbi, which reaches its goal in the ordination that makes the pupil a rabbi in his turn.
[768]Michel, *Heb.* 355, points to the *parnām*.
[769]Affirmed and vigorously evaluated theologically by Dix, *Ap. Min.* 228 ff.
[770]Reid, *The Biblical Doctrine of the Ministry* 40; G. W. H. Lampe, *Some Aspects of the NT Ministry*, 1949, 9; Holl, *Gesammelte Aufsätze* II 52, n. 1.
[771]Michel, *Röm.* 27, n. 4.
[772]Rengstorf, *TWNT* I 414 ff., esp. 419.5 ff. (*Apostleship* 12 ff., esp. 21 ff.).
[773]Craig, *The One Church* . . . 57 f. Cf. especially also Ehrhardt, *The Apostolic Succession* 16 ff., and G. Klein, *Die zwölf Apostel* 26 f.
[774]*Yesôdôt* 1QSa 1.12, and on this H. N. Richardson, *JBL* 76, 1957, 108 ff.; but there everyone who is not less than 25 years old is counted. For the rabbinic use cf. R. Mach, *Der Zaddik in Talmud und Midrasch*, 1957, 142. But C. K. Barrett in *StudPaul* 1 ff. plausibly relates the image to the early Christian idea of the eschatological temple.
[775]E.g. in Linton, *Das Problem der Urkirche* 23. See also n. 99 above.

k. Thus the New Testament agrees[776] that God does not bestow all the gifts of grace on every Church member; and Paul expresses this quite clearly when he warns his hearers not to run after other people's gifts. Everyone must think within God's limits (Rom. 12.3).[777] God orders the different ministries, both side by side (I Cor. 14.26 ff.) and in sequence (I Cor. 3.5 f., 10; cf. also II Cor. 3.9). But he assigns different geographical spheres of action even to ministries of the same kind (Gal. 2.7;[778] II Cor. 10.13[779]). This thought is clearly echoed in Eph. 4.7, 16; I Peter 4.10; Heb. 2.4. Thus there is in the New Testament no monarchical Church management; such a thing is known only to opponents.[780] But this means, not only that everyone who is in the Church's service has people alongside him who are endowed with other gifts, but that no one carries out his ministry except in co-operation with other people. The apostle, indeed, is marked out from the rest by his special call from the risen Lord; but he is the one who regards his ministry as team-work with fully authorized fellow workers.[781] Paul knows that he is a link in the chain of tradition (I Cor. 15.3; cf. 3.5 f.); this is not changed till the sub-apostolic period.[782] Except for the apostolic ministry, therefore, which is unique through a special call, no ministry in the New Testament is forbidden to any member of the Church. It is only in the Pastorals[783] that women are excluded from preaching,[784] and that

[776]It is only in the Johannine writings that this is somewhat qualified. The exceptional position of these writings is apparent here, as that of the Pastorals was previously on the other side.

[777]See 7l.

[778]This too is not merely human arrangement, but God's disposition: πεπίστευμαι.

[779]Κανών probably does not mean 'limitation of the sphere of work', but should rather be regarded as the measuring scale that becomes manifest through God's blessing (Beyer, *TWNT* III 603.15 ff.). It is therefore not the case that any such demarcation is fixed from the beginning and can be legally observed, but rather that God's affirmation of Paul's work continually provides him with a new and wider sphere for it.

[780]See 24g and n. 743 above.

[781]See 24g; also I Peter 5.1.

[782]See 24b.

[783]I Cor. 14.34 f. is presumably a marginal gloss that was put into the text by a copyist. DG feel that the context is badly upset, and correct accordingly. The passage can hardly be accepted, especially in view of 11.5. Such regulations of Church order were the most important thing to later periods, and so it is here that interpolations are most easily made (cf. e.g. the addition

an age limit is fixed for widows. Otherwise only God decides by his gift what ministry is to be performed by one, and what by another. The Church can confirm this by its order, but it must remain open to God's correction, and must not, through its order, completely exclude others from that ministry. So in the Church there are feelings neither of inferiority (I Cor. 12.15–20) nor of superiority (12.21–25), but only 'joy in the other's gift'.[785]

l. Freedom of the Spirit and formal order were at first seen as mutually exclusive opposites; one was seen in the Pauline churches, the other in Jerusalem. We have seen that that is to some extent correct, as there was a difference of emphasis between these places. Yet the antithesis cannot be maintained in that form.[786] Even looking at it purely historically, we saw that Jerusalem was probably strongly influenced by the activities of ecstatic prophets, and that Paul was indebted to tradition.[787] The question is, however, what kind of order was thus understood in the Church. What has been shown to us especially in the letters of Paul[788] is valid for the New Testament generally:[789] it is God's Spirit who marks out in freedom the pattern that Church order afterwards recognizes; it is therefore functional, regulative, serving, but not constitutive; and that is what is decisive.[790]

---

of fasting in some MSS. in I Cor. 7. 5, or the changes in Luke 22.17–20). In view of 33b, ἐν ταῖς ἐκκλησίαις is at least very hard, as it means in the first case the various local churches, and in the second the Church assemblies. Elsewhere in the Pauline sphere of influence ἐπιτρέπω is found only in I Cor. 16.7 (traditionally of the κύριος); I Tim. 2.12. The reference to ὑποτάσσεσθαι is significant in I Tim. 2.11, but not here. Cf. Weiss, *I Kor.* 342.

[784]But in the ancient Church women baptize: Nauck, *I Johannesbr.* 164.

[785]O. Schmitz, *Die Vorbildlichkeit der urchristlichen Gemeinden*, 1921 (reprinted from *Volkskirche*), 41.

[786]Cf. also Bartlet, *Church-life and Church-order* 12 ff.

[787]There order and the Spirit's vitality by no means exclude each other (J. A. Robinson in *The Early History of the Church and Ministry* [ed. H. B. Swete], 1921, 60 ff.: all those who minister in the early Church are charismatic). Cf. also R. Meyer, *Der Prophet von Galiläa*, 1940, 70 ff.: the patriarchal council of Sepphoris provides charismatic leaders of the people for generations.

[788]See 7m.

[789]For the Pastorals see 6g; for Luke, 51; and for John, 12c.

[790]Bultmann, *CJT* 1, 1955, 79; likewise Manson, *Ministry* 71 f. Also Dix, *Ap. Min.* 292, recognizes this quite clearly for the 'bishops and ministers', but sees the apostle and the second-century bishop in a different category; see ch. 26 below.

There are three ways in which Church order can thus remain open to God's active intervention. First, it can be broken through by God's giving an instruction to an otherwise uncommissioned church member (I Cor. 14.30; cf. Acts 11.27–30). Secondly, God's initiative creates new ministries not hitherto foreseen (Acts 13.1–3). This, of course, is true not merely in direct revelations by the Spirit, but equally so when the Church listens to God as it confronts a new situation (Acts 6.1 ff.[791]), or when a new ministry is at first simply carried out on someone's own initiative and is recognized afterwards by the Church (I Cor. 16.16). Thirdly, however, it is also possible that certain ministries have proved their worth and are being continued, but that the Church tries seriously later on to find out who has received from God the gifts of grace that are necessary for them (I Tim. 3.1 ff.). But there is no precedent in the New Testament for supposing that such ministry includes a whole list of different duties that the person chosen has to carry out.[792]

[791]It should be noticed here that, according to Luke's account, the rational reflection that leads to the creation of a new ministry is due to the right of the *minority*. The primitive Church, though strong and backed by tradition and by all God's previous activity in history, does not make light of the Hellenists' grievance, although theoretically this would have been understandable.

[792]Only in the Pastorals are there signs pointing in this direction. Although there is maintained here the literary fiction of a unique personality, of an apostolic pupil specially marked out by prophets, it is in fact clear that this model is to stand for all Church leaders. Thus there begins here (assuming that the letters are not authentic) a development in which more and more ministries are expected of the church leader.

25

ORDINATION

a. We have seen that fundamentally the New Testament knows no distinction between ministry and office. Certainly, the Church has to recognize and regulate certain ministries for the sake of order, particularly if they are regularly repeated and if the people who carry them out have to be known to the Church for practical reasons. If we like, we can call such ministry an office; but we must be clear that this is simply a matter of order, and that an 'office' is not on principle separated from a 'ministry' which, although it is not part of order, may in certain circumstances be much more important and fruitful. The concept of 'office' is today even fuller than in New Testament times, and is laden with the content that it has acquired in the secular sphere. Of course, in New Testament times too such ministries had to have definite names; but no comprehensive term 'office' was adopted, and even the special designations of individual ministries were by no means uniform. For these, moreover, biblical terms were not usually chosen—at any rate none that were related to cult and sacraments. 'Apostle' sounded quite new to Greek ears;[793] 'deacon' is unbiblical;[794] and 'teacher' occurs only twice in the Greek Old Testament.[795] Only in the case of 'elders' and perhaps 'bishops' was there a comparable ministry in the Jewish community; but neither has any ceremonial function, and both are also used in a non-technical sense.[796] Other expressions like 'pastors', 'evangelists', 'catechists', are purely functional terms.[797] Thus the Pauline view, which sees 'ministry' as synonymous with 'gift of grace' and 'manifestation of power', so that it keeps its character of an event (I Cor. 12.4–6), is essentially maintained throughout the New Testament.

[793]Rengstorf, *TWNT* I 407.29 ff.; 408.6 ff. (= *Apostleship*, 2f.).
[794]See 21c.
[795]Rengstorf, *TWNT* II 153.27.
[796]I Peter 2.25; 5.5; I Tim. 5.1.
[797]Goguel, *l'église primitive* 115 f.; also K. L. Schmidt, *TZ* 1, 1945, 310 f.

b. Proceeding from this, we have to ask whether there is ordination in the New Testament, and if so, what kind of meaning it is likely to have. We have seen that Paul does not know it. It is not merely that he does not happen to mention it. His statements show that there is in the churches of which he has the care no rite by which people are either installed or ordained for particular ministries, and that it would be impossible for him to regard any such rite otherwise than as a subsequent recognition of a ministry that had been bestowed previously.[798] The same is true of John's Gospel and Letters.[799] Thus in the New Testament there were large sections of the Church where no special action was performed to assign a particular ministry; but it is equally certain that there are within the period covered by the New Testament other sections of the Church that are familiar with such action. Acts and the Pastorals mention the assignment of a ministry by the laying on of hands; and when Matthew assumes the existence of Christian scribes it may be presumed that they were ordained, as Jewish scribes were. But we have to ask what exactly was intended by this action.[800] The laying on of hands[801] is a frequently used rite whose content can be very varied.[802] It appears in the healing of sickness, in benediction and baptism,[803] and perhaps also in the readmission of a sinner.[804] What is common to these passages is that the laying on of hands accompanies the imparting of God's power which heals, blesses, and claims; and that the question whether the rite must necessarily accompany the word can be answered only from the context. So we have at

---

[798]See n. 387.

[799]See 11i, 12c.

[800]On this cf. particularly E. Lohse, *Die Ordination im Spätjudentum und im NT*, 1951.

[801]Cf. J. Behm, *Die Handauflegung im Urchristentum nach Verwendung, Herkunft und Bedeutung*, 1911; J. Coppens, *L'imposition des mains et les rites connexes dans le NT*, 1925; Adler 62 ff.; Goguel, *op. cit.* 401–10; Kaiser, *Die Einheit der Kirchengewalt* 104 ff.; S. Morenz and H. D. Wendland in *RGG* III 52–54.

[802]See n. 285.

[803]Besides Acts 9.17 f., Heb. 6.2 should probably be so interpreted (cf. H. Strathmann, *Der Brief an die Hebräer* [NT Deutsch], 1949, 99).

[804]In I Tim. 5.22 this would suit the context best. This custom is attested by Cyprian, *ep.* 74.12; Eusebius, *Hist. eccl.* 7.2, as an 'old custom'; *Const. apost.* 2.18, 41, 43. This, of course, is no proof for the period of the Pastorals, which may be thinking of the appointment of elders; this would correspond approximately to Acts 6.1 ff.

first a whole list of possibilities, from the mere symbol to the magic act. The only passages that interest us here are those dealing with the matter in relation to the appointment to a task.[805]

c. First there is Acts 13.1–3, where Paul and Barnabas are sent out with the laying on of hands to their missionary task. Who lays his hands on them is obviously unimportant to Luke; he would probably like the reader to think of the other 'prophets and teachers' in the local church at Antioch.[806] Thus it is plain that it is not a matter of ordination,[807] as both already belonged to the company of 'prophets and teachers'. It is therefore an 'installation', i.e., a placing in a particular sphere of service which differs in some respects from that previously occupied.[808] The account is specially interesting, because in it a man whose apostolic status the later Church (unlike Luke himself) has never doubted, is the recipient, not the giver, of the laying on of hands.

In 6.6 the rite is described in just the same way.[809] Here Luke is presumably thinking of the apostles as laying hands on people, though it is not expressed clearly. We may infer from the parallelism of the two actions that the action described here is similar to that of 13.3; here too men are 'installed' for a quite definite ministry within the local church at Jerusalem, with no thought of any further activity beyond this definite task. In both cases the rite is one of blessing.[810] The churches which continue today the laying on of hands when a member is appointed to a particular service are therefore in the succession of the Church with Lucan characteristics, which may perhaps be found historically in Jerusalem and Antioch. Others, which do not practise the rite, are equally clearly in the succession of the Pauline Church.

[805]Corresponding to the Jewish leaning on of hands (see n. 285).
[806]See 5m, and n. 674.
[807]So also Roman Catholic scholars: Brosch, *Charismen und Ämter* 163; Kaiser 38 n. 44.
[808]Nor is there any evidence in Judaism that emissaries (*šᵉlīchīn*) were authorized by the laying on of hands (Lohse 63; Dix, *Ap. Min.* 228 f.). From the point of view of methodology it is very doubtful whether it can be inferred from Acts 13.1 ff. (Lohse 73).
[809]Here too προσευξάμενοι comes at the beginning. Cf. P. Gaechter, *ZKT* 74, 1952, 129 ff.
[810]See 5m. It cannot be maintained that Acts 14.23 also involves a real installation (Kaiser 94 n. 76) unless we transfer fourth-century language (J. H. Moulton and G. Milligan, *The Vocabulary of the Greek Testament*, 1929, 687) back into the first century.

d. The more material passages are those in the Pastorals. It is not absolutely certain that it is a matter of ordination here at all,[811] but in view of the Jewish parallels it most probably is. Nor is it clear who ordains. According to II Tim. 1.6 it is Paul, and according to I Tim. 4.14 the body of elders.[812] Behind this statement there is presumably the fact that in the writer's time any such appointment was made by the elders. It may also be presumed that the appointment was for a definite ministry in a local church, or at least for a ministry supported by the local church, so that it was carried through as an 'installation'. Of course, that consideration is not of itself enough, for in both passages there is a reminder of the charism that has been bestowed on the appointed person through the laying on of hands. As it is assumed in the case of Timothy and Titus that they will come back to the apostles from the churches in which they are now working, it can hardly be supposed that the writer thought of the charism as being limited to the duration and the special nature of that particular ministry.[813] Speaking historically, there may have been in his time nothing but the laying on of the elders' hands for some ministry in the local church; but at any rate the writer of the Pastorals means more than that.[814]

e. Unfortunately we no longer know for certain what Jewish ordination was in New Testament times.[815] This much, however, is clear: in the Pastorals' reference to an appointment all the

---

[811]The laying on of hands might be the one that took place at baptism. Presumably I Tim. 6.20 f. is also thinking of baptism (see n. 324).

[812]We can hardly escape this conclusion (as does Jeremias, *ZNW* 48, 1957, 130 f.) by the translation 'ordination to eldership'. Of course, the expression 'the ordaining of the elders' can mean either that the elders ordain or that they are ordained (Str-B II 653, n. 2). But the expression 'the laying on of the hands of the presbytery' (I Tim. 4.14 in AV) in a letter that cannot suppose that its hearers knew anything about rabbinical rites can hardly be taken to mean 'the laying on of hands dedicating to eldership'. Jeremias certainly pointed out a variant of the Theodotion text in which πρεσβυτέριον indeed means the rank of elder (unless it is simply the erroneous substitution of the more usual word instead of πρεσβεῖον). But in any case, in the New Testament it means exclusively presbytery or elders (cf. Luke 22.66; Acts 22.5 for the Sanhedrin).

[813]Schlier, 'Ordnung . . . nach den Pastoralbriefen' 44 f., emphasizes the permanence of the charism in ordained people.

[814]It is quite possible that he wants to portray something like metropolitans; but where is that to be found in the text (*pace* Schlier 46 f.)?

[815]Lohse 64 ff. (also 53–55).

emphasis is on the imparting of the Spirit—a thing that, if it did play any part in Jewish ordination in New Testament times, was at any rate not the dominant factor.[816] On the other hand, there is no trace in the Pastorals of authorization on the ground of a prescribed course of study that had been completed at the required standard, such as is the essence of the Jewish scholar's ordination. I Tim. 1.18 proves that the charism is still taken seriously in the Pastoral Letters, and has not become simply an attenuated idea. That, of course, does not tell us how often or how seldom such phenomena occur; but the writer still knows, at least in theory, that it is not the permission of an authority but the 'event' of God's Spirit, that qualifies a person to serve. It is true that the laying on of hands acquires a special importance for him on that account. The writer certainly does not think that God's Spirit can be acquired only in that way, for he does not mention it at all in connection with the appointment of presbyter-bishops or others; but the idea that there was thus mediated to Timothy the charism that is of such importance for his ministry is clearly expressed. Side by side with churches whose sole concern is that every member shall possess the fulness of the Spirit (I John), and side by side with those that subsequently acknowledge the Spirit that is already at work (Paul), we also find in the New Testament others which, in view of the gnosticism in which the Church threatens to break up, join charism and office firmly together. The Johannine and the Pastoral Letters represent two extreme possibilities in shaping the Church's order. Throughout the centuries the 'institutional' church has laid the emphasis on the latter view, while the 'free' churches have laid it on the former. The Church would not become heretical, however, unless it saw only one side and completely forgot the other.

[816]E. Sjöberg, *TWNT* VI 384.20 ff.

26

APOSTOLIC SUCCESSION

a. The first question to be asked is whether the New Testament gives any ground for preferring an episcopal or a synodal system. Now it is quite clear that an apostle referred to as a pillar (Gal. 2.11 ff.) can fall into error just as a whole Church can (Gal. 1.6 ff.). A Church can call its apostle to account (Acts 11.1 ff.), and *vice versa* (Acts 20.17 ff.). Truth is guaranteed neither to anyone consecrated from the highest source of authority nor to a majority of voters (which means at least half a vote over 50 per cent). The essential thing, therefore, is simply the way in which an episcopal or synodal (or congregational) system is applied. Where there is a strongly articulated episcopal system, it is vital that the Church as a whole should be taken seriously and not disfranchised.[817] We saw that even an apostle can demand obedience for his message only because he himself is subject to it (I Cor. 15.3; Gal. 1.8), and that for him the only obedience is that which comes from conviction—an obedience given because the Church has realized that it necessarily follows from the gospel to which they are both subject.[818] The main emphasis of the episcopal ministry too must therefore lie, as in the New Testament, in the local church itself and its ministry.[819] Where, on the other hand, there is a strong synodal system, it is vital that the Church should really listen to the gospel, and not enforce the wishes of its own majority. Here it is relevant that in the New Testament there are no majority decisions, but that efforts are made to arrive at a right judgment, even though the discussions are by no means easy or harmonious, till those of differing views can unite. Where no such understanding can be reached, the matter is taken so

---

[817]Torrance (*Royal Priesthood*) argues for this, especially 97 ff.

[818]See 23c, and v. Campenhausen in n. 714 there. Dix, *Ap. Min.* 244 stresses that although the apostle is highly regarded, he has no actual right to command.

[819]This is supported particularly by Dix, *Ap. Min.* 293 ff. (cf. v. Allmen 13), and by A. M. Allchin in *Theology* 61, 1958, 149.

seriously in the New Testament examples that the Church has to summon up the courage to point out to the dissident(s) that they are repudiating the gospel, and to warn them of God's judgment, or even to pronounce it. Thus it is quite conceivable that a church that had hitherto had no episcopate should introduce it for the sake of order or unity with brethren in another denomination; but it could never be demanded for the church as an unconditionally necessary form of church order.[820] For there are undoubtedly New Testament churches without bishops, even in the later period of development; in fact, we find that there is probably nowhere a bishop in the modern sense, nor any attempt to create one, except possibly in the figure of Timothy or Titus in the Pastorals.

b. Can we then speak of apostolic succession at all in the New Testament? There is no doubt that the term 'apostle' here implies authority. Only for the apostle are the words 'of Jesus Christ' added, and so his relation to him is a more direct one than that of any other person.[821] His word is God's own word (I Thess. 2.13). But here we have to make a very careful distinction: this holds good for the 'gospel', for the fundamental message to which he himself, as we have seen, is subject (Gal. 1.8),[822] and for whose form he remains indebted to the tradition (I Cor. 15.3).[823] But where it is a matter of applying the practical conclusions to the actual situation, Paul can only claim to think that he 'also' has the Spirit (I Cor. 7.40; cf. 12). The Church has to realize for itself and on its own responsibility why this or that conclusion must be drawn from the gospel. The concern is clear: there must be no Church order—even in obedience to the apostle himself—through which a meeting with the living Lord is avoided. There is therefore no guarantee of a correct interpretation that would make possible an obedience that is simply law-abiding without listening to the gospel. For an obedience that conforms to the law, to the regu-

---

[820]Cf. Reid, *The Biblical Doctrine of the Ministry* 47, in view of the talks about union between the Anglican and Presbyterian Churches in England and Scotland, and also the theses of the theological commission of the Swiss Kirchenbund (Protocol of the Assembly of Delegates of 9 and 10 June 1958, pp. 35 ff.). See 26h.

[821]Selwyn, *First Peter* 117.

[822]On this W. Baird, 'What is the kerygma?' *JBL* 76, 1957, 181–91.

[823]The classification of the apostolate among all the other ministries is stressed by K. H. Rengstorf, *Apostolat und Predigtdienst*, 1934, 6f.

lations laid down by some authority—whether a bishop or the majority of the voters—is no obedience without a perception that the required action is a necessity derived from the gospel. What was shown in Jesus' own life[824] is also true here: faith is genuine only where the distress, difficulty, and tribulation of a direct meeting with God himself, as he comes to us in Jesus Christ, are not avoided. No law and no legally interpreted authority must excuse the believer from asking what is God's will and from subordinating himself to the Holy Spirit and the risen Lord.[825] There can and should be reminders of the message and its interpretation, as well as comfort, directions, and guidance, but never so that the Church is relieved of its own responsible decision.

c. We next have to ask in what way the apostle's ministry[826] is continued in the Church.[827] The historically unique testimony to the risen Lord cannot recur. Although the apostolic message is never a 'chemically pure' substratum, but an unfolding of the gospel into the thought and speech of a particular time and place, and therefore in constant need of reinterpretation, it is still the *first* proclamation, which cannot simply be reproduced. It is in that sense that the apostle lives on in the form of the New Testament in the Church of today. If the question is asked anywhere in the New Testament how the apostle's ministry lives on, it is in the Pastorals. But this is where it is most strongly emphasized that the essence of the ministry of Timothy and Titus and the men whom they appoint is to hand on the apostle's message unchanged.[828] That the apostle's ministry in its uniqueness is to be continued is not suggested here any more than elsewhere in the New Testament.[829] On the contrary, the Pastorals, like much of the

[824]See 2c.

[825]Cf. Rengstorf 39 f.: the Spirit's leading and the apostolate are not contrasted.

[826]K. L. Schmidt's argument that because there is no prophetic succession there can be no apostolic succession is unconvincing, because the nature of the call and appointment differs in the two cases (cf. F. M. Braun, *Neues Licht auf die Kirche* 165 f.).

[827]The answer is not as simple now as at the time of the Protestant 'Consensus'. On the history of this question cf. F. M. Braun 158–65.

[828]Dix's emphasis (*Ap. Min.*) on this, not on the position of the bishop in the liturgical-eucharistic sphere, is rightly welcomed by v. Allmen (Dix, *Le ministère dans l'église ancienne* 11 f.) and at least recognized as a basis of discussion.

[829]So too Reid 24 f.; C. K. Barrett, *ExpT* 70, 1959, 200 ff.

sub-apostolic literature in general, see the apostolate much more emphatically as a unique ministry of the past than does Paul himself. What cannot cease in the Church is preaching, and therefore the charge in Matt. 28.19 f. always applies.[830] That charge, however, is given to the whole Church.[831]

d. Historically too, however, the thesis that there was from the beginning an apostolic succession that was important to the Church is untenable. Even the relation of the New Testament concept of apostleship to the Jewish institution of the authorized 'envoy' is open to question.[832] Then, too, the synoptic tradition shows that the introduction of the term 'apostle' represents a later development and in any case does not go back to Jesus himself.[833] It was probably Paul himself who obliged the Church to develop a precise idea of apostleship.[834] But in this it is he himself who is the 'dangerous exception'.[835] His apostleship was never attacked by the twelve;[836] and that proves that in his time there was as yet no institutional apostleship in the sense of

---

[830]Cf. Cullmann in *Background* 409 ff.

[831]This is strongly emphasized in Torrance, e.g., 26. If it is stressed from the Anglican side that in *one* sense the apostolate remains unique and cannot be reproduced, so that the bishop of the second century is no apostle, and the Church remains God's continual creation through Christ working in the apostles (Farrer, *Ap. Min.* 171), there is another serious possibility here for conversations. This then raises the question where the apostles are to be found (on that, see 1d, e).

[832]See 24i.

[833]See 24a, b, and Farrer 120, 124. The explanation of this absence in the tradition cannot be solely that the 'messengers' were of no importance as long as Jesus himself was present (Dix, *Ap. Min.* 229 f.). For if Jesus had really ordained the twelve in the sense of the Jewish institution of the šālîaḥ, that would certainly appear in the tradition. In that case the different ideas of apostleship would be as difficult to imagine as the stressing (probably in the very early days) of the part to be played by the twelve in the coming kingdom.

[834]Perhaps himself compelled by Judaizers who cast doubt on his apostleship (H. Mosbech, *ST* 2, 1948/9, 194 f.).

[835]Davies, *A Normative Pattern of Church Life* . . . 8 f.

[836]Leuba, *New Testament Pattern* 69, 77, rightly stresses the 'miracle' that he was acknowledged by the first apostles (moreover without consecration or laying on of hands). Even if the opponents in Corinth had been associated with the first apostles—which seems to me very doubtful, *pace* E. Käsemann, 'Die Legitimität des Apostels', *ZNW* 41, 1942, 33 ff. (on the other side Bultmann, *Symb. Ups.* 9, 20 ff.)—that does not in any case hold good for the twelve themselves.

appointment and conveyance of authority by the historical Jesus.[837]
Indeed, the opening of the mission to the Gentiles probably had
nothing to do with the twelve, nor even, in its beginnings, with
Paul.[838] And beside him there stands James, at a later time the
leader of the church in Jerusalem, who was not appointed by
Jesus,[839] although the risen Lord appeared to him.[840]

e. Unfortunately we have no historically reliable witnesses at
all for the development of the primitive Church.[841] If we keep to
Luke, the thesis of the apostolic succession fails because he does
not include Paul among the apostles,[842] whereas in the Pastorals,
which alone approach the question of the continued existence of
an office after the apostle's death, Paul appears in fact as the only
apostle. It is logically inadmissible to acknowledge Luke as an
authority and then to refuse to follow him on this decisive point.
If we confine ourselves to him, it is clear how concerned he is to
present the apostolate—through his account of the choice of
Matthias and the conditions then laid down—as the historically
unique testimony of those who had seen and heard Jesus.[843]

There is no transfer of apostolic authority—in any circumstances,

---

[837]Menoud, *Eglise* 28. Goguel's thesis, *L'église primitive* 90 ff., that the charismatic apostolate is primary, and the institutional apostolate a later development,
cannot be disputed, *pace* Leuba 52 ff.; for the twelve are neither institutional
'apostles' nor 'directors of the Church' in Jerusalem. The idea that they
were appointed by Jesus as apostles and administrators of the sacrament
for the time after Easter, and were relieved of that duty only for the time of
his earthly life (cf. Leuba 56 f.) is possible at the most as a later construction,
and historically untenable (see 2k and 3n here). J. Munck, *ST* 3, 1949/50,
101 ff., also stresses that there was an older concept of the apostle, which did
not see in him the forerunner of the bishop.

[838]W. Telfer, *JTS* 48, 1947, 226.

[839]Farrer 119.

[840]I Cor. 15.7. It might be inferred from Acts 1.14 that this happened within
the forty days. But Luke, who is the only one to know of the forty days at
all (on this however cf. P. A. van Stempvoort in *NTS* 5, 1958/9, 30 ff.),
reports nothing of this, and mentions him only from Acts 12.17 onwards.
In I Corinthians he appears, like the 'more than five hundred brethren',
without the mention of any particular charge given to him by Jesus.

[841]See n. 92.

[842]See 5h.

[843]So Reid 13 f. G. Klein 175 thinks that Luke actually created the idea
of apostolic succession, but in such a way that Paul is not considered as an
apostle, but as the second link of the chain. There is, however, no real
ordination or authorization of Paul by the twelve. Thus we may see at the
most that Luke shows a tendency in that direction.

according to Paul's letters. [844] But how does the matter stand in relation to the accounts in Acts? Everything that we know from the Pauline letters argues against his having appointed elders in the churches (14.23). [845] But if we keep to Luke's view, it is obviously only a matter of someone's being appointed as leader in the newly founded churches. Nothing is said about the laying on of hands or the assignment of an office, and while 20.17 ff., where the departing apostle's farewell address clearly takes the Church's sub-apostolic period into account, contains a broad self-justification, and urgent admonitions to the elders to be faithful and unselfish after his good example, it makes no allusion whatever to the transfer to them of any authority of office. On the contrary, it is only by 'God and the word of his grace' that the building up of the Church is expected (20.32).

f. We hear nothing of the appointment of elders in Jerusalem. Regarded historically, their rise is most probably connected with James' taking over the direction of the Church. It is likely that James' position (working towards a monarchical leadership) and also the company of elders (corresponding to the organization of the Jewish community) originated when the twelve were no longer in Jerusalem. [846] But by that time things had developed so

[844] See 25b.

[845] See 7i.

[846] On Schoeps' theory see n. 130. In Jerusalem the high priest is at the same time the president of the Sanhedrin. That may have an analogy in James' position in relation to the elders (Dix, *Ap. Min.* 235 f., 250), but not previously. The grouping together of 'apostles and elders' appears first (six times) in connection with the Council at Jerusalem. As Gal. 1.19; 2.9 coincides with what is found in Acts (n. 840), this Council at Jerusalem presumably implies a transition from the original guidance by Peter (and the sons of Zebedee?) to that by James; and so it is possible that 'apostles and elders' once worked side by side for a very short interval. But it cannot be maintained that these are the only real offices (Dix, 237 f.), even for this period. Of course, not everyone can be an apostle, but that is because not everyone has met the risen Lord and been commissioned by him. Similarly, not everyone can be a prophet, but only the person whom God has endowed and commissioned for the purpose. It might rather be said that everyone can become an elder if the Church chooses to make him one; but here too God's gifts are presupposed. We may perhaps say that in the case of apostles and elders the ministry lasts for life; but is it otherwise in the case of prophets and teachers? It should be remembered that Eph. 2.20; 3.5 regards apostles and (New Testament) prophets as the Church's foundation, and that in Luke 11.49 (Acts 15.32?); I Cor. 12.28; Eph. 4.11 they stand very close together.

far that that body could no longer exercise even a moral right to supervise the Hellenistic churches and their elders—these were independent of each other and of Jerusalem,[847] and so the elders in Jerusalem never played the part of the Jewish Great Sanhedrin.[848] If, however, we heed Luke's evidence, we can say simply that there is never any mention of the appointment of elders in Jerusalem by apostles. It may well be impossible to see the origin of elders in the seven of Acts 6.1 ff.[849] Historically they have nothing to do with the twelve, but are a (competing?) parallel organization,[850] and Luke certainly does not regard them as elders, as they have to take over the service of tables as distinct from the apostles' ministry of the word.

But even if there had been anything like an appointment of elders in Jerusalem by the apostles, could that ministry really be separated from others, especially that of the bishop? Is it not a fact that the appointment of elders and the choosing of overseers or bishops from within the Church go on side by side without any regulations,[851] and that this ministry of the elders can nowhere be traced back in any special way to the apostles and so distinguished from other ministries? Even less can we find anywhere an indication that there were from the very beginning two kinds of elders, one corresponding to the members of the Great Sanhedrin in Jerusalem and being continued in the bishop (in the sense of

[847]Dix, 236 f.

[848]See n. 130. It should be remembered, with Brunner, *The Misunderstanding of the Church* 33, how completely Jerusalem's pride of place disappears after 70.

[849]Against Farrer 133 ff., especially 143. I cannot see that the choice of the seventy in Num. 11.24 f. (as against the twelve heads of the tribes in 1.4) is supposed to be repeated symbolically in Acts 6; because there are not seven, but seventy (who, moreover, seem to be taken from a larger group of elders), and because the heads of the tribes play no part there, but Moses acts alone. Michaelis, *Ältestenamt* 35-39, is much more cautious, but his opinion too seems to break down on the fact that the seven belong to a separate group of the church in Jerusalem (see 3 o).

[850]Which may have been formed in a way comparable with the Jewish *local* elders (see 3 o).

[851]F. M. Braun 172. Farrer 143 f. pictures the development as being either that the apostles were replaced by men who were closely connected with them (such as Barnabas in Antioch), or that only locally active elders were appointed, who then remained subordinated to any apostles who might arrive. See n. 853. According to Brosch 121 f. the appointment by an apostle would give an official character to a charismatic ministry.

the metropolitan),[852] the other corresponding to the members of the local Sanhedrin and found as elders of local churches.[853] But where should we find the first group? In the apostles, whose pupils Mark, Timothy, and Titus would in that case correspond to the 'pupils of the wise' (= of the members of the Great Sanhedrin)?[854] But of that the New Testament knows absolutely nothing, apart from the fact that the circle of the twelve, called by Jesus to be judges in the eschatological kingdom of God, is something totally different from the Great Sanhedrin, and that they probably never had the management of the primitive Church. Where we hear anything at all of 'Christian scribes'—namely in Matthew— they are very clearly distinguished from the twelve.

g. If we go beyond the New Testament, then, of course, documents like the *Didache*, I *Clement*, Ignatius' letters, and the *Shepherd* of Hermas give us information about the further historical development; but the same is also true of the *Letter of Barnabas*, the *Odes of Solomon*, the *Acts of Thomas,* and many others.[855] When, at the close of the second century, the Church did not receive these writings into its canon, this was either an objective judgment by which it kept aloof from them in respect of their contents, or a decision on principle which clearly separated the apostolic writings from all later productions, and which can therefore hardly be understood against the background of a belief in a continuing apostolic office. But even in these other writings the preservation of the original apostolic preaching is treated as a matter of importance; it is also assumed that certain people take over the guidance of the Church, and that after their death others will do the work; but it is never suggested that the apostolate is

[852]Of course, the fact that ἐπισκοπή is related in Acts 1.20 (though in an Old Testament quotation) to the service of Judas (!), but in I Tim. 3.1 to that of the bishop (Spicq, *Les épîtres pastorales* 93) does not prove that the later bishop takes the apostle's place.

[853]Thus Palmer, *Min. and Sacr.* 378–81 (on the other hand Michaelis 41); Lockton, *Min. and Sacr.* 375, goes further by thinking that the apostles had already established a metropolitan organization (Rome, Antioch, Alexandria), while the bishop had stood out among the locally appointed elders. In the New Testament nothing is said about either; and how little this came into being generally in the early part of the following period is shown by v. Campenhausen, *Kirchliches Amt*, e.g. 131, but also 91, 103 f., 110 ff., 117.

[854]So Palmer 373 f., similarly Farrer 142.

[855]See 1c, d.

to continue in a special way, separated from other ministries, with apostolic successors.[856]

h. So if we consider that the office of bishop, as understood in modern times, is a good institution which has stood the test of centuries, then it is at least worth discussing.[857] Only then we must be quite clear that it belongs, at most, to the Church's *bene esse,* not to its *esse.*[858] Where the institution is regarded as an unconditional necessity,[859] the same situation exists as in Gal. 2.3 ff. For the Church that does not possess the apostolic succession it would mean, not the renunciation of cherished ideas for other people's sake, but a declaration that something for which it can see no basis in the New Testament is necessary for salvation. Here the concern of the Church to which the apostolic succession is important must certainly be heard, for continuity is essential to the Church of Jesus. But it is the succession of believers, in which the message is handed on from generation to generation.[860] A person will hardly attain to faith unless a living witness of the message mediates it to him by his words or by his whole existence. The only way to guarantee that this handing on does not wander away from the original gospel is, indeed, to go back constantly under the guidance of the Holy Spirit, and ask what is the witness of the apostles themselves in the New Testament.

[856]See chs. 15–19.
[857]The celebration of Sunday, too, has no authority in the New Testament, but it is a good institution (Craig, *The One Church* . . . 42 f.).
[858]So too Torrance, *Royal Priesthood* 107.
[859]As in the view discussed by Newbigin 85, who is opposing an understanding which implies that even a church filled with all the fruits of the Holy Spirit is no part of the one Church unless it has the apostolic succession, whereas even the most corrupt and depraved church within the apostolic succession remains a church under God's forgiveness. However correct on principle are the question of continuity and the assertion that it is not the church's worthiness that makes it a church, the thesis of the apostolic succession, in that sense, is none the less untenable on New Testament grounds. See n. 820.
[860]Craig 65.

27

THE CHURCH SERVICE

a. If Church order is understood as a manifestation of the
Spirit, and a witness to the Lord who lives in the Church, it must
be apparent particularly in the worship of the Church. [861] If we ask
first about the New Testament's terminology for this, we again
have to note the absence of all religious and ritualistic concepts; [862]
and the Sunday service is therefore not separated as a holy event
in a sacred sphere from everyday service. So in the Pauline
enumeration of charismata, gifts that are exercised in the meeting
for worship stand side by side with those that are exercised in
everyday life—prophecy, for instance with the gift of liberality
(Rom. 12.6, 8). There is no longer in the New Testament Church
a cult such as existed in all contemporary religions. [863] Yet there
can be no doubt that to a great extent worship is the centre of
the Church's life. [864] It is only in connection with it, and particularly with the Lord's Supper, that Paul uses the concept 'body of
Christ'. There the Church represents itself as the Lord's body.
But how?

All the expressions used in describing the service stress the
impulse of coming together, and are also used purely secularly. [865]

[861] I am briefly summarizing here what I set out at greater length in *Der
Gottesdienst im NT* (Zwingli-Verlag, Zürich, 1958). The literature (cf. in
particular Delling) is noted and discussed there. Cf. also *The Reformed and
Presbyterian World* 24, 1957, 196 ff. I am using the word 'service' here in its
narrower meaning of the meeting for worship.
[862] Λειτουργία, λατρεία, θυσία. These denote, on the contrary, the Church's
everyday service!
[863] It is to be found only in 'heaven', where, according to Hebrews, Christ
rules as the only high priest (M. Dibelius, *Theol. Blätter* 21, 1942, 11).
[864] This is true in the sense of the image in 20f. Of course, God may so lead
the Church that the martyr's witness in prison, for instance, becomes the
real centre.
[865] Paul uses συνέρχεσθαι, Acts συνάγεσθαι. συνάγεσθαι ἐπὶ τὸ αὐτό appears too
in Acts 4.26 = Ps. 2.1 f. in the usual sense (for συνέρχεσθαι ἐπὶ τὸ αὐτό cf. the
Koine reading in I Cor. 7.5). The same holds good for the word ἐκκλησία,
cf. Acts 19.32, 39, 41.

It is therefore essential for the service and for the Church order that it expresses, that the Church is actually physically together,[866] and that is emphasized, as far as we can see, by the fact that everywhere it comes together in one place.[867] This is shown by the expression, which has become a technical one, 'to come together ἐπὶ τὸ αὐτό (= to the same)',[868] and also by the New Testament writers' natural expectation that their letters would be read to the whole assembled church.[869]

b. We no longer know in detail what took place in those assemblies; but it is clear that they were characterized by the abundance of gifts.[870] This is true of the church in Rome, not founded by Paul (Rom. 12.3–11), of the Johannine[871] and probably also of the Palestinian[872] churches, as well as of Thessalonica and Corinth.[873] It is not till the later period of the Pastorals that we find a form of service resembling ours, though even there it is still open to all the men to speak.[874] Prayers too were certainly offered during the service at an early period.[875] The short confessional formulae of the

---

[866]This suggests a church building in which the congregation sits at least in a semicircle in which people can see each other.

[867]Gal. 6.16 does not contradict this; nor is G. Schrenk (in *Judaica* 5, 1949, 81–94 and 6, 1950, 170–90), who relates the expression 'God's Israel' only to the Jewish Christians, thinking of a special group. On the problem of II Thess. see E. Schweizer in *TZ* 1, 1945, 90 ff.

[868]Acts 1.15; 2.44, 47; I Cor. 11.20; 14.23 and in the Apostolic Fathers (J. H. Moulton and W. F. Howard, *Grammar of NT Greek* II/3, 1929, 473 f.).

[869]Does I Thess. 5.27 point to threatened dissensions? I Cor. 11.18 shows how very much the service is a gathering together of the whole church; it is there that all tension and disunity is bound to be seen.

[870]See 7k–m.

[871]See 11i, 12c.

[872]See 3 o.

[873]I Thess. 5.19–21; I Cor. 12–14; for post-Pauline developments see Eph. 5.18 f.; Heb. 6.5; *Did.* 11.7; Ign. *Philad.* 7. In the New Testament it is only in missionary preaching and in special cases, such as Acts 20.7 ff. and 18 ff., that only one person speaks.

[874]I Tim. 2.8–12; 4.13. Cf. 6g, h (nn. 338 f.). Bible reading appears here for the first time (n. 11), although the letters habitually assume some knowledge of the Old Testament (or of collections of testimonies)—on the strength of instruction in the catechism?

[875]I Cor. 11.4 f.; 14.14–16; Eph. 3.14–21; I Tim. 2.8; John 4.23; Acts 4.24 ff. etc. To that the congregation says the Amen, and perhaps a doxology (such as is added to the Lord's Prayer: Cullmann, *Early Christian Worship* 12 f.).

New Testament probably belong rather to baptismal teaching,[876] whereas hymns are typical of the church service.[877] In them the lordship of Jesus at God's right hand is the central theme, while the formulae 'for sins' or 'for repentance and remission of sins' are absent. Thus in singing the Church joins the ranks of those who bow the knee and worship the Lord, and its singing is an act confirming its subordination to the Lord who has been exalted into heaven. The service is therefore meant in the first place to acknowledge the present lordship of Christ, whereas in the confessional formulae of baptismal teaching the emphasis is laid more on God's saving acts which have already been accomplished.[878]

c. The decisive gift, however, is that of the Word. What is promised in it is beyond telling. Everything that can be said realistically about Christ's presence can be found in the New Testament much more clearly in relation to the Word than, for example, in relation to the Lord's Supper.[879] It is meant, indeed, in the first place to refer only to the unique first message which must be accepted or rejected once for all—that is, to the *kerygma*, the 'message', not to the *didache*, the 'doctrine'.[880] That is why Paul gives a typical illustration of the power of the Word by the example of the Gentile who goes into the assembly and is so effectively reached by the preaching that he falls on his face and declares that 'God is really among you' (I Cor. 14.24). But the preaching to the Church, as far as we can now see, is largely of a similar nature.[881] In the name of the risen Lord the prophet con-

[876]I Cor. 15.3–5; Rom. 4.25; 10.9 etc. Luke regularly brings it into missionary preaching. Cf., however, I Cor. 12.3. But it is scarcely possible to regard them as texts for sermons (E. Käsemann in *Verkündigung und Forschung* 1953/5, 162 f. against Delling, *Der Gottesdienst im NT*).

[877]Phil. 2.6–11; I Tim. 3.16 etc. Revelation too contains some. Of course, we must not equate with earthly worship what is deliberately described as heavenly.

[878]The laying by of money for collections is likewise an important ministry. According to I Cor. 16.2 this is more likely to be done privately, so that perhaps only the total sum is presented at the service (cf. Acts 5.1–11).

[879]I Thess. 2.13; Luke 10.16; John 20.23; Matt. 10.12–15 (a town to which the Word has been preached is a different town afterwards, even if it has refused to believe).

[880]This distinction is made by C. H. Dodd, *The Apostolic Preaching and its Development*, 1936, 3 ff., although in too one-sided a way.

[881]Cf. I Cor. 14.1 ff.; Rev. 2 f., and the fragments of sacred law in the New Testament (E. Käsemann, *NTS* 1, 1954/5, 248 ff.). For the nature of the New Testament Church's preaching cf. G. Friedrick in *Wort und Dienst*, 1959, 70 ff.

fronts the Church and says what he has to say in the actual situation. It is not instruction, but a straight talk demanding a 'Yes' or 'No'. But the imperative is rooted in the indicative, the call in the message of the salvation that has been accomplished.[882] On the other hand, no confession of sins by baptized persons appears in the service.[883]

d. Finally, the Lord's Supper plays a large part, though the thesis that it was the climax of every meeting for worship[884] is very much open to question.[885] It is the proclamation of Jesus' death, and it tells every individual that that death took place for him.[886] But it is above all the event in which the Church continually presents itself as the body of Christ; and therefore a sacramental Lord's Supper at which there is not actually a common meal is for Paul a misuse of the service.[887] The Lord's Supper is, after all, an anticipation of future table-fellowship with the risen Lord, and is therefore celebrated in exultation.[888]

e. Here again we can see the twofold nature of the New Testament's view of the Church. In all its expressions the service is in the first place a witness for the freedom of God's grace which continually becomes anew a living reality. We can put it in an extreme form: the Church is in itself only part of the world; but it is part of the world allowed to assemble repeatedly for worship and there to become the body of Christ through the Word of the

---

[882]This becomes clear in Paul's writings (see 23c), and also in the Pastorals, where the set phrases reminiscent of Pauline expressions prove how well the Church knows that all admonition must be based on the gospel, even when the latter is no longer given an original wording. But this combination is found in the other letters too.

[883]On this see 28d; so also Delling 116.

[884]Cullmann, 29.

[885]Luke pictures in the early period what is presumably a daily breaking of bread; but in any case, this period has for him its own laws. From I Cor. 11.17–22 it only seems clear that the Lord's Supper was in any case not the conclusion, but at most the beginning of the service, for it is the conclusion of the common meal, at which the Corinthians no longer waited for latecomers—probably the slaves who were not free to come earlier. This is also supported by the placing of chs. 12–14 after 11.

[886]On the question of 'representation' cf. E. Bizer, *EvTh* 16, 1956, 1–18. The events in God's plan of salvation do not become present in time, but Christ does—in a way quite analogous to what takes place in the Word.

[887]G. Bornkamm, *NTS* 2, 1955/6, 202 ff.; *ZTK* 53, 1956, 312 ff.; also E. Schweizer, *RGG* I 11 f.

[888]See *ibid.* 11, 16 f., and notes 84 and 646 above.

Redeemer which comes to it, and through the bread and wine distributed to it, both of which unite it as a Church. But at the same time the Word that is uttered today rests on the message on God's saving actions that took place once for all; and the Lord's Supper is the proclamation of Jesus' death as well as the fact of constantly renewed table-fellowship with the risen Lord. So, again in an extreme form, we can also say that the Church is lifted clear of the world by something that was done for it long ago and that now in no way depends on its religious vitality. Of that its baptism is the sign. Thus the Church service is characterized by these two things: by the new and living preaching that testifies to the freedom of God, and also by the set liturgical formulae and hymns that testify to God's faithfulness.[889] Neither must remain without the other.[890]

[889]Cullmann, 32 f.

[890]Today there is a widespread inclination towards a liturgical order of service. The risk of allowing all church members to speak at will is hardly ever taken—it seems too great. But can a Church that is not thought mature enough for all to be free to speak be thought capable of liturgical singing and speaking, which probably needs a good deal more maturity if it is not to degenerate into mere words? Thus, however much we may agree to a meaningful liturgy, we may ask critically whether it is not a lazy way out as long as the Church is deprived of the right to speak freely. On the other hand it might be asked whether the Church was not simply in quest of itself if it merely aspired to the right to speak freely with no subordination to liturgical discipline.

28

CONCLUSIONS

a. Both free and fixed forms can be seen together only where people build the Church, or rather allow it to be built, on the basis of faith in God's freedom *and* in his faithfulness. Both are therefore most clearly attested in the Church order where the Church can make it clear in the most unmistakable way that it is what it is solely through God's action, and not through any guaranteed means of salvation, or through its imposing size or order, or through its own religious vitality, impressive prophetic utterances, or ascetic achievements; and that it is thus neither an institution to provide salvation nor a religious club. It therefore knows that it is in itself only part of the world, which must always simply wait for God's grace to be bestowed. But at the same time it knows that God is faithful and will therefore not withhold tomorrow what he gives today. Thus it is a Church as long as it believes and because it believes. But such faith is not its own achievement, but is the knowledge that it can expect nothing from itself, or even from the intensity of its faith, but everything from the freedom and faithfulness of its Lord. What separates it from the world is therefore the gift of God—namely that it has been allowed to hear that Jesus Christ came for the world, lived, died, and was raised from the dead. Only 'in Christ' is it essentially the Church. [891]

b. What the Church has to stress most strongly in its witness will vary from country to country and from century to century. It may emphasize the obligation imposed by God's call in Jesus Christ, and thus make it clear in its own self-understanding and order that it lives only through that act of God for the world. This will be true in every possible detail of life, in the confession

---

[891]See n. 365 above, and H. D. Wendland, *Die Kirche in der modernen Gesellschaft*, 1958, 57 f. (also 39 ff., 45 ff., and on the other side 54 ff.). He shows quite clearly how being separated off from the world is the presupposition for the Church's spreading into the world (60).

with which it praises God's act, in the conduct of life in which it testifies that it does not now live by its own perfection, but by God's actions in baptism and the Lord's Supper in which it receives God's gifts. Then what happens is neither more nor less than what is described in Luke 17.15–19 and Mark 6.10–13. But as soon as the Church begins to identify its special nature with the power of its enthusiasm, with its moral achievement, or with a Church order that gives it a guarantee, whether through the orthodox creed that it teaches, the sacraments that it administers, or its own particular hierarchy—then it has overstepped the bounds of the New Testament. The openness of the disciples' circle certainly never means that the world is to be left in any doubt of the fact that God's call in Jesus Christ is final and urgent, and that anyone who passes it by is bound to make a failure of his life. It does mean, however, that the Church that knows this knows at the same time that even in its religious phenomena, its ascetic achievement, and its centuries-old order it is in itself only part of the world, because only the miracle of God's grace, continually repeated in freedom for the sake of God's faithfulness, is its life. This miracle, however, never becomes the Church's own property by allowing it either to guarantee the miracle to anyone who complies with the Church order or fulfils certain prescribed religious or moral requirements, or to forget that God can completely by-pass the Church's organization in calling people to himself.[892]

c. For that reason the man from outside, the fringe member or the Gentile, is for Paul the proper yardstick by which the whole proclamation must be measured (I Cor. 14.16 f., 23–25). For the same reason, language that edifies only the initiated is inadmissible. For the same reason Paul will in the last resort allow no distinction to be drawn between prophetic preaching to church members and to those from outside. What is specially striking when it happens to these people according to I Cor. 14.25 is really nothing fundamentally different from what happens to every church member when he really hears; the difference simply is that the church member hears afresh what he has already heard before, and, in hearing, accepts again what he has already learnt.

[892]See 15f, 16c, 17c–e; on the other hand Matt. 25.37–39, 44; Rom. 11.19–21; Luke 11.31 f.

d. This is taken so seriously in the New Testament that the Church has no confession of sins—none, at any rate, that is to be said regularly at the Sunday service.[893] This by no means implies that the Church regards itself as perfect; no New Testament witness is a perfectionist. The Church's sins are spoken of quite clearly, but also in quite a concrete way; nor are the sins that were committed before baptism and have been forgiven through Christ simply forgotten (Rom. 7.7 ff.; I Cor. 15.9; I Tim. 1.15 f.). But the *tone* is quite different from that in a Church that is taken every Sunday from a confession of sins to absolution. The Church *has* heard that God's action has been carried out, and this is so central for it that it can never act as if every Sunday the whole drama of salvation began all over again from the very beginning. That it lives in principle by hearing this justifying word means that it has renounced sin once for all. Of course, it knows that it must continually be hearing anew what it was once told, and so again and again in the service it will hear the call to live anew, and better, by what it has been told there. But for all that, it is always looking forwards, always at the open door to the new week in which once again it may live—and much better than in the week just gone— on what has been given to it. It does not look back full of remorse. It has renounced sin by building its life on God's gracious action, and so it is no longer possible for it, even if there were time, to revolve pharisaically round its good deeds, or penitently round its bad ones. That, and again only that, separates it from the world.

e. This ought to have certain practical consequences.[894] Witness both to freedom and to God's faithfulness is given in the following ways:

[893]On I John see 12a above. We may also refer to James 5.16; Matt. 6.12; 26.28. But there is not the slightest sign that the service was anything like a repetition of the drama of salvation with preaching of the law, confession of sins, blessing, and absolution. Indeed, apart from the passages mentioned there are hardly any that speak of the forgiveness of sins for believers. This is not seen as a problem until Heb. 6.4 ff.; I John 2.1 f.

[894]If I repeat here in essentials what I wrote in my essay (now out of print) on 'Geist und Gemeinde im NT und heute' (*Theol. Existenz* n. F. 32, 1952, 47 ff.), I am fully aware that I can only offer suggestions, which must not be torn out of the context of what has already been said. I think, however, that the exegete must not wholly withdraw from the task of at least giving such suggestions towards the present-day shaping of the Church.

1. The Church has a definite order, which, however, is never an inflexible law, but always open to amendment.[895] Where God clearly shows a different way, the letter will never be allowed to be an obstacle. But it really is order, and when it is broken through, the Church must earnestly try to find out whether it is God's direction and not its own arbitrary act.

2. The preaching of the great acts of God is central. In this it becomes clear that it is not a matter of awakening and promoting the life of one's own soul. But the preaching must at the same time always speak to the existing situation; and it therefore takes shape in ministries of many kinds.

3. Every church member is to minister by means of his particular gift;[896] but no one must ever push himself forward with his own special charism. The Church therefore takes the ministries that do not appear openly (silent intercession, for instance) as seriously as it takes the public ones.

4. The Church service for all believers living in the same place is the centre and goal of all Church life, because no single group must content itself with its own charism and the people whom that can reach. But the Church knows at the same time that it may please God to bring about decisive things in any such special group; and so it bears the responsibility for all the groups, even if they have to work independently. And the latter see the Church service as their goal, even if there is as yet no practicable way to it.[897]

[895]So too e.g. Wendland, *Gemeinde* 9 and *Kirche* 58; v. Campenhausen, *Bindung und Freiheit in der Ordnung der Kirche*, 1959, 5 ff.

[896]This may work out in practice in a circle of responsible church members, who prepare the sermon and the whole service. Individuals among them may also take over liturgical and extempore prayers, and perhaps also a free statement of, for instance, the problem that the text meets. At least occasionally a non-theologian should undertake the sermon; and short supplementary testimonies are also possible. There may sometimes be special occasions when a well conducted course of Bible study, in which everyone could take part, would be possible and very suitable.

[897]See n. 708 above. This is relevant to the question, which is so topical today, of the relation between occupational or age groups (e.g. Christian doctors or youth groups) and the local church. Here we have to recognize that the local church of today is often quite incapable of constructing a service in the New Testament sense; and so it may well be that many people can be reached today only through the service of particular groups seeking their own form of worship. To deny this would be wrongly to take the local church's present organization as a guarantee of the Holy Spirit. That must

5. The Church knows that the gospel remains the same through all the centuries, and that it therefore gives rise to certain clear requirements; but it knows that God's directions can never be taken over as legal regulations, but have to be heard anew today by the Church. Important decisions are therefore taken neither by direction of an authority nor by a simple majority decision.[898] It is true that the Church will not manage without any such decisions, especially where it can no longer meet together; but it testifies to its faith by striving, on important questions, for a right understanding till the one group can declare that it is convinced, or at least that it is prepared to assent.

6. Because Church order is gospel testimony, whether one wishes it or not, matters of election and administration that concern the Church as a whole are carried out in meetings that are in the nature of worship. That, of course, does not guarantee that all those taking part listen to God's directions; but it does testify that that is what the Church would wish.

7. In its choice the Church considers what gifts of grace God has bestowed on one of its members, and decides the limits of his ministry accordingly. It knows that in this connection the natural circumstances (e.g. age, sex, studies) have to be taken into account just as seriously as others. It may therefore provide one of its members with the necessary training, or relieve him, either wholly or partly, of anxiety about his livelihood.

8. The Church knows of the need to regulate individual ministries; but it also knows that a ministry that it does not regulate may be just as great and important. It therefore makes no distinction between 'office' and 'ministry', beyond the purely practical need of division.

f. A wrong development may, as we have seen,[899] lead to a gnostic group just as well as to an institutional Church. It makes

---

be conceded to Brunner, *The Misunderstanding of the Church* 91 f. But it must be said at once that this situation is one of exigency, and that everything possible must be done on both sides so that the aim of a common divine service offered by all is achieved. To neglect this would be to construct a church on a few people of religious genius, or even on special gifts, so that everyone could pick and choose what he found specially congenial.

[898]See 26a.
[899]See 1c–e and 20e.

no final difference whether the official or the ecstatic—or as a variant, the ascetic—is made absolute, whether the view of the Pastoral Letters or the Johannine writings—or as a variant, that of the Matthean fulfilment of the law—is developed one-sidedly. Whether the presence of God's Spirit is guaranteed by the group of regularly ordered persons or by a company of complete pneumatics or ascetics, any such idea is merely a form of a wrong concept of the Church. The Church will therefore have to seek a way through between Rome and Sohm;[900] and it will be able to do so successfully only where it lives, with the utmost determination, on *God's* freedom and faithfulness, and not on its own order or on its own religious vitality. How it can do this and give its witness effectively it must continually ask anew.

[900]Here we must reaffirm what was said in 20f above.

INDICES

Numbers followed by letters refer to chapters;
numbers alone refer to notes.

I. BIBLICAL REFERENCES

2. SUBJECTS

Altar, 18

Apostles, 2k, 3n, 5hi, 7ghi, 8f, 10b, 11ci, 13e, 15e, 16c, 18c, 19a, 21a, 22ac, 23b, 24abik, 25a, 26bcd

Apostles—prophets—teachers, 15e, 22bc, 23d

Apostolic succession, 1c, 5h, 6c, 16c, 18d, 24b, 26b–h, 562

Asceticism, 15f, 17bc, 18b, 20e, 28b

Asia Minor, 14a

Baptism, 3g, 5f, 7e, 11a, 15c, 22g, 27e, 28b, 478

Bishops, 5i, 6h, 12c, 14a, 15d, 16cd, 17cd, 18c, 22b, 23b, 24ghi, 26afh, 489

Body of Christ, 7b, 8c, 11b, 16b, 17a, 18a, 19b, 20f, 27ade, 447

Catholicism, early, 1bc, 5b, 335

Charism (cf. Ministry), 6g, 12c, 21fg, 25e, 27a, 340, 377

Church,
    authority, 4f, 5m, 23b–e
    building (cf. Temple), 866
    characterization, 3b, 5e, 6b, 11g, 12c, 13a, 16b, 23a, 350, 590, 707
    corpus mixtum, 4d, 15c, 18a
    discipline, 4e, 6f, 15c, 23e
    growth, 8be, 9a, 11f
    historical, 6cdi, 7ach, 9a, 10a, 11d, 12a, 13f, 15b, 16b, 20 a–f, 361
    history, 1de, 5ad, 20e
    law, 3 0, 24l, 28e, 687
    local, 22b, 23a, 25cd, 28e, 595, 708

    open circle, 2ad–f, 3gl, 4d, 5f, 6ef, 11e, 27e, 28ab
    pre-existent, (17a), 18a, 19b
    relation, mutual, 11h, 14b, 20f
    relation to disciples, 2beh, 3d–g
    separated from the world, 2g, 3egkl, 7e, 11bc, 12be, 13f, 15c, 17a, 27e, 28ab
    sufferings, cf. 717
    tertium genus, 5ben, 19ac
    united with Christ in the present, 7ch, 8ac, 9a, 10a, 11ci, 13f, 17a, 19a–c, 20a–f
    world-wide, 8bg, 9a, 15c, 17e, 20f, 22b, 23a

Collection, 5k, 878

Communism of early Church, 107

Confession of sins, 27c, 28d

Conventicle, 14ab

Deacons, 5im, 6h, 15d, 16cd, 17d, 18c, 21c, 22b, 23b, 24gi, 25a, 283

Deaconesses, 6h

Disciples = office-bearers?, 2ik (see also Church's relation to)

Doctrine, false, 6bei, 12ab, 596

Doctrine, right, 6b, 12ade, 28b, 596

Ecstasy, 15f, 17f, 18bd, 20e, 21f, 22f, 28f

Elders, 3m, 5il, 6h, 7i, 9b, 12c, 14a, 16c, 17d, 18c, 22af, 23c, 24fgi, 25ad, 26ef, 379, 394

Eschatology, 2f, 3n, 6c, 10b, 11a, 12d, 13a, 15b, 24a (see also Parousia)

Event, nature of, 7m, 21eg, 23a, 25a, 27e

3. AUTHORS

Marxsen, 100, 101
Masson, 411, 412
Maurer, 546
Médebielle, 701
Menoud
  Eglise, 165, 496, 612, 638, 668,
    673, 837
  Judaïsme, 114, 451
Meyer, 177, 787
Michaelis
  Ältestenamt, 296, 270, 329, 332,
    333, 420, 741, 756, 849, 853
  TWNT, 258
Michel
  Hebräer, 426, 427, 428, 430, 433,
    435, 437, 768
  Römer, 630, 771
  Zeugnis, 96, 117, 165, 353, 358,
    485, 497, 582
  other works, 72, 131, 295, 377,
    416, 447
Molland, 529, 581
Morenz, 801
Mosbech, 834
Moule, 25, 127
Moulton & Howard, 868
Moulton & Milligan, 634, 810
Munck, 126, 130, 165, 174, 731,
  837
Mundle, 165
Mussner, 353, 398

Nauck
  I Johannesbr., 131, 475, 478, 495,
    784
  ZNW, 273, 335, 336, 422, 538,
    640, 644, 751, 762
Neugebauer, 361
Newbigin, 357, 594, 595, 859
Niebergall, 11
Nigg, 32
Nötscher, 456, 640, 644
Nygren, 357

Odeberg, 583, 641
Oepke, 43, 98, 100, 352, 364, 462,
  484

Palmer, 765, 853, 854
Passow, 603, 604, 622
Percy, 357, 361, 362
Peterson, 501, 590, 674
Philonenko, 763
Poland, 590
Preiss, 464
Preuschen, 420

Ramsey, 284
Rankin, 11
Rawlinson, 707
Reicke, 92, 102, 280, 710, 764
Reid, 1, 4, 6, 209, 259, 770, 820,
  829, 843
Reitzenstein, 548
Rengstorf
  Apostolat, 823, 825
  TWNT, 525, 772, 793, 795
Renié, 73, 261
Reuss, 362
Rich, 690
Richardson, 94, 774
Riesenfeld, 79, 739
Robinson, J. A., 501, 787
Robinson, J. A. T., 181, 353, 357,
  447
Robinson, J. M., 104, 397
Romanides, 566
Rost, 94, 95, 96, 97, 640
Rozemond, 545, 556
Rüsch, 546

Sasse, 473, 522
Scheel, 671
Scheidweiler, 107
Schierse, 424
Schille, 78
Schiller, 574
Schlatter, 14, 17, 20, 357
Schlier
  Past., 302, 813, 814
  other works, 416, 596
Schmid, 507, 578
Schmidt, 37, 587, 590, 702, 707,
  797, 826

16 cl. 20 = 19.20

STUDIES IN BIBLICAL THEOLOGY No. 32

Church Order
in the New Testament

Eduard Schweizer

SCM PRESS

About the author

EDUARD SCHWEIZER has been Professor of New Testament in the University of Zürich since 1949. Immediately before that, from 1946–49, he was Professor of New Testament Interpretation and Theology at the Universities of Mainz and Bonn, lecturing at the same time at the University of Frankfurt. From 1936–46 he was a minister of the Reformed Church of Switzerland. He is a Doctor of Divinity of Basel and, *honoris causa,* of the Theological Faculty of the University of Mainz. From 1959–60 he was visiting Professor at Colgate Rochester Divinity School, Rochester, New York. He has contributed articles to *Religion in Geschichte und Gegenwart* and Kittel, *Theologisches Wörterbuch für das Neue Testament,* and is the author of *Ego Eimi, Das Leben des Herrn in der Gemeinde und ihren Diensten,* and *Erniedrigung und Erhöhung bei Jesus und seinen Nachfolgern* (a translation of which has already appeared in the Studies in Biblical Theology (No. 28) under the title *Lordship and Discipleship*).

Studies in Biblical Theology

A SERIES OF MONOGRAPHS designed to provide clergy and laymen with the best work in Biblical scholarship both in this country and abroad.

The Advisory Editors for this series are:

C. F. D. Moule, M.A., *Lady Margaret Professor of Divinity in the University of Cambridge,* J. Barr, M.A., B.D., *Professor of Old Testament Literature and Theology in the University of Edinburgh,* Floyd V. Filson, Th.D., D.D., *Professor of New Testament Literature and History, McCormick Theological Seminary, Chicago,* G. Ernest Wright, Ph.D., D.D., *Professor of Old Testament History and Theology at Harvard University.*

8 GOD WHO ACTS—*Biblical Theology as Recital*
by G. ERNEST WRIGHT   8s 6d net

9 STUDIES IN DEUTERONOMY
by GERHARD VON RAD, translated by David Stalker   8s net

10 EARLY CHRISTIAN WORSHIP
by OSCAR CULLMANN, translated by A. S. Todd and J. B. Torrance   8s 6d net

11 ORAL TRADITION—*A Modern Problem in Old Testament Introduction*
by EDUARD NIELSEN   8s net

12 THE MISSION AND ACHIEVEMENT OF JESUS
by REGINALD H. FULLER   8s 6d net

13 LIFE IN CHRIST
by THÉO PREISS, translated by Harold Knight   8s net

14 STUDIES IN THE BOOK OF LAMENTATIONS
by NORMAN K. GOTTWALD   8s 6d net

15 CONSCIENCE IN THE NEW TESTAMENT
by C. A. PIERCE   9s 6d net

16 GALILEAN CHRISTIANITY
by L. E. ELLIOTT-BINNS   7s 6d net

17 AN APPROACH TO THE THEOLOGY OF THE SACRAMENTS
by NEVILLE CLARK   8s net

18 THE MESSIAH IN THE OLD TESTAMENT
by HELMER RINGGREN   7s 6d net

19 EARLY ISRAEL IN RECENT HISTORY WRITING
by JOHN BRIGHT   9s 6d net

20 THE SERVANT OF GOD
by W. ZIMMERLI and J. JEREMIAS   10s 6d net

21 THE PROBLEM OF HISTORY IN MARK
by J. M. ROBINSON   8s net

22 ESSAYS ON TYPOLOGY
by G. W. H. LAMPE and K. J. WOOLLCOMBE   7s 6d net

23 PROMISE AND FULFILMENT—*The Eschatological Message of Jesus*
by W. G. KÜMMEL, translated by Dorothea M. Barton   12s 6d net

24 JESUS' PROMISE TO THE NATIONS
by J. JEREMIAS, translated by S. H. Hooke   7s 6d net

25 A NEW QUEST OF THE HISTORICAL JESUS
by J. M. ROBINSON   9s 6d net

26 TEN YEARS OF DISCOVERY IN THE WILDERNESS OF JUDAEA
by J. T. MILIK, translated by John Strugnell   12s 6d net

27 MYTH AND REALITY IN THE OLD TESTAMENT
by BREVARD S. CHILDS   9s 6d net

28 LORDSHIP AND DISCIPLESHIP
by E. SCHWEIZER   10s 6d net

29 THE POWERS THAT BE
by CLINTON D. MORRISON   9s 6d net

30 NEWLY DISCOVERED GNOSTIC WRITINGS
by W. C. VAN UNNIK, translated by Hubert Hoskins   7s 6d net

31 HUMAN ACHIEVEMENT AND DIVINE VOCATION IN THE
MESSAGE OF PAUL
by W. A. BEARDSLEE   10s 6d net

32 CHURCH ORDER IN THE NEW TESTAMENT
by E. SCHWEIZER, translated by Frank Clarke   16s net

SIXTEEN SHILLINGS NET

2400